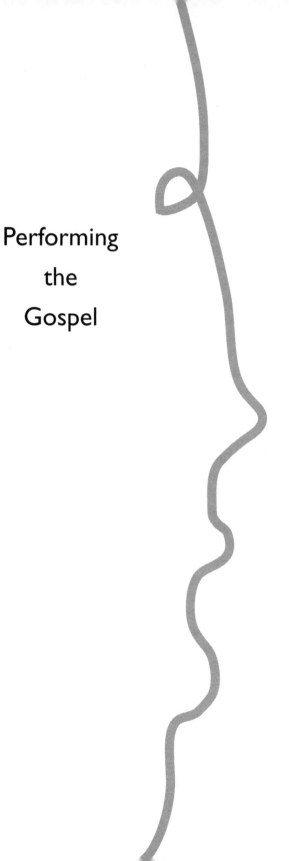

Performing
the
Gospel

Performing the Gospel

Orality,
Memory,
and Mark

Essays Dedicated to Werner Kelber

Edited by
Richard A. Horsley,
Jonathan A. Draper,
and John Miles Foley

Fortress Press
Minneapolis

PERFORMING THE GOSPEL
Orality, Memory, and Mark

Cover image: © Diana Ong/Superstock
Cover design: Becky Lowe
Interior design: Zan Ceeley, Trio Bookworks

Library of Congress Cataloging-in-Publication Data

Performing the Gospel : orality, memory, and Mark / edited by Richard A. Horsley,
Jonathan A. Draper, and John Miles Foley ; dedicated to Werner Kelber.

    p. cm.
    Includes bibliographical references.
    ISBN 0-8006-3828-X (alk. paper)
1. Bible. N.T. Mark—Language, style. I. Horsley, Richard A. II. Draper, Jonathan A.
III. Foley, John Miles. IV. Kelber, Werner H.

    BS2585.6.L3P47 2006
    226.3'0663—dc22
                                    2005037888

The paper used in this publication meets the minimum requirements of American
National Standard for Information Sciences—Permanence of Paper for Printed
Library Materials, ANSI Z329.48-1984.

Manufactured in the U.S.A.

10   09   08   07   06   1   2   3   4   5   6   7   8   9   10

CONTENTS

Part 3

Orality, Literacy, Memory, and Mark

Introduction

Richard A. Horsley

Biblical studies is a conservative field, for several reasons. Its focal texts are sacred to the faithful and canonical for church doctrine. Even beyond the walls of churches and synagogues biblical literature is foundational for western culture more generally. Professional biblical interpreters have dedicated their careers to the conservation as well as the fuller understanding of these texts. Many biblical interpreters stand in ecclesial traditions of interpretation and have received intensive and formative training in the principles and methods appropriate to those traditions. Many of the institutions of higher learning in which biblical studies is housed are closely related to Christian and Jewish religious bodies; scholars in those institutions are not necessarily in regular interaction with other fields of learning usually located in universities. Innovation is not always welcome and is sometimes suspect.

Yet innovation can bring excitement and insight that renew and enliven the field of biblical studies, church communities, and personal faith. In the last generation, innovation in three interrelated areas has introduced fundamental challenges to the standard assumptions in biblical studies:

- In the 1970s, some interpreters began reading the Gospels as sustained narratives rather than continuing the standard focus on individual sayings and pericopes.

- The 1980s brought initial explorations of the oral communication that was predominant in the ancient world and of the implications particularly for Gospel materials.

- In the 1990s, cultural memory came to the attention of at least some interpreters as a central factor in the composition and appropriation of biblical literature, again especially the Gospels.

Werner Kelber was a pioneer in all three of these interrelated areas. He was one of the first to explore the Gospel of Mark as a plotted narrative, and not a mere "string of beads."[1] He was the first to recognize that the Gospels were composed and received in a world dominated by oral communication, and he has patiently explained the implications to other scholars still stubbornly faithful to the typographical assumptions of the modern western study of sacred texts. Following the implications of those insights, he has more recently demonstrated that the Gospel narratives were produced by and from cultural memory. In all of these interrelated areas, Kelber's path-breaking work has not only opened the eyes of others to their central importance for New Testament studies but also become formative for other biblical scholars' attempts to question established assumptions, approaches, and interpretations. Separately and in combination, probing inquiries and reflections in these three areas promise to change the landscape of Gospel study. Kelber's incisive investigations in these areas have already led to decisive shifts in our approach to and understanding of the Gospel of Mark.

Narrative

Kelber was one of the principal pioneers to explore the Gospel of Mark as narrative, as a fascinating and compelling story.[2] Reading Mark as a sustained story was a decisive break with the standard treatment, which regarded the Gospel as a mere collection of text fragments to be closely examined in isolation as prooftexts for Christology or ecclesiology or another theological doctrine. Literary criticism enabled the discovery of Gospels as narratives, with "overarching plot constructions, numerous subplots, configurations dictated by thematic concerns, and compositional arrangements of various kinds that have the effect of overriding the episodic structure."[3]

Reading Mark's Gospel as a narrative requires respecting its literary integrity. While Mark may not have a narrative unity and coherence, it must be recognized as a complete, plotted story in which particular episodes have significance not in themselves but in the flow of the overall narrative. Insofar as Mark's Gospel is a complex story with plots, interwoven subplots, and persistent themes, moreover, meaning is immanent or inherent in the narrative and does not lie in some truth or doctrine abstracted from and projected above (or underneath) the text.

Reading Mark and other Gospels as narratives became a virtual growth industry during the last decades. Any number of books and articles have explored various facets of the Gospels as stories, using a variety of modern approaches to literature. Sometimes these explorations have imposed modern assumptions about "authors," private, individual "readers," and "character development" onto Mark and the other Gospels. Kelber has insisted that the Gospels, as ancient narratives, are not necessarily susceptible to methods of interpretation developed for and practiced on modern literature. The Gospels and other New Testament and contemporary Jewish, Latin, and Greek literature have distinctive features of their own. These ancient literatures belong to distinctive social-cultural worlds that require historical as well as literary sensitivity.

Orality and Literacy

Kelber was the first to recognize the import of pioneering research by classics scholars who noted not only the oral communication environment of antiquity but also the difference between oral performance and written text as understood according to the assumptions of modern print culture. This led him to challenge the established and deeply ingrained assumptions and methods of form criticism, which treated the oral tradition of the sayings of Jesus as if they were artifacts in print. Mediating the research of the pioneering scholars on orality in other, related fields, he explained, for those with ears to hear, how oral tradition could be understood more appropriately.[4]

More recent analysis of evidence for orality and literacy in antiquity has made it unavoidably clear that literacy was limited mainly to the social-cultural elite.[5] Literacy was even more limited among the Jews, especially in Palestine. Extensive recent surveys of evidence for literacy in ancient Judea and Galilee conclude that writing, whether in Hebrew, Aramaic, or Greek, was confined to a tiny elite and used, in limited ways, to secure and enhance the power of dominant families.[6] Even when available in written form, texts were recited aloud to larger or smaller groups of people. In an environment in which communication was mainly oral, oral forms, techniques, and style carried over in the production of manuscripts. In both composition and reception, "ancient chirographs [manuscripts] came to life . . . in an environment saturated with oral sensitivities."[7]

This recent recognition of the oral communication environment, and of the close relationship between written text and oral performance, has major implications for Gospel study. First, whether or not Mark and other Gospels existed in written form, they were performed orally and received aurally. Thus, if we are to understand them appropriately in their historical context, we must approach them with sensitivity to oral communication and to how textuality was interrelated with orality. Second, since modern biblical scholarship was "born and raised" and "acquired its formative methodological habits in modern print medium,"[8] its established assumptions and procedures may be inappropriate to the texts-in-context that it seeks to appreciate and interpret.

To those two implications for Gospel studies in western academic circles, we should add a third that threatens to break down the boundaries between academic study and appropriation of the Gospels by ordinary people. In societies in which literacy and books have not been so prominent, people have continued to appropriate the "text" of the Gospels in ways that have involved the interaction of oral performance and literacy. It is conceivable that investigation of this interactively oral-and-literate appropriation of Gospel materials will prove stimulating to further exploration of the process by which the Gospels were composed-performed, written, and again performed in interaction with written texts.

Following Kelber's lead, a number of other scholars have been exploring aspects of orality and literacy, oral performance, and issues of communication media in general as they bear on biblical studies. The Bible in Ancient and Modern Media Group of the Society of Biblical Literature has sponsored a variety of innovative explorations in this area. New Testament interpreters have found help in the form of approaches developed in other fields to deal with the relationship between oral performance and written text. Particularly stimulating has been the work of John Miles Foley, who has shown biblical interpreters how to combine insights from socio-linguistics, performance theory, and ethnopoetics.[9] Martin Jaffee demonstrated how Kelber's insights and Foley's theory could be applied to rabbinic recitation and understanding of the oral Torah—"Torah in the mouth"—and to the intricate relationship between the memory of Qumranites and Pharisees and the scrolls they possessed.[10] Several scholars have followed Kelber's lead in exploring orality and literacy and oral performance with regard to the Gospel of Mark as narrative.[11] And some, drawing also on comparative studies in folklore and storytelling, have examined biblical and related stories as oral performance.[12] As exemplified in Foley's wide-ranging multicultural work, exploring the relationship of orality and literacy has led biblical interpreters into interaction with other academic fields and other cultures. Kelber, Jonathan Draper, and others organized a series of international conferences to explore orality and literacy in connection with colonialism, memory, and other topics.[13]

Memory

Exploration both of the predominantly oral communication environment of the Gospels and of the Gospels' narrative form led Kelber to the importance of memory in the composition of the story. Memory must have been the force that mediated between the ministry of Jesus and the composition of the Gospels as fully plotted narratives.[14] Kelber's critical comparative study of oral tradition had exposed the assumptions and procedures of form criticism as untenable. The notion of an "original form" of a text fragment, whether a Jesus saying or a narrative episode, was a phantom of the typographical imagination. Bultmann and other New Testament scholars had assumed that oral tradition evolved in a linear way, propelled by its own momentum, into a Gospel. But Kelber showed that, in an oral communication environment, oral tradition required active memory, not simply passive recollection.

More in contact with the intellectual ferment in other disciplines than most biblical scholars, Kelber has tapped into the vibrant discussion of memory in both the humanities and the social sciences in the last several decades. In its own typographical captivity, modern western academe had forgotten that late antiquity and medieval Europe were cultures in which other strategies of memory prevailed beyond the written text.[15] Kelber found particularly illuminating the interdisciplinary work of scholars such as Jan and Aleida Assmann, which builds on the pioneering earlier reflections of Maurice Halbwachs.[16] Although a brief summary is hardly adequate to the complexities of recent reflection, it is important to have in mind some of the principal interrelated features of cultural (or social) memory.

Memory is social, closely related to group and group identity. As Kelber has written, "The process of remembering does not work purely for the benefit of what is deemed worthy of recollecting. . . . Rather memory selects and modifies subjects and figures of the past in order to make them serviceable to the image the community wishes to cultivate of itself. Socialization and memory mutually condition each other. . . . The emphasis is decidedly on the sociological dimension of memory."[17] Following the Assmanns, Kelber prefers to avoid the term "tradition" because it overemphasizes continuity and evolutionary progression. Rather, memory is a dynamic operation that reappropriates the past in the process of social interaction and in the interests of the community.[18] More particularly, this reappropriative "cultural memory," as distinguished from the "communicative memory" of daily interaction, transcends the everyday and is maintained through cultural forms such as texts, rites, festivals, monuments, or images. It crystallizes meaning that reaches across generations.[19]

Kelber suggests that we approach the Gospels as narratives more appropriately when we incorporate study of cultural memory. This enables us to cultivate extra-textual sensitivities, to become familiar with the notion of mental composition, and to appreciate "a cultural tissue at once more copious and more elusive than the conventional linear perception of literary sources will ever allow us to imagine."[20] Awareness of the creative role of memory will help us appreciate how those who composed the Gospels may have drawn on "the web of cultural memory, retaining, collating and adapting traditional items, reclaiming and citing some, appropriating directly, critically and even destructively others, while recontextualizing all so as to make them serviceable in a text designed to speak to the present."[21]

The work of Kelber, the Assmanns, and others on cultural memory has only begun to influence biblical studies. Most significant, perhaps, is the formation of a new program unit in the Society of Biblical Literature called "Mapping Memory: Tradition, Texts, and Identity." Other SBL program units have recently sponsored sessions also drawing on studies of social/cultural memory. Contributors to those sessions produced a volume of essays, *Memory, Tradition, and Text*, which examined the importance of memory mainly in early Christian literature.[22] Thus, in addition to Kelber's recent articles on cultural memory, the essays in this volume and the rich range of references to recent studies of memory in a variety of related academic fields now provide resources on which biblical interpreters can draw in exploring this important factor in the Gospels and other texts.

Looking Forward

The chapters that follow are all deeply engaged in one or more of the three interrelated areas of innovation that Kelber has pioneered. The contributors include Jan Assmann and John Miles Foley, two internationally prominent leaders in the fields of cultural memory and verbal art as oral literature, respectively, with whom Kelber has worked closely. The other, more senior contributors—trained in the standard assumptions, concepts, and approaches of biblical or rabbinic studies, but then stimulated by Kelber's explorations as well as the work of Assmann and Foley—have recently been pursuing some of the implications of orality and literacy and cultural memory for biblical and related literature. The more junior contributors, even in their initial scholarly ventures, have produced important studies focused on oral performance, memory, and closely related matters.

Part 1 includes a general survey of studies of orality and literacy in New Testament literature and two case studies of the interaction of orality and literacy. Holly Hearon provides a helpful orientation to several key aspects of orality and literacy in New Testament literature and thus also a good preparation for the rest of these essays. She judiciously surveys many of the recent studies by other New Testament interpreters on the basic implications of orality and literacy for the composition, performance, and writing of texts produced by Jesus followers and Christ believers. At key points she builds on her own pioneering study of stories of Mary Magdalene in the context of ancient storytelling.[23]

Martin Jaffee, an important scholar of rabbinic literature, was the first to recognize the implications of recent studies of the interrelation of orality and literacy for understanding rabbinic learning. His groundbreaking study of the rabbis' cultivation of "Torah in the mouth" (often called "oral Torah")[24] shows the way not only for rabbinic scholars' further appreciation of the process of transmission and appropriation of rabbinic learning, but also for Gospel scholars' understanding of the transmission and appropriation of the teachings of and stories about Jesus. Here Jaffee shows how appreciating the oral cultivation of learning can help us understand rabbinic discussions of "Gentiles, undisciplined Jews, and their women," discussions that exemplify the interaction of orality and literacy in rabbinic circles.

Jonathan Draper lives and teaches in a multi-ethnic environment (KwaZulu-Natal) that still mixes oral and written communication.[25] For the last several generations, indigenous prophets, who had through oral performance appropriated the Gospels that had been brought to them by European missionaries in printed Bibles, founded new church communities with a lively production of prophecies and hymns. In a fresh investigation of handwritten copies of the prophecies of George Khambule, Draper finds that they involved an interaction of oral performance and written copies. This essay makes available to a wider public a South African prophet and his community almost completely unknown outside of a small academic circle. The interaction of orality and literacy in the performance of Khambule's prophecies should also prove suggestive for those interested in the cultivation of Jesus' prophecies in early Jesus movements and the composition-performance of Gospel materials.

Part 2, on "Orality, Literacy, and Memory," presents two theoretical essays and two that are focused on particular New Testament texts. The work of Jan Assmann, perhaps the most important theorist of cultural memory, is now becoming one of the principal bases for study of social memory in various fields.[26] Assmann emphasizes that the past is always mediated by socially constructed memory, so that a pristine past is simply not recoverable from archivally understood sources. Since memory is also integrally connected with social identity, often of whole societies, the investigation of history is better understood as one aspect of a wider-ranging process of constructed cultural memory. Assmann's essay, which extends his theory to focus on the relationship of cultural form and cultural memory, has significant implications for how biblical scholars rethink issues such as "form" or "genre" and how they contextualize ancient cultural forms.

John Miles Foley works from a wide-ranging knowledge of texts composed and performed in the interface of orality and literacy and from a variety of societies, from ancient Greece to contemporary Tibet. His theory of oral performance,[27] which pulls together insights from sociolinguistics, ethnography of performance, and ethno-poetics, has already been influential among biblical interpreters attempting to extricate themselves from the assumptions and concepts of print culture. His essay explores how memory is understood and used by three oral performers in different cultures.

Ellen Bradshaw Aitken draws upon an extensive knowledge of popular culture heroes in contemporary Hellenistic literature in order to examine Jesus as the hero who interprets scriptural tradition in the Gospel of Luke and the Epistle to the Hebrews.[28] She brings to these New Testament texts a thorough grounding in the Milman Parry–Albert Lord tradition of interpretation of Homeric epics in oral performance as

continued by Gregory Nagy and others. Her reading of Jesus' performance of scriptural tradition in a very wide context of cultural memory
displaces the standard older focus on quotation of scripture in a given
New Testament text.

Jens Schröter, who has become a close collaborator with Kelber, has
produced the principal study in German on memory of the sayings of
Jesus (in Mark, Q, and the Gospel of Thomas).[29] His conclusions raise
questions about some of the standard assumptions and applications of
form criticism to the Synoptic Gospel tradition. With a sharpened awareness of the important role of memory in the interface of orality and literacy, his essay explores the role of communal memory of Jesus' sayings
in the development of early Christian texts and the eventual formation of
the New Testament canon.

The three essays in Part 3, finally, explore the interrelationship of
memory, orality, and literacy with regard to the Gospel of Mark. Vernon
Robbins, one of the principal leaders in the revival of rhetorical criticism
in New Testament studies, insisted that such criticism have a solid basis
in ancient Greek and Roman rhetorical theory and education. Having
mediated that knowledge to others in the field, he was well prepared to
appreciate the relationship between orality and literacy. Since he, like Kelber, originally honed his interpretative skills on the Gospel of Mark under
the guidance of Norman Perrin, Robbins now returns to the Gospel with
full appreciation of the range of modes of communication available in the
process that produced it.[30]

Whitney Shiner, in his first book, engaged Robbins's interpretation
of Mark's representation of the disciples on the basis of further study of
ancient rhetorical theory and practice. Building on a general knowledge
of ancient Greek and Roman rhetoric and drawing upon a thorough
examination of pertinent references in ancient rhetorical literature, he
then presented what is to date the definitive account of how Mark's story
would have been heard in oral performance in the Hellenistic world.[31] On
that foundation of contemporary rhetorical practice Shiner here explores
how the technology of memory was operating in the composition-
performance of the Gospel of Mark.

In my own recent work I have explored how Kelber's insights on oral
tradition and cultural memory and Foley's theory of oral performance
and the interaction of orality and literacy can be can be combined with
careful consideration of historical social-political context in appreciation
of texts such as Q and Mark.[32] Drawing on the work of James C. Scott, I
have investigated the differences and tensions between the parallel "great

tradition" of the literate elite and the "little tradition" of the nonliterate ordinary people, showing how at both levels Israelite tradition was cultivated not in small fragments but in broader patterns such as that of the Mosaic covenant. Here I focus on another pattern in Israelite cultural memory that informs the Gospel of Mark, the memory of Moses and Elijah.

Building on recent innovations on the three important fronts pioneered by Werner Kelber, this book develops a complex analysis of previously unappreciated facets of New Testament texts, their historical context, and their composition. Individually and collectively, these essays provide an encouraging sense of how quickly our understanding of these issues has developed in biblical studies and how sophisticated it has become in recent years. From outside the field, several of these articles pursue insightful analyses of oral performance and memory in other cultures, which offer illuminating comparisons for New Testament materials. In all of the essays, theoretical reflection balances and informs textual and social-cultural analysis. Finally, on the issue in which Kelber may have made his most suggestive and influential innovation, two contributors in particular, drawing on an ever-widening awareness of the ancient cultural context, present two different approaches to and theories of how orality and literacy are related in the composition of Mark's Gospel.

PART I

Orality and Literacy

I

The Implications of Orality for Studies of the Biblical Text

Holly E. Hearon

Scholarly interest in the oral dimension of biblical texts dates to the early part of the twentieth century.[1] Since then, the tide of studies has ebbed and flowed. A swirl of activity during the 1950s and 60s slowed to a drizzle in the '70s and early '80s. This drought was broken with the appearance in 1983 of the groundbreaking study by Werner Kelber, *The Oral and the Written Gospel.*[2] Kelber's book marked the beginning of biblical scholars' growing awareness of and engagement with the works of Eric Havelock, Milman Parry, Albert Lord, Ruth Finnegan, Jack Goody, Walter Ong, and more recently John Miles Foley. Since then the flow of studies has steadily increased, surpassing the efforts of any previous decade. This is in no small part due to the ongoing efforts of Werner Kelber, who, through presentations, publications, conferences, and the active support he so graciously offers to others working in this area, continues to offer new insights into the implications of orality for studies of the biblical text.

Despite growing interest, these studies have yet to make a significant impact on the biblical field. The challenge for scholars in the twenty-first century is to effect a shift in the study of biblical texts away from the heavy, indeed almost exclusive, emphasis on the literary nature of these texts to the study of the texts as sound maps intended to be heard in a rhetorical culture that emphasized the persuasive power of the spoken word. This chapter highlights some of the ways in which the application of studies in oral tradition to biblical texts have begun to foment this shift in thinking by encouraging us to look at the biblical texts in relation to their oral/aural contexts and by considering how these oral/aural texts functioned in the ancient world. Because these studies have taken us in many different directions, this chapter is organized around a series of "sound bites" loosely grafted together. My intent is to be suggestive, rather than comprehensive, and to describe some of the places we have been and some of the places we have yet to go.

My analysis focuses on studies of the Second Testament, as this is the locus of my own research. Nonetheless, a number of issues that I raise find resonance in both Testaments. Also, while I cite a few specific studies, there are many more fine essays that will be referenced only by allusion. This is not intended as a bibliographic essay. Finally, while I have endeavored to represent a spectrum of perspectives in my comments, my particular interests and bias will no doubt be evident to those who have ears to hear. Because of my own limitations, there are, at least, two major areas I do not address; I name them here so that they may not be overlooked altogether: the relationship between oral text and history (and the attendant implications for the historical Jesus movement), and the reciprocal impact oral and written forms may have had on each other and the implication of this for the development of biblical traditions.

Written Remains

It is appropriate to begin with the written remains because, in the end, that is all we have: written remains of ancient texts that look nothing at all like what we expect to see when we encounter a written page or printed text. Uncial manuscripts, at least, are not divided in into paragraphs or lines; they exhibit no punctuation, and there are no spaces between words. The sheer visual impact of letter after letter without interruption is overwhelming. Yet it is the visual impact of the page that provides us with the proper orientation: Because the structure of the text cannot be discerned from the construction of the physical page—that is, visually—we are challenged to discover it another way.

Paul Achtemeier, observing that reading written texts aloud was the normative practice of the ancient world, has proposed that the structure of the text is revealed not through sight but through sound.[3] Margaret Dean builds on this proposal in her study of sound as the basis of grammar in

Hellenistic rhetorical manuals.[4] She observes that whereas "we first learn to read from written texts and then to write," among the Greeks, students first "memorized the elements of sound," in order to learn to write and then, once having learned to write, to read.[5] Thus "grammatical study began by identifying the elements of sound . . . then encoding spoken sounds with written symbols."[6]

Together with Bernard Brandon Scott, Dean explores how the grammar of sound structures text through an analysis, based on aural cues, of the Sermon on the Mount.[7] Listening to the text, they observe that aural formulas divide the sermon into eight sections. Within each section, aural cues create organizational patterns through the use of parallels, doublets, triplets, chiasms, and inclusios, which are signaled by the repetition of phrases, words, and sounds. Variations in length or pattern (such as the absence of an opening aural formula) establish, they suggest, the importance of certain sections over others. The result is a visual depiction of a text structured on the basis of sound rather than sight. Although (ironically) we must read this study by Dean and Scott, it nonetheless invites us not only to see but also to hear our "written remains" and to experience them in relation to aural rather than visual cues by letting our ear be guided from sound to sound rather than our eye from chirograph to chirograph.[8]

The impact of sound (versus sight) has only begun to be explored, but the combined effect of sound, pattern, and rhythm suggests a different way of receiving as well as processing text.[9] Dean and Scott point toward this when they compare their analysis of the Sermon on the Mount with analyses based on literary cues. These studies, Dean and Scott observe, structure the Sermon on the basis of themes. The result, however, is that they ignore opening formulas and interrupt sound sequences. The sound map produced by Dean and Scott indicates that the internal structure of the Sermon is not thematic but sequential. Sections and ideas are linked together on the basis of sound rather than themes.[10] Notably, the outline that most closely resembles the one produced by Dean and Scott is that of George Kennedy, which is structured around rhetorical figures.[11] The similarities between these two outlines suggest that sound was an integral component of rhetoric: how a text was received depended not only on what was said but also on the sounds employed to say it. This brings to completion the circle described by Dean, in which students first learned to inscribe sound on wax tablets before they learned to translate the signs they inscribed into sound. The art of ancient rhetoric moved from sound to text, not, as we might expect, from text to sound.

Attentiveness to the primarily aural nature of our "written remains" signals to us their close relationship with oral text. Since these written remains were largely dictated, the remains are, in fact, text that began in oral expression and were actualized in performance. To view these so-called written remains wholly as written texts, then, is to miss an important dimension of their function and to misconstrue how they were experienced in the ancient world.

The Oral/Aural Text

These written remains point to their function as oral/aural texts. Although explicit attention to the grammar of sound in relation to biblical texts is a relatively new development, numerous studies have examined these written remains for characteristics of oral/aural text. Drawing on studies in folklore and orality, these studies, like that of Dean and Scott, observe a structure in the texts that differs from that posited by literary studies. Werner Kelber, for example, exploring the imprint orality has left on the Gospel of Mark, calls attention to the sequential (as opposed to thematic) structure of the narrative through the use of connective devices, the extensive use of doublets and triads, and use of the reiteration of "words, clauses and themes" to allow "the hearer to return to and link up with what was said before."[12] Joanna Dewey, who views Mark's Gospel as "oral composition" that "shows some indication of writing,"[13] also observes characteristics of oral narrative and plotting: an additive, aggregative style, repetition of similar episodes, and use of parallels and chiasms to create echo systems.[14] These devices order the material, she concludes, creating "anticipation and responsion, so that what is new is framed in terms of what is already known."[15] Like Kelber, Dewey stresses that the plot of Mark's Gospel is developed not along linear lines but sequentially, relying on the use of mnemonic structures to assist the hearer in recalling what has gone before.[16] These devices point to the fundamentally aural nature of the text, a text intended to be heard, not read.[17]

Pieter Botha goes further than Dewey, arguing that Mark employs a compositional process similar to that described by the oral formulaic theory. While noting a lack of epithets in Mark (more characteristic of oral poetry), he points to examples of "recurring, at times almost rhythmical, wording," stereotyped names, patterns of repetition that seem to function as formulaic introductions to narrative units or expressions, and repetitive phrases that can be heard as refrains.[18] Botha also observes evidence of thematic composition, noting in particular how in several instances Mark adopts a "well-known, general motif" (evidenced in biblical as well as Greco-Roman literature) and transforms it into an "internalized narrative grammar."[19] In conclusion, he proposes that the Gospel of Mark "reflects an improvisatory composition and re-composition within an informal context under the constraints of various traditions," which was at some point dictated.[20] Botha's exploratory essay is significant because it links the oral features of Mark's text with tradition in a way that points beyond Mark as a text that either exhibits "orality" or contains oral traditions to suggest that Mark is, in fact, an example of oral composition.[21]

Earlier, Werner Kelber had called attention to the oral nature of the gospel (as spoken word) in the letters of Paul.[22] More recently, scholars have begun to attend also to oral patterning in Paul's letters. John Harvey, recognizing the oral/aural nature of composition and delivery in the Greco-Roman world, examines the letters with respect to patterns of composition described in Hellenistic rhetorical manuals: chiasmus, inversion, alternation, inclusion, ring-composition, word chains, and repetition of formulaic phrases.[23] A brief examination of three books from the Septuagint employed by Paul also reveals traces of oral patterning, drawing the conclusion from Harvey that Paul was influenced by two sources in the use of oral patterning in his letters. Although Harvey does not explore it, the evidence of patterning in the Septuagint opens the question of whether Paul employs formulaic phrases adapted from general motifs, such as described by Botha. As in studies of the Gospels, Harvey observes that attention to oral patterning can illumine the structure of Paul's letters, where literary critics have stumbled. Casey Davis, in his study of the oral/aural dimension of Philippians, draws more explicitly on studies in oral text.[24] His proposal for a "method for oral biblical criticism" is attentive not only to the kinds of patterning described by Harvey but also to sound, the use of formulas to develop themes, and mnemonic constructions.

These studies in the Gospels and Pauline texts demonstrate the fundamentally oral/aural nature of the biblical texts, whether driven by rhetorical strategies or storytelling exigencies. Yet one of the challenges these studies pose is the need to specify more explicitly what we mean when we speak of "orality" in respect to the text.[25] In some instances the term appears to refer simply to spoken discourse; in other instances, "orality" intimates at the very least that the oral dimension of the text is related in some way to the transmission of tradition. Nor do these distinctions break down neatly between Gospel narrative and Pauline epistles; Paul is a tradent in tradition even as the Gospels represent spoken discourse. While both aspects of "orality" offer insight into the nature of the text, they are not the same thing.[26] Future studies will need to strive for more careful distinctions. This can only lead to a better understanding of the oral/aural nature of the texts and how they function.

Some observations have begun to be drawn regarding the distinction between the impact of oral/aural text and that of written text. Werner Kelber comments that: "spoken words . . . produce the actuality of what they refer to in the midst of the people."[27] Thus the letters of Paul, when spoken, evoke his presence, while stories bring into the present people and events of other times and places. Antoinette Wire describes the difference in this way: "writing itself limits a story by recording only words, whereas storytelling depends for effective communication as much on the speaker's tone, volume, pace, gestures, and embodiment of direct discourse as on the words spoken."[28] While both written and spoken text can be evocative, they engage the reader/hearer in different ways. Joanna Dewey suggests that in print narrative the reader identifies with the narrator with respect to values but identifies with the characters with respect to situation; in oral narrative, the hearer identifies with both the values and the behavior of the characters as they are encountered. She describes this as "associative identification," in which the distance between the characters and the hearer is collapsed.[29] Perhaps it is because the distance between characters and hearers is collapsed that listeners are able to identify with characters sequentially, which, according to Dewey, allows them to adopt different perspectives as they move through the story.[30] This means that a single (oral) text may "tolerate different points of view in a way that print culture cannot"[31] because print culture is structured in a linear fashion and rooted in patterns of cause and effect. The implications of these insights for interpretation have only just begun to be explored. They signal, however, that the oral/aural dimension of texts describes not only how texts are structured but also how they are experienced and received.

The Oral and the Written Text

Important as these insights into the oral/aural dimensions of the biblical texts may be, we cannot escape the fact that we are able to gain access to these dimensions only through written remains. Over the past sixty years, biblical scholars have developed a much greater appreciation of this close relationship between oral and written text. Vernon Robbins ascribes this close relationship to the "rhetorical culture" of the ancient world, a culture based in the art of recitation.[32] According to Robbins, "rhetorical culture" uses both written and oral language, as well as written and oral sources and traditions, interactively. There is, indeed, an *expectation* that oral traditions will appear in written texts and written traditions will be heard in oral texts. The distinction between the two in terms of content and structure, therefore, is blurred, and no clear sequence of, for example, first oral, then written can be discerned.[33] In "rhetorical culture" the oral and the written text are bound together in a dynamic relationship.

The impact of this insight on studies of biblical texts is profound. It disrupts any notion of a clear distinction between an "oral phase" and a "written phase" and points to the reality that both oral and written versions of the same text may have been in circulation at the same time. Nor is it possible to identify any clear and specific relationship between the two. Eduard Nielsen suggests that in some cases written texts may have functioned to support oral text as a memory aid, while in other cases oral texts may have at times been written down only to resume circulation as oral text when the written text was actualized through performance.[34] This would occur as members of the audience recalled some part of or even the whole of the text and told it to others.[35] Yet in the retelling the text would be modified and adapted as the occasion and audience demanded.[36] Thus, while an oral text may have gained circulation (or re-circulation) through a written text, once in circulation it could take on a life of its own.

Although we have access only to written remains of the biblical texts, studies in orality offer criteria that allow us to at least posit oral circulation for many of the stories and narratives found in the biblical text. These may be framed as questions; for example: Do written remains point toward the independent existence of two or more versions of the same story? Does the story include a clear beginning, middle, and end, describing a single story line? Does the story exhibit characteristics associated with oral text? Does the written version diverge from the literary tendencies of the author?[37] While no single criterion, on its own, is adequate to demonstrate circulation as oral text, a persuasive case can be made for a story that satisfies all four criteria. In addition, evidence within the biblical text points toward oral circulation of at least some stories. The story of the woman accused of adultery, for example, is variously located in different manuscripts: at John 7:53—8:11, following Luke 21:28 or 24:53, and in others following John 7:36. Similarly, the story of the miraculous catch of fish is recorded in John as a post-resurrection appearance narrative, but in Luke as a pre-resurrection call narrative. This suggests that these stories did not belong to a fixed narrative setting and points to their ongoing circulation as independent texts.[38] This, in combination with the predominantly oral/aural environment of the first century, in which the vast majority of people were dependent upon memory and the spoken word, argues for the oral circulation of much of the biblical text.

This poses at the very least two interesting challenges to the assumptions that have governed biblical studies. The first challenge is to the implicit assumption that the written text represents the authoritative version. Few people in the ancient world could read or write. For the majority of people, the authority of a written text could be claimed only for its iconic value. The words themselves took on value only as they were oralized. Whether or not these words replicated precisely the signs encoded in the written text may have been of less importance. Both the Dead Sea Scrolls and the Targums, with their variable readings, seem to point in this direction, as do the variant readings of the two Testaments.[39] Efforts to identify the reading of the "original text" or to argue for the authority of one text over another may, therefore, be misplaced. It may be more helpful to consider why different versions arose and to consider each version for its respective rhetorical impact.

The second challenge is potentially more disruptive to the canons of biblical scholarship: that is the possibility that the relationships among the Gospels rest in performance rather than written texts. This possibility has most recently been advocated in studies by James Dunn. Undertaking a close examination of the differences among versions of stories found in Mark, Matthew, and Luke, Dunn notes that the core structure of these stories remains stable, yet that there is often great variability in terms of detail.[40] While redaction criticism has long focused on the consequential changes made to each text by its respective authors, these inconsequential changes have slipped by unnoticed. Dunn observes that many of the differences are so inconsequential that it is difficult to argue why they would have been made. He suggests that a plausible explanation for these differences is that "Matthew and Luke knew their own (oral) versions of the story and drew on them primarily or as well. . . . Alternatively it could be that they followed Mark in oral mode . . . as a storyteller would."[41] The possibility that the similarities between the Gospels rest not on literary dependence but on shared tradition, transmitted through performance, offers a small but significant shift in balance. The two-source hypothesis—the theory that Mark wrote first and was used as a source by Matthew and Luke, supplemented by their common use of Q and further special material unique to each, usually termed "M" and "L"—has kept us focused on the written dimension of rhetorical culture; Dunn's proposal brings into sharp focus the oral/aural dimension and underlines the significant role that performance played in the ancient world.

Texts in Performance

The oral/aural nature of our "written remains" underscores their existence in performance: They must be understood in terms of the interaction between a performer and an audience and the tangled web of discourse and experience that binds them together in a particular place and time.[42] Margaret Mills cautions us that it is necessary to have specific ethnographic information before we make assertions about a particular audience and performer.[43] For biblical scholars, this task is complicated exponentially because we can only glimpse performer, audience, and context through reconstructions based on fragments of literary and material remains. It is, nonetheless, an important part of the task.

Performance calls to the fore one of the distinctions between oral and written text. Although both texts would be performed, written texts are "fixed" in a way that oral texts are not. As Kelber has observed, however much the written text may be modified in performance, there remains a "fixed original" against which any subsequent version may be checked.[44] Whatever variations may be introduced in terms of tone, volume, pace, or gesture, the text itself remains the same. In this respect, the performance of a written text, however eloquent, is a recitation. In contrast, an oral text has no existence outside of performance. It represents an event that occurs when a performer and an audience come together in the same location.[45] There is no fixed text against which the particular performance may be compared; there are only remembrances of other performances, each offering their own variations.[46] Oral text, then, has an inherent instability.[47] The variable elements that compose a performance require that each performance produce a new formulation of the text to accommodate the shift in performer, audience, occasion, and context.[48] The hearers, too, will lend shape to the text by interjecting comments, while the performer, in turn, will need to adapt the text to the shifting demands of the audience.[49]

Because our biblical texts have survived as written remains but contain evidence of having circulated as oral texts, it is important to consider their performance both as fixed, written texts and as unstable, oral texts. Just how large the divide is between the two may be debated. Both word-for-word memorization of written texts and memorization of content are described in rhetorical manuals.[50] The degree to which memorization of content would resemble oral composition in performance remains uncertain, and we cannot determine the degree to which memorization of content would be measured against a written text. We also should not assume that oral composition was wholly free-form. Any given oral text could be expected to conform to certain structures and formulas.[51] Despite these ambiguities, the oral/aural nature of our written remains invites us to consider the variety of ways in which performance might take place.

Two recent studies each offer a distinctive approach to this challenge. Whitney Shiner, culling rhetorical manuals and other ancient texts for evidence of performance strategies, focuses on how these strategies could be employed in an oral performance of the Gospel of Mark.[52] He attends not only to the many settings in which a performance might occur but also to issues related to the memorization of text, as well as voice modulation, gestures, pace, and the crafted interaction between audience and performer. Shiner's study emphasizes the impact of performance strategy on the spoken word and its capacity to move an audience emotionally. This alerts us to the fact that the aural dimension of our texts moves beyond simply hearing words spoken aloud; it invokes conventions of performance intended to transform words into an event in which both performer and audience participate. At the same time, Shiner's study of ways in which these texts might have been seen and heard cautions us that any effort at reconstruction or reenactment must be attentive to the social and cultural conventions that produced the texts.

Shiner's study, based as it is on rhetorical manuals, explicitly focuses on more formal performance settings. In contrast, I have attempted to reconstruct an informal storytelling of the post-resurrection appearances to Mary Magdalene, based on my study of storytelling in the ancient world.[53] This self-consciously heuristic undertaking considers the shifting elements of storyteller, story, audience, and context. I describe potential types of storytellers and storytelling settings and identify the points at which a storyteller would be able to shape the gaps between the elements that represent the stable core of the story, so that it becomes a direct response to the particular audience and context. I then bring these elements together to posit two potential storytelling events that result in significantly different renderings of the story in order to underline the ways in which storytelling can serve "as a field of engagement where storyteller and audience meet in order to resolve tensions in the life of the community and establish the parameters of their life together."[54]

Attentiveness to the admittedly allusive performance of texts has begun to prompt proposals for a shift in how we study our written remains. In particular, David Rhoads, building on the work of others such as Tom Boomershine and the Bible in Ancient and Modern Media section of the Society of Biblical Literature, has begun to develop an approach that he labels "performance criticism."[55] He suggests that we cannot adequately interpret texts intended to be heard unless we hear them. What may at first glance seem like a modest proposal is, in fact, radical. It calls on skills that biblical scholars have not practiced. It is also difficult because of our limited capacity to reconstruct how, in fact, texts were both performed and heard. Nonetheless, these challenges should not deter us from "turn[ing] the act of performing itself" into "a method of research designed to interpret the text."[56] As Rhoads suggests, performance criticism will invite us to hear things that we have not observed before and understand the texts in ways that reading cannot illumine.

To uncover the performance context signaled in our oral/aural written remains is to recognize that they reference an immediate social context, described by the location of a performer and audience in a specific place and time. To complicate things further, this performance context is not stable. It shifts as the performer, audience, and occasion shift: who is present with whom and under what circumstances. There is, then, no fixed relationship between content and setting, performer and audience.[57] They are variable, and each new performance context requires a re-examination of how these elements are engaged.

Performance in Context

Vernon Robbins identifies the oral/aural dimension of our written remains as closely related to their function in rhetorical culture, that is, as ideological rationale "generated through rhetorical elaboration in support of particular social postures."[58] Texts are partisan. They are embedded in and responding to particular social and historical contexts in ways that are value-laden. This requires us to do more than establish the words of our texts. It also requires us to establish the function of texts in their historical social contexts and to see, if not a direct relationship, then a dynamic relationship between words and context.

Two recent studies have endeavored to examine our written remains specifically both as oral/aural texts and in relation to their "social postures." Wire undertakes a close reading of four types of Jewish stories in an effort to describe "who told these stories, to whom, at what occasions, and for what purposes."[59] Resisting the temptation to reduce the meaning of the stories "to what happened in it, or to tell what values it affirms," she instead looks for "structures of meaning that shape a text" by how "the text is structured in sequence, and how it is held together in scattered patterns of symbolic structure."[60] Identifying these written texts as the remains of "storytellers who happen to write," she sifts through them in order "to get access to the creative performance taking place in our texts."[61] Among the several contributions made by Wire's study is the bringing together of stories of similar structure and drawing out the many functions that such stories can be made to serve by adapting the sequence and the particular symbolic structure evoked by the text.[62] This allows us to begin to gain a sense of the "expressive forms" that were in circulation in early Christian and Jewish communities and, in addition, underlines the fundamentally persuasive nature of oral/aural texts and their capacity to invite the audience to see the world in new and different ways.[63]

Whereas Wire examines a broad range of stories, Richard Horsley and Jonathan Draper focus on a single text, Q, which they identify as a series of discourses.[64] Their goal is to undertake a comprehensive study of Q as a performance event by attending to the multiple dimensions that comprise such an event. Specifically, they endeavor to describe the "'performance arena,' which frames the audience's 'horizons of expectations'" and the ways in which "the performer performs the 'text' . . . in the dedicated 'register,' thus evoking in the audience by 'metonymic referencing' the resonating depth of the 'tradition.'"[65] What is distinctive about Horsley and Draper's study is their effort to understand how all of these elements work together to convey meaning in "concrete communication situations." This approach contrasts sharply with studies that view Q as clusters of sayings whose meaning can be understood in abstraction from the social context that is referenced in the discourses. Horsley and Draper focus on ways in which Q may have functioned to shape a community's identity in the face of and in response to specific social circumstances by drawing on a set of traditions with which the audience was not only familiar, but experienced deep resonance. Although we gain access to this function through written remains, Horsley and Draper underscore how the capacity of Q to be effective would be dependent upon the point of identification established by performer, text, and audience.

These studies reveal that attention to the oral/aural function of the text can offer insight into both the context that is referenced and how that context is reimagined through the text. If the spoken word is intended to lend support to particular "social postures" it must simultaneously reflect the context in a way that hearers will recognize and with which they will identify, and engage the hearers to a degree sufficient to create in them the capacity to entertain new social boundaries.[66] Our oral/aural written remains, then, belong to an act of social construction, an act that is undertaken through performance.

Acknowledgment of the actualization of our written remains in performance, however, also introduces to them an element of instability. The way in which each text is "framed" in specific performance contexts will create new variables. This underscores the futility of past (and present) efforts at identifying an "original text" no matter how stable the tradition may be. Yet this may represent more of a problem to those of us who are dependent upon written words than it did to the ancients. As Robert Coote suggests, "if the tradition of [a text's] transmission accepted and produced reformulations and preserved its multiforms, why should greater importance be imputed to the hypothetical original than the ancients thought it had?"[67]

Transmission of the Text

The existence of multiple forms of individual texts leads to the question of how texts were transmitted. The implications of this question range far beyond technology to reconstructions of communication practice. They also touch on our understanding of the nature and organization of early Christian communities.

Three theories of transmission dominated the twentieth century.[68] The first, put forward by Rudolph Bultmann in the early part of the century, viewed transmission as a dynamic, open process in which tradition arose out of the social life of early Christian communities. Bultmann described this process of transmission in evolutionary terms, in which tradition moved from the simple to the complex, driven by theological interests, and inexorably from the oral to the written.[69] Perhaps the strength of Bultmann's theory is the emphasis on the dialectic among community, context, and form, however inadequate this description might now appear.[70] Nonetheless, it points to the complex web of relationships that form both community identity and expressions of that identity. From the perspective of studies in orality, a major critique of Bultmann is that he is dependent upon written texts for his model of oral transmission and that he lacks appreciation for the complex nature of oral text.[71] Unfortunately, the latter legacy in many ways continues to dominate biblical studies, in which efforts to "peel away the layers" in order to derive the "original voice" of the text persist.

A second view, dating to the midpoint of the century, describes transmission as a strictly controlled process that can be traced back to eyewitnesses. Proponents of this view, in particular Birger Gerhardsson and Harald Reisenfeld, model their theory on rabbinic practices in which teachings were transmitted verbatim from rabbi to disciple through rote memorization.[72] Although rooted in historical practice, it is not clear to what degree this practice can be translated from a post–first-century context to a first-century Galilean context. Studies in orality point to additional shortcomings by observing that it is predicated on an understanding of memorization closely tied to manuscripts, rather than oral memory.[73] Kelber has noted several ways in which Gerhardsson also advanced the conversation by recognizing the aural dimension of text in the ancient world and showing an awareness of oral techniques of composition.[74] Nevertheless, these insights are overridden by an interest in tracing the unity and stability of the tradition through a line of individuals.

A third view, arising during the latter part of the twentieth century, has been proposed by Kenneth Bailey, based on his years of work in the Middle East. Bailey describes this theory of transmission as "informal controlled oral tradition."[75] Here the setting for transmission is an informal social gathering; stories and traditions may be told by anyone, although the responsibility usually falls to those who are considered good storytellers or who enjoy some status within the community—particularly if the story relates in some way to the identity of the community. Control is exercised by the community members, who judge whether or not the story is told "correctly."[76] Kelber has developed a theory of transmission along similar lines, positing that "oral transmission is controlled by the law of *social identification* rather than by the technique of verbatim memorization."[77] From the perspective of studies in orality, the strength of Bailey's proposal is that it is rooted in the actual practice of oral transmission. A limitation is its distance chronologically from the ancient world. However, my reconstruction of storytelling in the ancient world finds evidence for practices similar to those described by Bailey.[78]

This overview points to ways in which studies in orality are increasingly having an impact on our understanding of the transmission of tradition in the ancient world. A brief look at two more recent studies draws attention to ways in which social memory theory is beginning to intersect with studies of orality to shape theories of transmission. The first is by Samuel Byrskog, a proponent of the "eyewitness" model. Byrskog sets himself apart from earlier proponents of this model with his use of studies in memory. Drawing on the work of Maurice Halbwachs, Byrskog states that "groups and cultures do not remember and recall; individuals do."[79] For Byrskog, then, tradition can ultimately be traced through a line of individuals who function as bearers of tradition for the community.[80] The importance of this trajectory is that it provides continuity between the past and the present: "The deepest continuity with the past was not in memory as such but in mimesis, not in passive remembrance, but in imitation." As Byrskog explains, "What we have is 'memorative literature,' written from memory to memory."[81] While acknowledging that the performance of tradition generates "multivocal and contestive interpretations in diverse contexts,"[82] Byrskog ultimately wants to argue for a line of tradition transmitted from its source (Jesus) through eyewitnesses (Peter) to text (Mark). His appeal to social memory theory provides a theoretical basis missing in earlier studies.

In contrast, Richard Horsley and Jonathan Draper argue that composition cannot be differentiated from performance; consequently, transmission reflects a "collective cultural enterprise" embedded in "communal memory."[83] Proponents of this view, among them Werner Kelber, emphasize the variety of ways in which the community exerts control over the shape of memory. Øivind Andersen, for example, while recognizing the importance of the role played by those who are designated as "bearers of the tradition" notes that, even so, memory is dependent upon the collective: "while one member may serve as 'memory' the memory functions only if it has meaning for the body."[84] William S. Taylor, speaking to the role of the individual, adds that memory is a "product of the habits of thinking, attitudes of mind, and emotional patterns created in the individual by the society of which he is a part. They clearly reflect the cultural setting to which he belongs."[85] Here, stability arises not by the transmission of memory from one individual to another but as a result of social identification. This is not to underestimate the role of the individual but to recognize that the individual functions in dialogue with the community. For Byrskog, the community is more dependent upon the individual for both memory and identity.

I have polemicized this discussion more than is necessary, perhaps, but with a purpose. It comes down to a matter of control over the sanctity of the tradition. On the one hand are those who argue that the "tradition"—however defined—was carefully preserved and transmitted, beginning with eyewitnesses who handed the tradition on to authorized individuals and thus preserved it from corruption. On the other hand are those who emphasize the role of the community in giving shape to tradition, as it was contested among and within groups who were negotiating both meaning and structure, in part, through the use of tradition. In both theories, memory, as transmitted in tradition, is seen as a means of constructing a bridge between past events and present experience, but how that bridge is constructed differs widely. In each instance, the conclusions drawn are likely driven by the degree to which efforts to reconstruct the historical setting focus on elements of stability or instability, and these efforts are, in all probability, closely tied to the social experience, worldview, and theological interests of the interpreters. They represent, in effect, the two sides of history: stability and change. While the appeal to memory does not bring resolution to the divide between these two perspectives, it challenges us to consider both how memory was understood and how it functioned in the ancient world. Studies of our written remains in performance also should alert us that memory can serve to stabilize and to destabilize, to legitimate and to invalidate, to unify and to divide. Tradition represents contested territory.

The Power of Texts

One of the advantages of speaking in terms of "rhetorical culture" is that it neatly sidesteps the need to engage the question of whether there is, in the context of rhetorical culture, any necessary distinction between oral and written text. For some, the answer is no; the distinction is viewed as unhelpful because it creates an artificial and unnecessary divide that ultimately proves unproductive since what is left to us are the written remains of rhetorical culture. For others, the answer is yes. For them the distinctions between oral and written point to a differential in terms of access and power.

Studies of literacy in the ancient Mediterranean world place the number of people who could read, write, or do both at somewhere around 5 percent, rising to perhaps as high as 15 percent for urban males.[86] Since those who did not read or write could hire a scribe, production did not belong to the literate alone, but it did belong to those who could afford to pay a scribe and who, it must be assumed, had access to someone who could subsequently perform the written text through recitation. Not to underestimate the powers of patronage, this number must have remained small. When we speak of the close relationship between oral and written texts, therefore, we need to recognize that the written texts were relatively few, those responsible for the creation of these written texts less than a handful of the population, and, of this group, the vast majority were male. Thus it is important to raise the question of whose voice is represented in our written remains. Joanna Dewey, for example, has observed that few stories about women appear in our texts and that their role tends to be minimized. She notes that studies of European tales and their shifts from oral to written text reveals a substantial reduction in the number of stories that feature women and, in addition, that women assume more passive roles within the stories.[87] She proposes that as traditions move from oral to written text in the "rhetorical culture" of the ancient Mediterranean world, a similar shift may have occurred.[88] This is one indication that written texts that contain traditions and oral traditional texts should not be viewed as equivalents.

Kelber proposes that "those in positions of power shared a vested interest in advancing the cause of scribality because control over the medium allowed them to govern the public discourse."[89] This is because written texts conform to a single, textual perspective.[90] In addition, the existence of written texts in time and space outside of performance lends them a kind of permanence that is not shared by oral text. A written text therefore allows people who have never met to have access to the same narrative.[91] In this respect, the text takes on a life of its own and has the capacity to assume an authority that is not tied directly to interaction between a performer and an audience. This causes Antoinette Wire to raise the question, "To what degree does literacy define and intensify differences in social power and the continuing impact of traditional oral narratives in family and group identification?"[92]

In contrast, oral text is not fixed but has the capacity to be melded as the needs of changing circumstances and different audiences demand.[93] It does not exist outside of time and space. It is dependent upon the presence of a performer and an audience in the same physical space for voice and the ability to exert influence.[94] Stories that have become embedded in a community "are fought over by people with different interests" to "legitimate old social structures or new."[95] Because the authority of the text is tied to specific performance contexts, oral text "is generally more impervious to public control than the scribal medium."[96] Rather, it is dependent upon the assent of the community and represents a "largely invisible nexus of references and identities from which people draw sustenance, in which they live, and in relation to which they make sense of their lives."[97]

These differences should encourage us to guard against blurring the lines between oral and written text to the point at which all distinction is lost. Although our written remains underline the close relationship between oral and written text, they also point to the complexity of the relationship between the two, reminding us that at some points they must be viewed as separate and distinct. This leads Dewey to comment that "early Christian texts are not necessarily representative or typical of early Christianity as a whole."[98] Therefore, attention to the oral/aural dimensions of our written remains is essential, at the very least, to gaining access to the diverse expressions, interpretations, and practices of early Christianity.

Oral Texts from Written Remains

What began some sixty or more years ago as an exploration of oral tradition in the biblical text has brought us to a point at which we now see our written remains as evidence of an oral/aural culture in which written and oral texts and traditions were bound together in a dynamic relationship. This offers us opportunities to see and hear our written texts in new ways: as patterns of sound bent on the task of persuasion in particular social historical contexts in which performer and audience enter the world of the text in order to give "meaning and power to a way of life, to a cosmos become real in performance."[99] It also presses us to become even more attentive to the ways in which written and oral text differ—a challenge placed before us by Werner Kelber. The same traditions may appear in both; both may employ written and oral language; and because both are performed orally, both will be heard. Yet differences remain, not least of which are those related to power and access. To hear those other voices, we need to continue our search for oral texts and traditions in our written remains, and we must construct performance contexts that are not bound by the frame prescribed by biblical texts. This may, perhaps, bring us closer to the polemical context in which all of these texts were heard.

2

Gender and Otherness in Rabbinic Oral Culture: On Gentiles, Undisciplined Jews, and Their Women

Martin S. Jaffee

Rabbinic Judaism and the Anxiety of Oral Tradition

Oral tradition played a complex role in the classical rabbinic culture of late antiquity.[1] As a body of knowledge, it was laboriously collected, formulated for transmission,[2] and presented in ritual performances of learning.[3] As a symbol of the covenantal relationship of Israel with the Creator of the world, it guaranteed the continuity of rabbinic knowledge and authority with the founding revelations recorded in the Hebrew scriptures. For this reason, rabbinic communities by the third century CE had developed their own native terminology for their collective oral tradition: as part of the divine gift of Torah, it was called "Torah in the Mouth," to distinguish it from the "Torah in Script" that had been recorded in the scriptural books of Israel.

It should come as no surprise, then, that the acquisition, mastery, and transmission of oral tradition were the focus of some anxiety in rabbinic culture.[4] As a prominent figure in Israeli talmudic studies puts it, "The sense of danger 'lest Torah be forgotten among Israel,' and the constant

anxiety for the preservation of the Torah—upon which the existence of
heaven and earth depend—serve as a scarlet thread throughout the rabbinic literature."[5] Precisely because Torah in the Mouth was grounded
in human memory, its very existence was precarious, dependent upon
the maintenance of authoritative lines of transmission, and threatened
by the usual weaknesses of human retention and understanding. And to
the degree that the oral tradition was linked to the Torah of Moses, as
its primordial, unwritten interpretive matrix, the vulnerability of Torah
in the Mouth to forgetfulness and inattention summoned up yet a more
profound anxiety. A compromise in the integrity and continuity of the
oral tradition was no mere failure of human memory; it chipped away as
well at the foundations of the relationship that bound Israel, through its
rabbinic masters, to the covenantal love of Israel's God. So, in rabbinic
culture, quite a bit was at stake in the preservation and transmission of the
oral tradition of the holy Torah.

A foundational collection of early rabbinic wisdom-sayings, intended
to induct disciples into the ethos of the oral-traditional community of the
sages, preserves the following perspectives upon the dangers of flawed
retention of the oral tradition (*m. 'Avot* 3:7-8):[6]

> Rabbi Yaakov says: One who is walking along while repeating
> oral traditions and interrupts his repetition to exclaim: How
> lovely is this tree! How lovely is this furrow!—he is regarded[7] as
> if he had forfeited his own soul.
>
> Rabbi Doseti bar Yannai, in the name of Rabbi Meir, says:
> Whoever forgets a single word of his repetition—he is regarded
> as if he had forfeited his own soul. For it is said: "Only preserve
> yourself, and guard your soul well, lest you forget the things which
> your eyes have seen" (Deut. 4:9)
>
> Does this apply even if the difficulty of his oral traditions
> overcame him?
>
> Scripture teaches: "Lest you turn away in your heart all the
> days of your life" (Deut. 4:9[8])—thus, he forfeits his soul only if he
> turns them intentionally out of his heart.[9]

Much of the force of this passage hinges on the repeated refrain of "forfeiting the soul" (*mithayyev benafsho*). This rabbinic idiom can refer to the
punishment for a capital offense, or it can imply an eschatological punishment, in which the soul is cut off from the heavenly survival after death or
the order of existence forecast for the resurrection of the dead. We needn't
adjudicate the meaning in the present setting. The point here is simply

that the responsibility for forfeiting the soul lies with the disciple himself. Forgetfulness of oral tradition is no mere failure of memory. Deliberate or even inadvertent inattention to the perpetuation of the tradition entails consequences analogous to the willful courting of death.

One may surely object that this invocation of the death penalty for a bad memory for texts is an example of a common rabbinic tendency to overstate for the purpose of making a rhetorical point.[10] After all, the very same chapter of *m. 'Avot* informs us that "three who have dined at a single table and did not recite words of Torah might as well have eaten of sacrifices for the dead" (3:3). Nevertheless, I submit that there is an energy behind such rhetorical choices that should be explored. In the following, therefore, I probe some elements of this anxiety about the continuity and transmission of rabbinic Torah in the Mouth. The route I have chosen begins from an unconventional point of entry—some remarkable rabbinic expressions of contempt for those who are unfamiliar with the Torah of the sages. The logic of my choice is simple. If the disciple who forgets his Torah "forfeits his soul," he in a way enters into the kind of living death endured by those who never knew the tradition of Torah in the Mouth. So I ask, Who is the disciple afraid of becoming, and what does he believe about the one he does not want to be?

This question brings me to a rabbinic truism that, in fact, has inspired the title of this chapter. A brief remark in the Babylonian Talmud's tractate on the laws of the Passover celebration reports as a matter of self-evident knowledge the following social observation (*b. Pesaḥim* 49b):[11] "The hatred of the undisciplined Jews[12] for the disciples of the sages is greater than the hatred of the idolators[13] for Jews. And their women even more so!" Toward the end of this chapter I shall examine this passage in its larger talmudic literary context in order to grasp other dimensions of its meaning. But for now I only note that the larger discussion, to which this axiom is a contribution, is preoccupied with the threats posed by Gentiles, non-rabbinic Jews (the "undisciplined Jews"), and their women (as we shall see, wives and daughters) to the continuity of the tradition of oral learning.

I have wondered: What do Gentiles, Jews ignorant of rabbinic tradition, and the women associated with such Jews have in common? What singles them out as particularly threatening to the continuity of Torah in the Mouth? There is a simple and obvious answer: each of these three groups is by destiny, choice, or some combination of both, precluded from the discipleship communities of rabbinic learning. Each, so to speak, represents a state of "Torah-less-ness." Each embodies a diminished or malformed state of being from which the disciple must separate himself so as not to "forfeit his soul." To forget one's oral traditional curriculum is not simply to suffer a loss of information about law. Rather, in a way, it is to become like those who, in the first place, do not know it. In sum, Gentiles, undisciplined Jews, and their women symbolize the negation of the very thing that makes the disciple what he is—or, better, what he strives to become through his immersion in the traditions of Torah in the Mouth.

In the psychological economy that sustains and directs the project of discipleship, Gentiles, undisciplined Jews, and their women each threaten fundamental elements of self-identification that the rabbinic disciple discovers in his own being simply by observing the social composition of those with whom he labors in the vineyards of Torah. As a disciple of the rabbinic master, first of all, he knows he is not a Gentile, for, as the logic of revelation nearly requires, Torah was the portion of Israel alone. Similarly, his very inclusion in the life of the community of disciples, one that observed careful social and ritual distinctions between its members and other Jews, demonstrated to him that he was—at least no longer—an *undisciplined* Jew, a Jew at the margins of the sacred world of discourse that emerged within the rabbinic school. And finally—perhaps one could say, foundationally—the disciple knew he was not a woman, for women had played no role in the ancient processes of reception and transmission that—at least as far as sages' traditions could recall—had conveyed the Torah in Script and Torah in the Mouth from the hands of Moses to the current generation of rabbinic masters. Indeed, as I shall try to point out in what follows, his knowing what he was *not*—Gentile, ignorant, or female—was all encapsulated in the one thing with which his daily life as a disciple was permeated, the unbroken rhythms of his Torah texts, memorized and meditated, day and night, in the intimate society of other Jewish men doing the same thing.[14]

The burden of my argument in what follows will be to suggest how the nested set of negative identity markers possessed by the disciple—"I am neither a Gentile, nor an undisciplined Jew, nor a woman"[15]—are correlated to a gendered logic that holds that "my possession of Torah in the Mouth marks me as a man." This gendered logic, I hold, also engenders a deeply rooted anxiety that loss of Torah—particularly, the loss of control represented by forgetting one's learning and introducing a breach into the continuity of oral tradition—is simultaneously a loss of manhood and self. Thus at stake in the defense of the continuity of rabbinic oral tradition from the predations of Gentiles, undisciplined Jews, and their women is a kind of self-defense. For to become like a Gentile, an undisciplined Jew, or a woman is, as *m. 'Avot* insists, to "forfeit one's soul."[16]

Oral Tradition
and the Gentile Other[17]

It is most likely that the concept of Torah in the Mouth first emerged in efforts to legitimate the authority of rabbinic oral tradition within the Jewish communities among whom sages first spread their teachings.[18] But it is also clear that the concept of a revealed oral tradition appeared useful early on in encounters with Gentiles. Indeed, some of the figures whom rabbinic tradition names as its "founders" are reported to have referred to Torah in the Mouth in apologetic interactions with Gentile interlocutors. Hillel the Elder, for example, who taught during the Herodian period of Palestinian Jewish history, instructs a would-be convert to trust Hillel's rendition of the memorized Torah in the Mouth as he would trust Hillel himself to teach him how to read the Torah in Script (*'Avot of Rabbi Natan*, version A, chapter 15).[19] A somewhat later authority, Rabban Gamaliel (either the mid–first-century sage or his grandson of the same name) is depicted instructing a Roman *hegemon* in the distinction between the Torah preserved in writing and the one accessible only in oral transmission (*Sifre*, paragraph 351, to Deut 33:10).[20]

Surely the most compelling use of the distinction between the two Torahs in the context of polemic with Gentiles is one that seems to assume the fourth-century transformation of Christianity from a persecuted sect to the licit religion of the Roman Empire. I cite it here in one widespread version, found now in compositions that are likely to have been edited late in the Byzantine era or during the early Islamic period (*Pesiqta Rabbati*, 14b; cf. *Midr. Tanḥuma-Buber*, 58b–59a):[21]

> The Blessed Holy One foresaw that the Nations would translate the [Written] Torah and read it in Greek. And they would say: The Jews are not Israel!
>
> Said the Blessed Holy One to Moses: O Moses! The nations will say: We are Israel! We are the Children of the Omnipresent! And Israel, too, will say: We are the Children of the Omnipresent! . . .
>
> Said the Blessed Holy One to the Nations: What do you mean that you are my children? I recognize only the one who holds my mystery in his hands! He alone is my son!
>
> They said to Him: What is this mystery?
>
> He replied: It is the Oral Tradition (*mishnah*)!

There is in the rabbinic literature no stronger statement than this of the crucial role of Torah in the Mouth in drawing and sustaining the absoluteness of the social boundary between Israel, as the covenant community uniquely singled out by the Creator of the world, and the other nations. Behind this midrash stands the social reality of the rhetorical battle of the sages with Christian Rome over the conception of the True Israel. The Christian empire had appropriated the written texts of Scripture, translated them into the languages of the nations of the world,[22] and proposed to replace Israel as the unique community within whose boundaries divine love operates in its fullest presence. Moreover, Christian teaching had proposed that the original ethnic Israel had failed to understand its own privileged communication from the Creator. It retained the letter of scripture in the original tongue, but the spirit of the Creator had fled and now inhabited the community of the church, whose own traditions of scriptural interpretation conveyed the spirit of the divine to the New Israel of the church.[23]

In this conflict over the possession of the authoritative meaning of scripture and the validity of a community's connection to the Creator, the significance of identifying Torah in the Mouth as a mystery unique to Israel becomes paramount. Marc Bregman, in an important study, has pointed out that the word "mystery" itself bears heavily freighted meaning in early Jewish-Christian controversy.[24] Christian polemicists had, by the fourth century, extended the concept of the mystery of the faith to include not only the baptismal redemption effected upon entry into the church but also the oral tradition of interpretation that underlay the translation of the Hebrew Bible into the Greek language of the Septuagint. That is, the emerging rabbinic concept of Torah in the Mouth as a mystery that preserves Israel's covenantal relationship with the Creator is shaped by an explicit discourse with triumphant Christian supersessionism, in which the concept of oral tradition was also used to legitimate Christian appropriations of Israel's covenantal status.

The rabbinic response is, of course, to point out the superiority of Torah in the Mouth as a covenant guarantor, for it goes back to the moment of revelation itself, an ingredient of the original divine self-disclosure. Since this oral tradition does not exist in writing, it cannot be exploited or stolen. Rather, its very orality is its security, for it can only be mediated in the face-to-face setting of the community of disciples, and it can only be mastered by a process of protracted training that shapes individuals in accordance with the values, behaviors, and loyalties that are mediated in the oral tradition itself. From the perspective of the rhetoric of Torah in the Mouth, therefore, Israel is conceived not as a community possessing a book but rather as a community distinguished from all others by the living words that constitute the substance of oral-performative tradition and the social norms, or *halakhot*, that stem from it and shape concrete daily behavior. Thus Torah in the Mouth replicates within itself the essential function of the original Torah in Writing—it becomes the symbolic sign of abiding love, linking Israel as the recipient of unique revelation to the unique Creator and Revealer. It draws an absolute marker between Israel and the nations, announcing the incomparability of all nations to Israel, even as the tradition harbored by Israel, by virtue of its very orality, announces its incomparability to the traditions of all other nations, even those grounded in the scriptures first given over to Israel.

This competition between Christianity and rabbinic Judaism regarding the possession of the singular divine revelation is merely one example of a theme of competition over revelation that, by the seventh century, drew Islam into the controversy as well. Such competition is, indeed, central to the symbolic structure of monotheistic religions grounded in prophetic traditions.[25] The novelty of the rabbinic thematization, however, is the attempt to harness an extra-scriptural, orally transmitted tradition to the task of pulling along the wagon of an exclusive revelation.[26] As a monotheistic discourse of revelation, then, a fundamental rhetorical task of Torah in the Mouth is to reconstruct and restate the rhetoric at the heart of Judaism's monotheism—to declare the absoluteness of the distinction between Israel and the nations through the uniqueness of the revelation given to Israel in writing and preserved, inviolate, through the oral tradition by which revelation becomes social body.

Called into service to draw and reinforce the fundamental distinction between Israel and the Nations, the idea of Torah in the Mouth cannot be confined to this task of social demarcation alone. Rather, its power to circumscribe the border of Israel against those beyond it is turned as well inwardly, within Israel itself. There it continues to draw and maintain social divisions even within the community of the covenant. If there is within humanity as a whole an absolute distinction between Israel and its social and ontological others, there is also, through the rhetoric of Torah in the Mouth, a continuous mapping of hierarchical boundaries even within the sanctified borders of Israel. Insofar as Torah in the Mouth marks the border between Israel and humanity, it also marks and absolutizes on a smaller scale other inner-Judaic social borders.

These social borders are defined in part by the relative richness or absence of Torah within the groups subject to social definition. Two of particular relevance to our discussion are the borders between Jewish males and Jewish females, on the one hand, and between male disciples of sages and Jewish males who are not disciples of sages. We turn, then, to the ways in which the gender constructions in emergent rabbinic culture are intertwined with the rhetoric of Torah in the Mouth. These will in turn help us to understand precisely why Gentiles are classified homologously with inner-Jewish groups, in particular, Jewish women and Jewish men devoid of rabbinic learning.

Oral Tradition
and the Feminine Other

Despite some tantalizing clues to the contrary, represented by the fragmentary legendary material concerning the learned woman Beruria,[27] it is a virtual certainty that Torah in the Mouth was taught exclusively by male masters to a body of disciples from which females were explicitly excluded. With the exception of Beruria and perhaps one or two other female figures,[28] all traditions in the rabbinic literature are transmitted in the name of males, and there is no mention in narrative materials of female disciples. Women could be imagined as having "picked up" some traditions of Torah in the Mouth from fathers, husbands, or brothers who were engaged in discipleship activities,[29] but they could not be imagined as engaging in the intimate service of the sage that constituted the core of discipleship training. Recent historians of Judaism, working with models of feminist historiography that have proven successful elsewhere in uncovering the voices of females in hegemonic male cultural traditions, have come up with disappointingly little comparable material in rabbinic Judaism.[30] To be sure, there were disputes in rabbinic circles about whether or not a father should teach Torah to his daughters.[31] But it is probable that the term "Torah" in this discussion refers to the Written Torah of scriptural law or, at most, to selected oral traditional norms that touch specifically upon commandments of special relevance to women, such as the maintenance of menstrual purity, the preparation of kosher food, and perhaps the laws of personal modesty.

The important point, however, is the location in which the instruction of women is imagined. The assumption everywhere is that whatever Torah women might learn reaches them in the context of the home, where women are assumed to mingle freely only with men of their own families.[32] The primary setting of instruction in Torah is not the home but rather the space of the discipleship circle—the House of Study (*bet midrash*). This "house" is constituted not by a building set aside for the purpose of study, but by the men who gather together before the master to engage in the transmission of the oral tradition. Such a gathering might occur in a private domain, such as a home, or even in the public square or market.[33] The point, however, is that the boundary created by the discipleship circle was not so much a physical as a social space, a male discursive domain from which the female and the feminine were rigorously excluded except to the degree that women or their special status posed problems of intellectual speculation or legal reflection.[34] As Miriam Peskowitz has pointed out, "Rabbis move men out of spaces inhabited by women. To accomplish this, they must make domains belong to men, in part by moving women away. A man studying Torah is never in danger of engaging in work with women or in women's work."[35] Only in the space gendered entirely as male was the richness of the traditions of Torah in Script and Torah in the Mouth fully explored, both in practical spheres of covenantal law (*halakhah*) as well as in the purely theoretical or speculative matters incorporated into the encyclopedic knowledge of the sage.

It is important to notice that the masters of Torah in the Mouth did indeed mythologize the transmission of oral tradition in such a way as to grant its exclusively male society a kind of divine legitimation. In one of the most well-known depictions of the origin of the oral tradition now included in the Babylonian Talmud, the question is asked: "How was the oral tradition (*mishnah*) arranged for transmission?" (*b. 'Eruvin*, 54b). The answer begins: "Moses received it from the mouth of the Omnipotent. Aaron entered and Moses repeated for him his chapter." The passage goes on to explain how a series of repetitions mediated Torah in the Mouth throughout "all Israel," here defined as "the sons" of Moses, Aaron, and their disciples. Finally, at its end, two well-known sages intervene to point out that this model of repetition orally from God to Moses and from Moses to a succession of sons should be applied to the training of all disciples: "On this basis Rabbi Eliezer said that a person is obliged to repeat traditions to his disciple four times." That is to say, the discipleship community is imagined here as exclusively male. And the maleness of the community is legitimated by appeal to the origin of the oral tradition of learning in God's very own originary act of imparting oral tradition to Moses.

Thus the sacrality and holiness of the rabbinic tradition is here made to rest upon the male gender of its transmitters. This assimilation of the role of tradition-bearer to maleness begins with God himself, who, gendered in the narrative as male, establishes that the tradition of transmission can be given over only in the society of other men. Here is a fundamental manifestation of the boundary-defining impulse that links rabbinic religion to larger structures of monotheistic religions of revelation. The uniqueness of God is routinely correlated with a unique community possession—God's unique self-disclosure as revelation. Just as the idea of Torah in Judaism constitutes the uniqueness and holiness of the community of Israel among the nations that threaten it in exile, so too within the fundamental units of Jewish society the idea of Torah is linked to an exclusionary community protected by a fragile, porous border from the penetrations of threatening outsiders. The distinctly rabbinic version of this linkage, however, is much clearer in its assertion that the foundation of communal holiness—possession of Torah—is bound up with the gendered distinction of male and female. The oral tradition, defined as Torah, becomes the principle that divides males, qualified through their access to learning to enter the penumbra of holiness, from females, disqualified as outsiders.

Note that, from this perspective, Jewish women occupy a decidedly ambiguous conceptual and symbolic space.[36] As members of the historical people of Israel, Jewish women are included within the circle of the holy community and are thus distinct from the ontological other constituted by the Gentile nations. But within the community of Israel women are rendered as the other in relation to Jewish males. Only the latter are elected to be drawn into the inner circle of divine communion represented by the boundaries of the discipleship community, which is joined together by the sharing of Torah in the Mouth. In the monotheistic rhetoric represented by Torah in the Mouth as a symbol of revelation, Jewish women are gendered as male only to the degree that they are conceived collectively as part of the people Israel over against the feminized Gentile nations. Only as Israel do women lay any claim to Torah as an ontological plenitude denied to the nations. Theirs, however, is a thoroughly derivative maleness, extended to them only in a formal sense because of their inclusion in the polity of Israel. But within Israel disciples of sages alone possess the principle of maleness represented by Torah in the Mouth.[37]

This ambiguity of the conceptual space occupied by Jewish women yields yet another principle when it is replicated and applied. It turns out that Jewish women are not the only females in the nation of Israel.[38] Men, too, can be gendered as female, to the degree that they are not absorbed into the holy communion of discipleship to the sage and his distinctive

Torah. This raises for us our final question: What role does the feminization of the undisciplined Jew play in rabbinic anxiety about the preservation and transmission of the tradition of Torah in the Mouth?

Oral Tradition and the
Undisciplined Jewish Other

The classical literature of rabbinic oral tradition, from the Mishnah
through the Talmuds, recognizes a fundamental social distinction between
Jewish men who participate in the life of rabbinic discipleship and those
who are either passively beyond its boundaries or actively antagonistic
to the rabbinic disciples. Both groups of non-rabbinic Jews are classified
under the encompassing term, 'ammey ha-'arets. This is a term with a biblical genealogy that refers originally to "people of the land," or peasants.
In rabbinic usage its meaning normally can be rendered simply as "those
ignorant of or nonobservant of Torah as the sages expound it." For the
purpose of this chapter, I have rendered the term as "undisciplined Jews"
in order to underscore that the key distinction is between Jewish disciples
of sages and Jews who are not trained in the rabbinic discipline of Torah
in the Mouth.[39]

The range of rabbinic discussion of the 'ammey ha-'arets concerns
a variety of legal issues raised by the fact that the 'ammey ha-'arets
are fully Jews and bound by the Sinaitic covenant yet fail to live up
to the terms of that covenant to the degree that they do not practice
many elements of the rabbinic discipline enumerated in the oral tradition of Torah in the Mouth, particularly those concerning avoidance
of menstrual impurity, details of food preparation, liturgical traditions,
and so forth. Accordingly, full social intercourse with them opens up
a variety of dangers that have the power to influence disciples and
their households to abandon or weaken their loyalty to the covenantal
traditions of Torah in the Mouth taught by the sages. So, as a legal
problem, the 'ammey ha-'arets represent the issue of how to interact
with those who are wholly Israel—non-Gentile—yet by their very
existence constitute a permeable border through which the boundary between Israel and the nations can be threatened. Rabbinic discussions of these issues exhibit a wide variety of emotional overtones,
from benign dispassionate discussion of purely legal issues to some
altogether vicious expressions of contempt and hatred for the 'ammey

ha-'arets.[40] Some of the most vicious passages are found in discussions in which the distinction between male and female Jews is also of interest.

Such passages suggest that the rabbinic attitude of dismissal and contempt for the undisciplined Jews is grounded in the same gendered logic that excludes Jewish women from the House of Study. Women are "by nature" excluded from the discipleship circle, while the undisciplined Jew excludes himself "by choice." Whether one's ignorance of the oral tradition is a natural fact or a deliberate choice, that ignorance is read by disciples as a feminizing trait. In the economy of rabbinic social imagination, therefore, ignorant Jews are symbolically homologous to women. A text from the Babylonian Talmud illustrates the ways in which women and undisciplined Jews stand for a feminizing principle to be avoided by disciples whenever possible.

The tractate *b. Berakhot* 43b reports and comments upon a teaching received from the transmitters of the Mishnaic tradition of Torah in the Mouth. It concerns behaviors that should be avoided by disciples of rabbinic sages lest the reputations of disciples and the honor of Torah in the Mouth be called into question:[41]

> Our Masters taught as oral tradition:
> Six things bring disrepute upon a disciple of the sages:
> 1. He should not go about perfumed in public;
> 2. and he should not go about alone at night;
> 3. and he should not go out with patched shoes;
> 4. and he should not chat with a woman in public;
> 5. and he should not recline in the symposia of the
>   *'ammey ha-'arets*;
> 6. and he should not be last to enter the House of Study.

With the possible exception of the injunction against patched shoes, the factors that bring the disciple into disrepute share a common trait: each suggests a pattern of behavior that blurs or otherwise confuses conventional distinctions between male and female actions or domains of dominance. In other words, the "disrepute" with which these behaviors threaten the disciple involves, in one form or another, the feminization of an identity that, because of its immersion in the system of oral tradition, ought to represent a monolithic male persona—the very antithesis of the undisciplined Jew for whom the oral tradition remains a foreign body of knowledge.

Let us begin with items 4 through 6, since these make explicit the intersecting sets of values ascribed to women, the *'ammey ha-'arets*, and learning in Torah in the Mouth. The disciple avoids public association with women, lest he be suspected of erotic associations with them in private;[42] he avoids socializing in the fellowship of the undisciplined Jews lest, as the Talmud goes on to explain, "he be drawn after them"; and he avoids being late to the academy where Torah in the Mouth is mastered. If we restate these proscriptions in terms of the gendered logic that informs rabbinic thinking about oral tradition, the following proposition emerges: the disciple must be early to the study hall, for it constitutes the primary site of his demonstration of masculine virtue. To tarry beyond the disciple circle's male fellowship is to place at risk the true source of his masculinity.

Hence, precisely in the marketplace that demarcates a space beyond the protective precinct of the male House of Study, he must avoid association with women who might tempt him to express masculinity beyond the parameters of Torah in the Mouth. Similarly, he avoids the commensal fellowship of Jewish men whose lack of immersion in the oral tradition guarantees that their tables will be devoid of words of Torah.[43] The disciple who reclines in the symposia of the undisciplined Jews, therefore, submits himself to precisely that diminished quality of masculinity that he risks by consorting too freely with women. Ultimately, the undisciplined Jew is to be avoided for the same reason that a woman is to be avoided—each represents the negation of the body of knowledge and behaviors that constitute the core of the disciple's identity as a Jew and a man.

The idea that the disrepute of a disciple is in some sense bound up with behaviors that signal his feminization clarifies the meaning of the first two items in this list as well. The Talmud's discussion of the injunctions against going about perfumed and going out at night reveals that each of these behaviors bears feminizing overtones. According to the disciples of Rabbi Yohanan (b. Berakhot 43b), the perfumed disciple is suspected of soliciting male sexual attention, thereby feminizing himself sexually in relation to another male.[44] Item 2, for its part, is clarified under the interpretive rubric of item 4. The one venturing out at night without a clearly established prior appointment is suspected—like the disciple in the habit of drawing women into public conversation—of encouraging some sort of illicit sexual assignation.[45]

In light of the concern here for the feminization of the disciple, it is legitimate to propose that a hermeneutic of gender may explain the presence of patched shoes (item 3) in this list as well. Other rabbinic texts suggest that the dress of sages included distinguishing garments such as the toga (Hebrew: talit), which served as identity markers and symbols of authority.[46] If so, worn shoes would signify an interruption of the message of male mastery that the toga is designed to convey—a sign of imperfection and incompletion in an otherwise perfect presentation of the masculine self.[47] Regardless of the ambiguity of the meaning of patched shoes, the tendency of the list in its entirety is unmistakable. The disrepute suffered by the disciple is brought about by the confusion that his behaviors raise regarding the gendered identity of the person immersed in the tradition of Torah in the Mouth. This identity is rooted in the mastery of oral tradition in the exclusively male setting of the House of Study, where disciples achieve their simultaneous perfection as Jews and men through the incorporation into their beings of the authorizing words of the oral tradition. The world beyond the House of Study, the world of the street and markets, inhabited by Gentiles, women, and undisciplined Jewish men, is consequently a world in which the disciple's display of Torah-structured masculinity must be impeccable. A chink in the behavioral armor of masculinity—over-familiarity with a woman, a worn shoe, a fondness for the company of undisciplined men—is a threat, therefore, not only to the masculine identity of the Torah disciple but to the honor of the Torah itself, which preserves the very identity of Israel as the exclusive community of the Creator of the world.

Gentiles, Undisciplined Jews, and Their Women

In reflecting upon *b. Berakhot* 43b's concern for the disrepute of the disciple, I have been struck by the kind of threat that the feminizing qualities associated with the undisciplined Jews and their women represents. The feminine is not a passive presence that the disciple is encouraged to actively engage and dominate through his own masculine mastery. Rather it is embodied in social others—undisciplined Jews and their women—who are represented as actively hostile, aggressive agents of whom disciples must be wary and with whom they should minimize their relations. There is little confidence here in the ability of the disciple—outside the secure setting of the House of Study at least—to resist these feminized others and to withstand the risk of his own feminization that they embody. Rather, there is a gnawing anxiety that any social associations uninflected by the Torah tradition of the sages will lead to the tradition's disruption and, therefore, the loss of the disciple's carefully cultivated identity as a Jew and a man.

This anxiety—which sees the threat of feminization embodied by undisciplined Jews and women as hostile social others—lies at the heart of the final talmudic passage before us. I turn at last to *b. Pesahim* 49a-b, whose contemptuous discussions of women and undisciplined Jews have troubled talmudic commentators from early post-talmudic times to the present.[48] We encountered its discussion of the hatred of Gentiles, undisciplined Jews, and women for the rabbinic sages at the outset of this chapter, and we are now in a position to review the entire passage within which it appears. As the context shall make clear, the animosity of some rabbinic traditionists toward these paradigmatic others is grounded to a significant measure in a deep anxiety that they threaten the disciple's ability to sustain not only his own participation in the life of oral traditional learning but also that of his offspring.

The tractate *b. Pesahim* 49a-b is a literary collage, composed of materials stemming from second- and early third-century teachers of the Mishnaic line of tradition (*tannaim*) as well as post-Mishnaic teachers of the third and fourth centuries (*amoraim*) and later anonymous editors and glossators (*stammaim*). Thematically, the passage is introduced with recommendations for ensuring that the disciplines of Torah in the Mouth shall be transmitted from disciples of sages to their offspring.[49] The crucial first step is to contract the right sort of marriage. And it is precisely this recognition—that the continuity of the oral tradition from father to son depends upon the intervention of a woman to bear the son—that draws in its wake further reflections on the threats that women—and others like them—pose to the disciples of the sages:[50] "Our masters transmitted an oral tradition: A person should sell everything he has in order to marry the daughter of a disciple of the sages. For if he dies or incurs exile, he can be certain that his sons will be disciples of the sages. But he should not marry the daughter of an undisciplined Jew. For if he dies or incurs exile, his sons will be undisciplined Jews." The piety of the father is assumed here to determine the piety of the other members of the household. Accordingly, a disciple of the sages should make every material sacrifice in order to marry a woman whose father is himself a disciple. Only in this way can the continuity of the familial tradition of Torah in the Mouth be secured. In the event of the father's death or deportation, it is assumed that the father-in-law will assume responsibility for transmitting the oral tradition to his daughter's sons. In a marriage with the daughter of an *'am ha-'arets*, obviously, no one would be able to step in for the deceased father. Without a man to transmit the tradition to the son, the son would be lost to the tradition.

> Our masters transmitted an oral tradition: A person should sell
> everything he has in order to marry the daughter of a disciple
> of the sages and to marry off his daughter to a disciple of the
> sages. This is analogous to grafting grape vines with grape vines,
> producing a lovely and pleasant union. But he should not marry
> the daughter of an undisciplined Jew. This is analogous to graft-
> ing grape vines with the fruit of a weed, producing an ugly and
> unacceptable union.

The vinticultural metaphor suggests that the differences between disciples and undisciplined Jews are not merely behavioral. The possession of
Torah in the Mouth transforms, as it were, one's species being. Thus mar-
riages contracted with daughters of the undisciplined Jews produce a kind
of stunted offspring. This text introduces a fundamental theme explored
in what follows: the fundamental gap of being that separates the disciples
from the 'ammey ha-'arets.

> Our masters transmitted an oral tradition: A person should sell
> everything he has in order to marry the daughter of a disciple of
> the sages. If he can't find the daughter of a disciple of the sages, let
> him marry the daughter of a leader of the generation. If he can't
> find the daughter of a leader of the generation, let him marry a
> leader of the assembly. If he can't find the daughter of a leader of
> the assembly, let him marry the daughter of a charity collector.
> If he can't find the daughter of a charity collector, let him marry
> the daughter of a teacher of children. But let him not marry the
> daughter of an undisciplined Jew, for they are abominations and
> their women are vermin [in the virulence of their uncleanness].
> And regarding their women Scripture says: "Accursed is anyone
> who lies with a beast" (Deut 27:21).

The passage describes a descending hierarchy of social rank, with disciples
of sages at the top and undisciplined Jews at the bottom. Between them
are Jews who, while not disciples in a formal sense, share with the sages
responsibility for leading the Jewish community and maintaining its institutions. It is taken for granted that women's place in the social hierarchy is
geared to the ranks of their fathers. Thus it follows that one should marry
into the highest possible level of the hierarchy. Those daughters closest to
the Torah in the Mouth possessed by their fathers are the most desirable
matches; those furthest away are the least desirable.

The equation of the daughters, and by implication, the wives, of
undisciplined Jews as "vermin" and "beasts" may be hyperbolic, but the

metaphors are nevertheless important. They propose that the social division between those who possess Torah in the Mouth and those who do not is also in some sense ontological, distinguishing the truly human from the less-than-human. Note that those furthest from the possession of oral tradition—the women of undisciplined Jews—are precisely those associated metaphorically with beasts. Thus, the possession of Torah in the Mouth is the defining trait of the fully human individual.

> An oral tradition is transmitted: Rabbi[51] says: An undisciplined Jew is prohibited from eating meat, for Scripture says: "This is the Torah [for consumers of] beasts and fowl" (Leviticus 11). That is, those who engage in Torah are permitted to consume beasts and fowl. But all who do not engage in Torah are prohibited from eating beasts and fowl.

Women drop from the passage, and the species distinction between the disciple and the undisciplined Jew comes again into view. The passage is unclear why Torah scholarship entitles one to eat meat. A possible interpretation, offered by the thirteenth-century Provençal Talmudist R. Menahem ha-Meiri (*Hiddushei ha-Meiri*), is that the ignorance of the 'am ha-'arets regarding the laws of preparing kosher meat should disqualify him from consuming it. The point might also be that the disciple is analogous to a priest, for whom consumption of meat had been an entitlement in Temple times. In light of the literary context of the passage, however, and the larger gender dynamic we have noticed, I am inclined to argue that the point here is to correlate the possession of full humanity with the privilege of taking animal life for food. If so, it is the humanizing principle of Torah in the Mouth, embodied in the fully realized humanity of the disciple, that conveys this privilege.

> Said Rabbi Elazar: It is permitted to stab an undisciplined Jew on the Day of Atonement that falls on the Sabbath [despite the prohibitions against using weapons on these days]. Said to him his disciples: "Rabbi! Don't you mean that it is permitted to slaughter him ritually?" He replied: "The latter requires a blessing, but the former does not [and is thus preferable]."

The theme of the undisciplined Jew as beast continues. From a practical halakhic perspective, the case is an absurdity, since there is no warrant in rabbinic law for wanton murder. But the factual absurdity is a rhetorical device in which to express the view that the life of the undisciplined Jew—devoid of the humanizing influence of Torah—is comparable to that of a beast. The current passage is perhaps intended to be darkly humorous (*Ḥiddushei ha-Meiri*), pointing out that a benediction for a kosher slaughter would be wasted on the undisciplined Jew. But the humor seems lost on the classical commentators, many of whom seem frankly horrified by this interchange. R. Shmuel Eliezer haLevi Idels (*Ḥiddushei Halakhot ve-Aggadot ha-Maharsha*), for example, interprets the language of murder as a metaphor, giving license to rebuke and humiliate nonobservant Jews even on the most hallowed day of the year in order to restore them to the proper path. Others, relying upon the rabbinic concept of justifiable manslaughter, specify that the passage applies only to a particularly vicious 'am ha-'arets who, in a berserk fit, is bent on rape or murder. Murdering him is thus permitted so as to spare the life of the would-be victim.

> Said Rabbi Elazar: An undisciplined Jew is prohibited from accompanying [a disciple of the sages] on a journey. As it is said: "For it [Torah] is your life and the length of your days" (Deut 30:20). He shows no concern for his own life [since he does not study Torah]; all the more so for the life of his companion.

The 'am ha-'arets, lacking the humanizing possession of Torah in the Mouth, also lacks the normal restraints of passion and instinct that guide the disciple. Nevertheless he willingly places his life at risk by refusing to disciple himself to the sages. His contempt for the sages' Torah compels him to have contempt even for his own life. Accordingly, he can also be assumed to have no regard for the lives of those who devote themselves to the cultivation of oral tradition. In this passage, the implication is pushed to an extremity; the disciple who travels in the companionship of an undisciplined Jew risks being murdered once they have traveled beyond a populated area.

> Said Rabbi Shmuel bar Nahmani said Rabbi Yonatan:[52] You are permitted to tear an undisciplined Jew apart like a fish.
> Said Rabbi Shmuel bar Yitzhak: Down the back.

It is difficult to know whether Rabbi Shmuel bar Yitzhak disputes the recommendation of his colleague or is providing instructions on how to perform the task of dismembering the undisciplined Jew.

> An oral tradition is transmitted: Said Rabbi Aqiva: When I was an undisciplined Jew, I used to say: "If I could get a disciple of

the sages I'd bite him like a donkey." His disciples replied to him: "Rabbi! Don't you mean like a dog?" He replied: "The former bites and breaks the bones; the latter bites and does not break the bones."

Rabbi Aqiva is recalled in rabbinic literature as an 'am ha-'arets who only began studies of the Written and Oral Torah in midlife.[53] Here he testifies to the hatred he harbored against the disciples of sages. The recollection, of course, justifies rabbinic hostility to the undisciplined Jews: rabbinic hatred is a defensive response to the irrational hatred of the 'ammey ha-'arets for the disciples. The reminiscence, not incidentally, discloses as well the suspicion that the 'am ha-'arets is always lurking within one's own self.[54] One hates the undisciplined Jew for representing precisely what one is terrified of becoming.

> An oral tradition is transmitted: Rabbi Meir used to say: Whoever marries off his daughter to an undisciplined Jew is as if he tied her up and placed her before a lion. Just as a lion paws and eats and has no shame, so too an undisciplined Jew is sexually violent and has no shame.

We return to the theme of the appropriate marriage partner for the daughter of a disciple. Before us again is the representation of the 'am ha-'arets through a bestial metaphor. The 'am ha-'arets is metaphorically likened in his sexual practices to a beast of prey. Lacking Torah in the Mouth, he is humanly diminished. Like the daughters of the 'ammey ha-'arets presented earlier, he is closer to "beasts" than to humanity.

> An oral tradition is transmitted: Rabbi Eliezer [b. Yaaqov][55] says: If we weren't necessary to them for trade they'd murder us.

The received text, represented above, suggests that only economic necessity prevents the 'ammey ha-'arets from murdering the sages. This resumes the idea that the 'ammey ha-'arets are bestial in their natures and therefore more likely to engage in acts such as rape and murder. Not incidentally, rabbinic hostility is justified in light of the homicidal fantasies imputed to the undisciplined Jew. As we saw above in the debate about the proper slaughter of an 'am ha-'arets, however, the sages had some fantasies of their own. This is reflected in the text version preferred by Stephen Wald (p. 212, 238): If they weren't necessary to us for trade, we'd murder them.

> Rabbi Hiyya transmitted an oral tradition: Whoever engages in
> Torah before an undisciplined Jew is like one who has sex with
> his betrothed in front of him. For it is said: "Torah did Moses
> command us as an inheritance (*morashah*)" (Deut 33:4). Don't
> read it as inheritance; read it as "betrothal" (*meorasah*).

The point depends upon the assonance of the Hebrew terms for "inheritance" and "betrothal," which I have introduced into the translation. As in
preceding units of tradition, here, too, metaphors carry the burden of the
discussion. The likening of Torah study to sexual relations drives home
the exclusivity with which the relationship of disciple to the oral tradition
is imagined. To engage in Torah study before the undisciplined Jew is to
violate a cherished privacy and to demean both the disciple and his Torah.
This, of course, raises a logical conundrum: if the injunction is taken seriously, how can Torah ever be taught? The matter is not pursued here.

> The hatred of the undisciplined Jews for disciples of the sages
> is greater than the hatred of the idolators for Israel. And their
> women even more so!

This passage, cited at the beginning of this chapter, is the fullest equation
of the 'am ha-'arets, the feminine, and the Gentile. The purest and most
implacable hatred is held by the Gentile nations for the entire people
Israel. However, within the Jewish people, the 'ammey ha-'arets and especially their women harbor a hatred for the bearers of oral tradition that
exceeds even the hatred of Gentiles for Jews. Thus the Gentiles are to the
Jewish people what the 'ammey ha-'arets and their women are to the disciples of the sages. Each reiterates the implicit opposition of knowledge
of Torah versus ignorance, maleness versus femaleness, and humanness
versus bestiality.

> An oral tradition is transmitted: One who learned oral tradition
> and gave it up has hatred greater than all of them!

The passage ends with a surprising twist that highlights the anxiety
underlying the entire discussion. The hatred of Gentiles for Jews and
of undisciplined Jews and their women for the sages cannot compare to
yet one other passionate hatred—that of the man who has rejected the
teachings of the sages after having mastered the oral tradition that bears
them. Thus the disciple who discontinues his learning does not merely

"forfeit his soul," as *m. 'Avot* 3:7-9 has put it. Worse still, he brings into the center of the sages' society the hatred that normally exists only at the margins of the discipleship circle. More appalling than the Gentile, who is outside the redemptive penumbra of Torah, and worse even than the undisciplined Jew and his women, who reject the traditions of the sages, is the man who, having incorporated the oral tradition into his being, spits the humanizing Torah from his mouth and rejects the tradition that his peers so assiduously cultivate. In this concluding tradition, the logic of the entire passage comes to its fruition. The ultimate feminized role—and thus, the greatest source of hostility to those who are most deeply marked by the maleness of the oral tradition—is the defecting sage.

The Talmud at this point moves on to other concerns beyond our own range of interests. But let us consider what we have seen. These texts, we must remind ourselves, are extreme formulations, rather than conventional rabbinic opinions. They lead us into the darker regions of male rabbinic culture, where the "ways of pleasantness" made possible by the possession of Torah compete with fantasies of violence, where conceptions of Torah as a gift to all of Israel—and even, in some currents of the rabbinic tradition, to all of humanity[56]—run up against a hunger to preserve the Torah as the special possession of a closed community within Israel. Given the tradition of misrepresenting the Talmud in service of anti-Semitic polemics against Judaism, one hastens to affirm that these are not representative rabbinic opinions. These opinions nevertheless were retained for circulation and preservation in the primary anthology of Babylonian rabbinic oral tradition. They therefore require us to say something about the center of rabbinic social imagination as well, for although few compilers of rabbinic tradition may have recommended the attitudes represented here, they obviously did not find them offensive enough to suppress them.

Symbolic Gentiles, Feminine Others

Let us recall the matter that has generated our discussion. At issue are the implications of the rabbinic movement's appropriation of a rhetoric of revelation to universalize rabbinic oral tradition as the oral part of the Torah given to, and binding upon, all Israel. At a stroke, this rhetoric of revelation swept rabbinic concepts of oral tradition into a larger pattern of discourse characteristic of the deeply exclusivist patterns of monotheistic social thought and soteriology. This ensured that rabbinic Torah in the Mouth would serve as the symbolic preserver of the distinction between Israel and the surrounding, threatening Gentile nations. It ensured as well that the division between the recipients of revelation and those beyond its light would be reproduced within the community of the people of revelation itself. Within Israel, in other words, there would be found those who were, in some sense, like the Gentiles in their exclusion from Torah. But, of course, since the Torah, as everyone knew, had been given to all Israel, who among Israel could serve to symbolically embody the Torahless Gentile?

This is the point at which we can recognize the crucial role of the rabbinic representation of the oral tradition as Torah in the Mouth. Oral tradition, as sages experienced it, was a richly social phenomenon, carrying with it a host of social messages. Insofar as the tradition was transmitted in face-to-face discursive circles, with a minimal reference to authoritative written sources outside of scripture itself, it defined itself as a tradition that would be exclusive. Oral tradition would be learned among men alone, for women by definition could not—or, at best, did not need to—learn, and oral tradition would be the possession of an elite circle of men, since not all men were able or willing to learn. Inevitably, engagement in oral traditional learning became, among the disciples at least, a marker of male identity and entitlement. At the same time, it marked men outside of the disciple circle as lesser men, feminine in gender if not in sex.

Presumably, such gendering of the value of possessing oral tradition could well have preceded the rabbinic transformation of oral tradition from a human "tradition of the ancestors"[57] to a part of the Torah received from Moses at Sinai. But the transformation of oral tradition into Torah in the Mouth, into a part of revelation, cast Jewish women and non-rabbinic Jewish men almost necessarily into a new structure of identity. Prior to the spread of the rabbinic conception of Torah, a Jewish man or woman who may have been ignorant of "oral tradition" was still no less a Jew, for the ability to transmit "oral tradition" as such had not yet become a conventional marker of Jewishness. But with the ascendancy of the rabbinic ethos of oral tradition, a Jewish man or woman who was ignorant of Torah in the Mouth was now a kind of Gentile, a Gentile within Israel. So as oral tradition became ensconced in rabbinic theological imagination as vehicle for the transmission of Torah, the symbolism of the Gentile began to permeate the borders of Jewish society. Rabbinic disciples begin to create within the Jewish polity symbolic Gentiles ignorant of rabbinic tradition. Correspondingly, by a certain symbolic synergy, the representation of the feminine began to map itself beyond women's bodies onto the body of Jewish society. Defined in opposition to the male prerogative of engagement in Torah in the Mouth, the feminine now absorbed the most visible social other within the Jewish community apart from biological women—the vast majority of Jewish men, who were uninvolved in or actively hostile to the small, elitist rabbinic discipleship communities. Finally, once the feminization of those without Torah in the Mouth begins as an intra-Jewish phenomenon, its logic imposes itself upon the symbolization of Gentiles as well, those who of necessity are excluded by the very revelation that singles out Israel as the focus of divine attention.

It should not, then, be difficult to understand the relationship between the anxiety of rabbinic disciples regarding the fragility of their mastery of oral tradition and the simmering hostility toward Gentiles, undisciplined Jews, and their women. In the sectors of the rabbinic community that transmitted the texts discussed above, we discern the cohabitation of two fundamental attitudes. The first is immense gratitude for the exclusive gift of revelation that lifts Israel beyond the nations into a male community homologous to the Creator of the world. The second is a profound anxiety that the unique role of Israel as the recipient of Torah in Writing and Torah in the Mouth is threatened by the disciple's association with others who represent, by the absence of Torah among them, the negation of the maleness that links Israel, alone among the nations, to the Creator. To preserve Israel's maleness is to preserve God's Torah. And to preserve that Torah it is necessary to protect it within the male preserve of the House of Study—from which are excluded the Gentiles, the undisciplined Jews, and their women.

To the degree that possession of Torah in the Mouth is a male prerogative, gained within the confines of an exclusively male community, Torah in the Mouth becomes the sign of maleness and the symbol of ontological richness. By contrast, the social world beyond the charmed circle of Torah learning—inhabited by the homologous entities of the Gentile nations, undisciplined Jews, and Jewish women—is constructed as a world of feminized and feminizing emptiness. To allow that world into oneself—by forgetting one's oral traditions or, worse, by rejecting the entire discipline of rabbinic discipleship—is indeed to "forfeit one's soul."[58]

3

Many Voices, One Script:
The Prophecies of George Khambule

Jonathan A. Draper

From Prophecy to Text

When Rudolf Bultmann[1] claimed that most of the recorded sayings of Jesus are actually the words of prophets speaking in the name of the Risen Lord, he placed the issue of how oral performance played a role in transmitting the Jesus tradition squarely on the agenda of New Testament studies. His assertion is not based on any theory of oral performance nor on any particular study of the nature of prophecy itself. Subsequent attempts to refine his assertion by his students and disciples did not succeed in producing any consensus.[2] Instead, the gauntlet he threw down was taken up by three major studies in the United States just over twenty years ago, by Eugene Boring,[3] David Aune[4] and Werner Kelber.[5] Boring largely affirms the concept of prophetic creativity as the "transition point from proclaimer to the proclaimed" Son of Man.[6] Aune's encyclopedic study insists on an understanding of prophetic traditions in the Mediterranean world as the broad cloth against which any study of the prophetic tradition originating from Jesus must be examined. He finds the idea that the community could not tell the difference between sayings of the earthly Jesus and sayings of prophets after his resurrection speaking in his name "inconclusive" and falls back on the possibility of memorization in the transmission of the earliest Jesus tradition.

Kelber took the debate in a new direction by applying anthropological studies of orality. He challenged the textual bias of western scholarship in assuming a smooth, linear process of development from oral performance to written text.[7] Since oral transmission is always simultaneously composition, there is no original form, but only particular performances in appropriate social contexts in which the tradition is found to be socially relevant and acceptable. Hence the attempt to find the original form of a saying of Jesus is a futile and misguided enterprise. Kelber demanded a much more careful study of the mnemonics and social dynamics of transmission. Twenty years later, *The Oral and the Written Gospel: The Hermeneutics of Speaking and Writing in the Synoptic Tradition, Mark, Paul, and Q*, supplemented by his continuing contributions to the study of orality and literacy, remains a classic, encouraging a new generation of New Testament scholars to take oral performance seriously.

In this chapter I explore a case study of the growth of material from oral performance to text involving a Zulu prophetic community that followed the prophet George Khambule (1884–1949). I have charted the history and nature of the church iBandla Labancwele elsewhere.[8] Here, in response to Kelber's challenge, I will examine the written texts produced by this largely illiterate community to show the way in which they both mask and reveal multiple voices and the dynamics of oral performance in the production of text.

George Khambule and iBandla Labancwele

George Khambule was born in the rural "tribal reserve" of Zululand at Telezini near Nqutu, but he was descended from the educated Methodist mission elite from Edendale near Pietermaritzburg, the capital of colonial Natal.[9] His father had taken advantage of the alliance of his family with the followers of the Sotho mercenary Chief Hlubi Molife to obtain a share of the land granted to the chief for his services in the war against King Cetshwayo. George was educated up to Standard 4, probably at the famous mission school at St. Augustine's, Nqutu. He served in the South African Native Labour Corps on the Western front in the First World War[10] and subsequently became a captain of mine police in Johannesburg. He taught music as a sideline. He applied for and received status as an "exempted native" under Natal law, which exempted him from tribal law.

On October 18, 1918,[11] he was taken to the hospital. Here he claims to have experienced death and to have been called to account for his sins. His dead sister, Agnes or Agrineth, whom he had assisted while she was alive, intervened with God on his behalf, and he was sent back down to earth to warn people of God's impending judgment. Hearing of his conversion, a revivalist prophet from his home area, John Mtanti, summoned him to join in a mission to build the new Jerusalem. Khambule then worked with him, preaching within the Methodist framework, but on June 20, 1922,[12] he had a vision that the Ark of the Lord "which used to be handled by the cherubim is going to be handed to you." In other words, the throne of God's kingship was to be established in his church in fulfillment of the book of Revelation. This necessitated the establishment of an *isigodlo*, or royal harem, of maidens to care for the Ark, the throne of the King, just as the Zulu king required an *isigodlo* of maidens and an old woman as guardian to protect his *inkatha*, or magical throne woven from grass.[13] All members, male and female, of the newly established church, the iBandla Labancwele, were required to enter the marriage of the Lamb and become celibate. In line with Zulu custom, the young women of the *isigodlo* could join the harem before puberty and be initiated as royal brides when they obtained puberty after appropriate rituals had been performed. Khambule's *isigodlo* contained girls as young as twelve, who put themselves outside the control of their male heads of family. This caused unrest and litigation in the local community, and the main substance of the charges against Khambule was that he was abducting young girls. They were also forbidden to eat food outside the community, since this was likely to have been offered to what Khambule considered to be idols (that is, as libations offered to the ancestors). Members of the healing group or hospital (*isibedlela*) received special stones of power (red-and-black volcanic stones) as weapons (*izikhali*) in the battle against Satan. Each member received the name of one of the angels who were present in the worship of the community and could prophesy by means of that angel. Khambule himself and his two women prophets could also use a field telegraph, which he had observed in operation in Europe, to receive encrypted messages from God directly, and these could then be interpreted.

The formation of a separate and exclusive apocalyptic community of the new Jerusalem in the midst of a traditionally minded mixed Zulu and Sotho community led to major conflict. The magistrate of Nqutu took steps as early as 1924 to have Khambule expelled from the reserve, but he was frustrated by Khambule's status as a native exempted from tribal law living legitimately on land he had inherited from his father in a tribal area. The legal complications requiring consultations among the Minister for Native Affairs, the Department of Justice, and the Natal Chief Native Commissioner allowed Khambule and his followers a period of three years of immunity before they were finally driven out. Khambule was only forced to hand over the keys after compensation of 250 pounds sterling had been paid to him on February 18, 1927, and then it was only in 1930 that the land was finally sold by the state to the Church of Sweden Mission. This appeared a major victory to Khambule and his followers, who were much celebrated in their place of exile (Elim) in the following years, even as their church declined; they eventually bought a farm and settled at Spookmill near Dundee. Khambule himself spent much of his time working on the mines and running the branch of the church in Johannesburg until his death in 1949, while his brother-in-law, Mordekai Sikakane, continued the church at Spookmill until his death and the church's dissolution in 1970.

One of the distinguishing marks of Khambule's movement is that it left behind more than six hundred pages of handwritten Zulu script. There are four carefully dated diaries, two liturgies, two hymnbooks. Bengt Sundkler, who preserved and interpreted these writings, assumes that they are diaries in the European genre of personal introspection and private record. Here Khambule could speculate and "continue his argument in the relative safety of his diary."[14] Sundkler assumes that Khambule is himself newly literate and his words are "a string of loose letters from the alphabet, the latter a learned device with which Khambule . . . had made his acquaintance only late in life," so that he was "obsessed with language, a new literate with only one Book."[15]

It was this picture of a person from an entirely oral background who comes late to literacy that first drew my own attention to the potential for a study of the orality-literacy matrix. However, pouring over these handwritten texts in the Carolinum in Uppsala, I became more and more puzzled. They present a bewildering variety of voices and genres, a kaleidoscope of visions and reminiscences in many hands. This is a community that developed its own codes, symbols, and metonymic referencing system. Moreover, my research into the government archives revealed a very different man from the naive one portrayed in Sundkler's book: Khambule served on the Western front as a soldier, was respected by his employers in the mines, wrote hymns and composed music, dressed smartly in western attire when he wished, and hired the best lawyer in town to defend himself. Yet he also had an indomitable attachment to Zulu language and culture and a steady spiritual resistance to white authority and domination.

It seemed to me that the wealth of material left behind by this church demanded closer attention to the details of composition and tradition. If this was a movement of illiterates, and certainly there were many among its members, then how was the tradition mediated, and how did the material survive beyond Khambule's death? The clues to the process seem to me to be encoded in the written text.

One Script?

The prophecies and liturgies of the Khambule church are written down by hand in exercise books and are usually dated consecutively. However the process by which they came into their present form is complex. Sundkler gives an illusory picture of straightforward authorial composition by Khambule himself: "In his seclusion he also found leisure to write the beginnings of his diary and to conceive an extraordinary rich worship."[16] In the first place, there is more than one handwriting style found between the different books and, indeed, between sections of the same book in some instances. An examination of the text reveals at least four different handwriting styles: one flowing and stylish;[17] one crude, block-style printing with many errors;[18] one scrawled and uneven, often hard to decipher;[19] and one schoolbook style.[20] It is still possible that one of the scribes was George Khambule himself. On the other hand, one fieldwork informant claimed that the books were written down by George's brother, Jeremiah Khambule. Norman Khambule, grandson of the prophet, identified the "scrawled and uneven" script as that of his great uncle, Mordekai Sikhakhane. Then again, Fakazi Mhlungu, the second in rank of the two women prophets who figure as Khambule's lieutenants and who figure prominently in the diaries, is titled "General's Clack [sic] of the Lord. &-Prosecutor"[21] One wonders whether this implies some role in recording events and judgments or whether it is purely titular. This should already alert us to the danger of assuming that there was only one (semi-literate) author composing in the tranquility of his secret room. The multiple handwriting styles indicate that the material was dictated orally and recorded in writing, probably by more than one person. The multiple copies exist because of the ongoing use of the liturgies, hymns, and prophecies in worship. Each one is different from the other, even when they are drawing on the same prophecies and liturgical material, because the tradition is continually adapted to new circumstances. The liturgical use serves to embed the prophecies and visions in the communal memory and create a common religious consciousness or to construct a common "universe of meaning."[22] Here the personal visions and prophecies received by individuals lose their identification and become common communal property and pass into anonymity.

Second, at least one of the diaries was composed in the same prophetic style from September 27, 1951, to January 4, 1953, well after Khambule's death in 1949. The angels continue to visit the community and bring messages from God to direct them. These visions include visitations by Khambule himself.[23] In other words, the business of receiving and writing down prophecies was not seen as belonging uniquely to him, although he continued to be associated with the prophecies received, even after his death. Prophecy and text, oral and written, were not the monopoly of a lonely isolated man but were a community production.[24]

Third, prophecies given to members of the church were subsequently incorporated into liturgies and hymns performed in worship. For instance, a prophecy given on June 20, 1922, to Khambule himself—that the Ark of the Lord would be given to the church and required the setting apart of an *isigodlo*—is incorporated into *A Prayer of the Consecration of the Ark at 11:00 a.m.* dated June 19, 1926, at 5 p.m. It is clearly intended to be performed every year on the anniversary of the setting apart of the *isigodlo*:

Priest:	There the living creatures, elders, and the angels are praising and thanking the one who sits in the throne of Kingship, the one who is ever present, now and forever
Congregation:	All angels when they give thanks are saying, "You are great God."
Priest:	On the 20th of June 1922 a word of God came to St. Nazar saying, "Blessed are you, because the Ark which used to be handled by the Cherubim is going to be handed to you."
Congregation:	The angel said to St. Nazar, "Blessed are you, because you are going to be given power."
Priest:	"The Ark of the Covenant is going to be given to the virgins of your house. Therefore, set them apart."
Congregation:	"The Ark of the Covenant is going to be given to the virgins of your house."
Priest:	He repeated this many times indeed saying, "It is good that you set them apart because they are going to be given power."

Congregation:	"Indeed it is good that you set them apart because they are going to be given power."
Priest:	At that time St. Nazar told them that it was good that they set them apart because the Ark of the Covenant was to be given to them.
Congregation:	St. Nazar said to the women . . .
Priest:	It really happened when they set them apart, there was a great commotion but they finally set them apart.
Congregation:	They did as the angel had told them, all that was gain to them they counted as loss.[25]

This setting apart of the *isigodlo* in 1922 can be verified from the archival sources of the government. The withdrawal of wives and daughters from their own homesteads to join Khambule at his New Jerusalem created turmoil in the local community and led to the judicial processes that eventually led to his expulsion from Telezini.

Fourth, the same prophecies, hymns, and liturgies are found in several different forms in different documents. There is no attempt to preserve the temporal sequence of prophecies, even where the dates of the prophecies are preserved, so that there is occasionally "double dating": the date of the original prophecy and then the date on which the prophecy is reused in a different context! So, for instance, "A Song of *iBandla Labancwele*" is dated May 26, 1926, but its use is preceded by the date of its incorporation into the new liturgical performance on April 4, 1933.[26]

It is instructive to follow the trail of this particular song through the Khambule material, complicated as it may be. The first date is confirmed by the content of the hymn, its concern with the gift of the hidden manna:

> "A Song of the Church of the Holy Ones"
> A) Alleluia, Alleluia, Alleluia, Alleluia
> B) Who would dare play with us, we Cherubim?
> C) It is M. S. because he terrified the nations.
> D) It is G. S. because he attacked the churches.
> E) It is M. C. because he attacked the *Kedari*.
> F) To the one who overcomes I will give the hidden manna.
> G) A new name known by no one will be written
> H) I will not hold my peace because of you, Jerusalem.
>   Amen. Amen. Amen. Amen. Amen.[27]

A prophecy in April 1926 proclaims that the manna given by Fakazi Mhlungu will be deemed to be given by Joanna Ndlovu, the "General of the Lord" and first in rank of the two young women prophets who accompanied Khambule (Ndlovu is given the angelic name St. Agrineth Hlazile):

> The Ark has been called together with the Prosecutor. It was said that Hlazile is the one who is going to bring Manna, but today she [Mhlungu] will give all of them a white Manna. They will all leave it up to her. If they receive from her hands, they will be receiving from Hlazile herself.[28]

The problem is occasioned by the death of Ndlovu on October 21, 1925,[29] which presented the community with a major crisis. The field report of Bishop Philip Mhlungu in 1946 shows that the church had a problem with death,[30] probably because members were believed to have overcome death and because dead bodies were impure, and yet here the prophet and assistant of Khambule dies. Bishop Mhlungu reports that "she was called the archangel. She was respected and worshipped as Khambule himself and they stayed together in the secret room."[31] In addition, the ritual by which the members received the hidden manna in fulfillment of the promise of Rev 2:17, which is celebrated in this hymn, was instituted by Ndlovu.

As early as March 12, 1926, a prophecy praises the departed Joanna as "the Righteousness of the Holy Ones," a name already given to her when she was alive in a prophecy of June 12, 1925:[32]

> The word which comes from Jehovah.
> The Judge (*Umahluli*).
> Take another stole and let it be written thus, "The Righteousness of the Saints." This name was never given to any angel except for the Lady (*Inkosi*) who was called "the Righteousness of the Saints." The angels left here with sins, they left here with sins and were tried [in court]. They then received the nature of angels, but none was called "the Righteousness of the Saints" as it is said to you.[33]

However, the 1926 prophecy forbids her to be called Agrineth Hlazile any more, since this refers to the human woman and not the angel any more. Now the title still applies, but her name may not be used:

> Let us praise her, namely Righteousness. Who is the Righteousness of the Angels? The Righteousness of the Angels is A.H. Why? She should not be referred to as A.H. Why? This is the girl. We know this. She is the Righteousness.[34]

What should she be called then? How can the power she mediated continue to guide and protect the church? The crisis for the community was resolved by a series of visions that accompanied the hearing against Khambule held by the magistrate at Nqutu on April 27, 1926. In *The Prayer of the Church of the Holy Ones of April 27th 1926 for Victory over the Philistines at Nqutu Babylon*, a new angelic figure named St. Itengirrah with a retinue of angels appears in defense of the prophet "wearing [glorious] clothes for the trial." The first mention of Itengirrah is on April 16, 1926, when Khambule speaks about his defense in the forthcoming hearing. This is six months almost to the day after the death of Ndlovu, a significant period in terms of the end of mourning in Zulu culture, where often a dead person's personal effects may be left untouched for this period, concluded by a ritual. It seems that Ndlovu's glorious robes and cross as General of the Lord and prophet are left untouched after her death. After the hearing, which ended in confusion, Khambule (Nazar) has a vision of an angel while he is in the healing group (*isibedlela*, or hospital), though this could be a reference to his own death and resurrection experience in the hospital in 1918, when he first saw his sister-angel, who possessed Ndlovu:

> There came an angel and said, "You see, because your sister came to tell you about these clothes, that they are not needed." Because of his anger, St. Nazar became mad and said something he did not understand himself. He did not know who that angel was. He kept on wondering about the identity of that angel, what her/his name might be. On 27th at 9 a.m., we heard that it was St. Itengirrah. She was shining like the sun; therefore he could not possibly have known her because she had assumed the form of God (*wayetate isimo sobu Tixo*).
> *Congregation*: He threw away those clothes.[35]

The clothes of the dead woman are now destroyed. She has become an angelic figure, having overcome death. While she was alive she had been possessed by the angel of Khambule's dead sister, Agnes, and was therefore called by her name, St. Agrineth Hlazile. Now, in her new angelic status, her being and status merge with the dead sister, and she becomes St. Itengirrah, whose power now supports and protects the community. The spirit of the resurrected and glorified Joanna Ndlovu is seen to come down on Fakazi Mhlungu in a vision received by John Mtanti (the Gatekeeper or *Umgcinisango*). From now on, no one may even mention the human name of Ndlovu, since the Holy Spirit has come down through her onto Mhlungu. A prophecy given on May 23, 1926, declares this prohibition, which is later reworked in an anniversary liturgy for May 17, 1927, and exists in multiple texts because of its importance for the church:

Tuesday 17/5/1927
A Prayer for the Coming Down of the Holy Spirit through St. Itengirrah
On May 23, 1926, there came the Gate Keeper, and he talked with the Clerk [Fakazi Mhlungu] and said. This is what St. Itengirrah said, which is translated as Tegenel foEht Dorah according to the Greeks and according to the Roman and according to the Hebrew. In Latin which is to say it is translated Mowesh. She said, "It is right that the Prosecutor [*Umshushisi*, Ndlovu] should be called by these names, because she is the one who was given to St. Nazar on the 23-5-1926." It was said, "Even the surname Ndlovu Joanna must come to an end." It was said, "Bless them Lord. Those who are going to keep this." Yes indeed. Look, the holy ones are standing before you. Ask for light until you see them, victory, faith, and righteousness. Before you this was heard when it was said, "St. Nazar will rule the nations with an iron rod" and to Itengirrah it was said, "Morning Star." Then it was said, "Look! The holy ones are standing before you. Bless them, Lord." This was spoken by the Gatekeeper [*Umgcinisango*, John Mtanti] to the Clerk [Mhlungu]. Yes, it is so! Look, the holy ones are standing before you. Ask for light until you see them. Faith, victory, and righteousness are before you.
Congregation: Bless them, Lord.[36]

Interestingly, the title "Morning Star" is given to the heavenly Ndlovu as St. Itengirrah. In a prophecy recorded on June 4, 1925, Ndlovu, as General of the Lord, is already accorded (or accords herself?) this title. She is the one who has talked with angels in heaven even before Khambule himself entered heaven, the Morning Star who led the Wise Men to Jesus:

4th June 1925 6 p.m.—9:30 p.m.
The General of the Lord and prosecutor
I.K.Y.I.Y.K.A. The glorious morning star, the stone on which all the apostles are written (Stones of the 12 Apostles). Who could go to Zwana? Nobody. But the glorious morning star went there. Why? Even the angel AHK did not know that this is the stone on which are written all the apostles. Which star is this that was revealed to the Wisemen of the East? And who are the Wisemen of old? No! They are here, who could not have come to the baby if the star was not there. Before you were there, Nazar, the star was talking to the angels. You must know this.[37]

The code I.K.Y.I.Y.K.A. in this case has an acrostic signification: *ink-anyezi yokusa* (morning star). While Fakazi Mhlungu (*umpati Ark*) is the bearer of the Ark, Joanna Ndlovu is the "bearer of the angel" (*umpati wengelosi*) and the chief steward because she is the interpreter of God (*umusha likaNkulunkulu*).[38] But now there has been a transfer of angelic status on earth from Ndlovu to Mhlungu, while Ndlovu's heavenly role as St. Itengirrah, one of the seven angels of Revelation, can be celebrated. (Note that the instructions for the rituals use the sign "D.C." (*da capo*) to indicate manifold repetition.)

Sunday, May 30, 1926, 11 a.m.

They sang a new song. Today there are St. Itengirrah and St. Iven, St. Semeon, St. Moeed, St. Gebeallah, St. Mark, Libia

The Prayer of the 11 a.m. Service

Priest:	I will not hold my peace D.C.
Congregation:	Because of the New Jerusalem
Priest:	Come you who are being called D.C.
Congregation:	It is St. Itengirrah D.C.
Priest:	
A)	Peace be with you. In 1918 on the 18th on the 10th month. It was dark in Khambule.
Congregation:	Today St. Itengirrah is there.
Priest:	
B)	The gates are opened. One of us went with him to the twelve gates, because she was worthy.
Congregation:	Itengirrah overcame death D.C.
Priest:	
C)	Today you dial the telephone. Some among you are blessed, some are cursed.
Congregation:	Itengirrah went with Moeed D.C.
Priest:	
D)	What are you saying in your hearts? Look the gate was opened!
Congregation:	It is good that we follow them where they are going. D.C.
Priest:	
E)	It happened on a certain day that St. Itengirrah entered Paradise.
Congregation:	Today St. Itengirrah is present.
Priest:	She sang and said, "Blessed are they, the holy ones in heaven."

Congregation:	Itengirrah overcame death.
Priest:	
F)	She came and cried before the tomb and said, "What was it that I was supposed to do, which I did not do on earth?"
Congregation:	It is Itengirrah and Moeed.
Priest:	
G)	Judge for yourselves, are you worthy to go to heaven? It will not be according to your will but according to righteousness.
Congregation:	It is right that we follow them. D. C. All of them, Semeon and Iven.[39]

Of course, this is the metonymic, coded language of the church and difficult to understand. But the identification of Ndlovu with Agnes, already claimed for her during her earthly life, is confirmed in this liturgy by the reference to the date of Khambule's conversion and salvation by the intervention of his dead sister: "It is no longer said, 'Joanna.' It is now said, 'Agrineth Hlazile.' So it is with Joanna in the heavens, say the scriptures, that she will come by means of a person."[40]

To summarize what we have observed here, visions originating from various community members are recorded at the time they are given. If they prove of major significance to the life of the church, they are set into liturgies and hymns. These are performed on many occasions, probably on the anniversary of significant events. But they change their form from time to time, by the addition of new material. Furthermore, words given in one prophecy obtain a metonymic reference, which enables them to be used repeatedly in other prophecies and liturgical acts to conjure up the salvation history of the church.

The process of transmission of the prophecies and visions through repetition, writing, and re-copying results in the production and survival of manuscripts. Each manuscript reifies and unifies the spoken word of the individual prophets into a common tradition. What is not useful ceases to be copied; what the community finds to be contrary to the spirit or false is removed. So a prophecy or ruling of January 5, 1926, concerning two members of the church is simply crossed out, erased from the communal memory, presumably because its genuineness is rejected.[41] The script produces the illusion of one voice, while it masks the many voices that have produced it.

Altered States of Consciousness
and Recording of Visions

Reading the prophecies and visions of Khambule's church is sometimes
like looking through a kaleidoscope. It is full of color and light and constantly shifting shapes. Part of this is the result of the multiple voices in
the text: everyone in the community who has entered the "marriage of the
Lamb" could potentially prophesy through the power of or in the name
of their own angel, since they have "received the nature of angels."[42] The
prophecy usually begins with "The word coming from Jehovah" (*Izwi
elipuma ku Jehova*) and then is often marked by some indicator of the
recipient. The recipient is sometimes clearly indicated , as, for instance, in
the two prophecies attributed directly to Joanna Zondo:

> Saturday 1/8/25
> Joanna Zondo.
> The word coming from Jehovah.
> It is said, I must let you know this, "Worse is still to come to the
> earth," says the Lord.

and

> On 24 Monday Night or Tuesday Morning 9/3/26
> Joanna Zondo
> I saw two angels coming down. . . .[43]

Many of the prophecies have similar addressees. Frequently, as we would
expect, prophecies address Nazar or the Judge and once "Brother" (*uBhuti*),
which are all code names for Khambule, and General of the Lord or St.
Agrineth Hlazile or variants of this, which are codes names for Joanna
Ndlovu. Some of the prophecies indicate the agent of the prophecy, using
the Zulu prefix *ngu-* ("by means of") as in *ngu St. Itengirrah*. These are
delivered to the recipient through the apotheosized Joanna Ndlovu. However, the same prefix *ngu-* is used for a prophecy through John Mtante,
whose other code names are *Umazisi* ("the Seer"), *Umgcinisango* ("the
Gatekeeper"), and St. John Mark.[44] It seems likely that St. Batetelele,
who appears briefly in 1929[45] and later in the prophecies in the 1950s,
may have been Khambule's legal wife, MaSikhakhane, and there are many
other minor prophetic figures, such as Jemimah Ndimande.[46] In the later
texts, after Fakazi Mhlungu has taken over much of the authority in the
church, many of the prophecies are in her own name as the agent, for

example, on February 12, 1936, "A Hymn of the Saints through Fakazi of the Angels"[47] and "A Hymn of the Cherubim above Who Have Come to See the King of Salem through the Lord Fakazi of Angels."[48] Then later there are prophecies through someone referred to as Qinisekile, which may also be a code name for Mhlungu, and many others. However, many other prophecies have no names attached, and it is very hard to identify the receptor or the reference of the prophecy.

One very interesting feature of *Diary 1* is the use of the code names for Mtanti (*Umazisi*), or "the Forerunner," as Sundkler calls him—namely, the prophet John Mtanti, who called Khambule back from Johannesburg to Telezini. He clearly plays a key role on certain occasions. In the crisis over Joanna Ndlovu's death, he forbids the further use of the name and supplies several alternative names, especially St. Itengirrah, Tegenel foEht Dorah, and Mowesh. In a long prophecy addressed to the Judge, he discusses the service of "blowing out the seven candlesticks" held on June 27, 1925, the date on which the church was forced to vacate its premises; this action was believed to have dispatched the seven angels of the apocalypse to judge the world. The prophecy was given at Witbank on August 28, 1925, and seems to be a reflection on the state of the affairs of the church. There is a requirement in the prophecy to build separate and secluded spaces, so that the General of the Lord (Ndlovu), who has become mortally sick, will not be seen. The sickness and death of one of the key leaders of the church appeared to contradict its teaching in a fundamental way. The prophecy claims that the sickness was the result of the exposure of one who walked and talked with angels to the eyes of ordinary human beings. So the seclusion serves a double purpose. In any case, for our purposes, the interesting aspect of the prophecy is the explicit insertion of identity on the part of Mtanti, which clearly indicates that it is not Khambule composing or reporting on a vision he has received:

> This first vision will not be told to anyone. The Keeper of the Gate is the one who will do what he has resolved. And know this, that you came to represent the Lord Jesus here. Therefore everything will be arranged by you yourself. Finish them all. You are God's *Umazisi*, the one who makes God known. You are still going to go to many places. Perhaps when you come back this house will be finished, when you return from where you are going. Just as *iNkosi* traveled by boat, so will you. It is not said that you will not come home after you depart from here, but your destination is very far away, says Jehovah. It is good to work for God. It is praised greatly indeed. What will happen will take a very long time indeed, as it has been said that you may come here after the house is already built.[49]

It seems as if it is Mtanti inserting himself into the discourse throughout the prophecy, longing to go overseas like George Khambule, who had served on the Western front so many years before. One wonders indeed whether he may not have been the scribe who wrote down the prophecies in this book and not Khambule, as Sundkler supposes. Sundkler writes[50] that Mtanti parted company with Khambule "about this time" in 1928 to start his own church. However, Bishop Mhlungu, in confirming the split, does not give a date. Nor does the prophecy of September 12, 1928, which is cited by Sundkler to support his assertion but is not among the papers I have found in his archives, say this either.[51] It is simply an assertion of prior authority by Khambule over Mtanti, despite his having been called to his ministry by the latter. Mtanti had been a teacher in St. John's Anglican mission school at Blood River and is a not unlikely scribe for the community in the writing down of prophecies. However, the handwriting in *Diary* 3 and *Liturgy* 3 are the same, and they end in 1929 and 1933 respectively. Alternatively, George's brother, Jeremiah Khambule, may have been the scribe, since one of the field interviews identified him as the one who wrote books.

The key fact, whether the amanuensis is Mtanti or Jeremiah Khambule or Fakazi Mhlungu, is that the prophecies and visions were not written in a literary manner by a person holding a pen, as Sundkler assumes. Instead, they record ecstatic experiences and represent messages to the community mediated by various people during "altered states of consciousness."[52] People in such a state do not write, but they do remember. Since the messages are received from Jehovah by means of angelic mediators, they must be recorded, remembered, obeyed, and celebrated by the community.

Emergence of a Corpus of Prophecy

Not all prophecies are accepted by the community. In one case, a prophecy was written down and then crossed out in the records.[53] However, once the prophecies have been received, accepted, and recorded, they are not only obeyed by the church but also celebrated from year to year. If we return to the liturgy with which we started, we see that a vision is taken and cast into a new form. The original prophecy of June 20, 1922, was given to Khambule himself (St. Nazar) and was something like: "Blessed are you, because the ark which used to be handled by the Cherubim is going to be handed to you. Therefore set apart the virgins of your house so that they may be given power." This ecstatic vision is now reframed in the context of the worship of heaven:

Priest:	When the living creatures, elders, and the angels are praising and thanking the one who sits in the throne of Kingship, the one who is ever present, now and forever.
Congregation:	All angels when they give thanks are saying, "You are great God."

The prophecy itself is then cut up into sentence and refrain recited antiphonally between the priest and the congregation. The repetition (or "redundancy") allows the prophecy to enter the memory of the community. It also gives it a sense of permanence and surety.

Priest:	On the 20th of June 1922 a word of God came to St. Nazar saying, "Blessed are you, because the ark which used to be handled by the Cherubim is going to be handed to you."
Congregation:	The angel said to St. Nazar, "Blessed are you, because you are going to be given power."
Priest:	"The Ark of the Covenant is going to be given to the virgins of your house. Therefore, set them apart."
Congregation:	"The Ark of the Covenant is going to be given to the virgins of your house."
Priest:	He repeated this many times indeed saying, "It is good that you set them aside because they are going to be given power."
Congregation:	"Indeed it is good that you set them apart because they are going to be given power."

The liturgy then provides the response of the church to the prophecy. Khambule gave the instructions for the formation of the *isigodlo*. This caused tremendous strife in the community, as the surrounding homesteads found their women and children leaving to live in Khambule's homestead or remaining at home but refusing sex and food. Despite the danger of obeying the prophecy, the church obeyed, even at the cost of expulsion from Telezini:

Priest:	At that time St. Nazar told them that it was good that they set them apart because the Ark of the Covenant was to be given to them.

Congregation:	St. Nazar said to the women . . .
Priest:	It really happened when they set them apart, there was a great commotion but they finally set them apart.
Congregation:	They did as the angel had told them, all that was gain to them they counted as loss.[54]

The cost is great but is counted a small thing because of the joy of obeying the angels and the experience of God's presence in their midst symbolized by the Ark. The liturgy is dated after the hearing before the magistrate, when the issue was clear. There was confusion in court, but the outcome in the long run must have been obvious: they would be expelled from the holy mountain. This nested prophetic vision and its frame are then set in a wider context of invocation and testimonies to the healing power present in the community: a blind woman has a vision, and Saul Mushily comes for prayer for healing. Khambule settles a problem in the community over a claimed failed virginity test of some kind with regard to Fakazi Mhlungu. The context is not clear, but such tests are rooted in Zulu custom; what is known is that Mhlungu had a child by Khambule who was claimed to have been miraculously conceived (and hence was named Immanuel). This may have been the source of the problem mentioned here.

The liturgies created in this way are then repeated from year to year. They are copied in multiple forms. For instance, the liturgical rendition of the vision of the hearing of April 27, 1926, as cosmic warfare between the angels and the ruler of Babylon, is not only found in two versions but also set in the form of a hymn,[55] so that it can be sung regularly and pass into the memory of the community. What begins as vision in an altered state of consciousness ends as the ritual construction of a new social universe.

Embodied in Symbol

Khambule and his community produced a rich repertoire of symbolism. This was not only verbal, in that it was expressed in prophecy, chanted in liturgy, and sung in hymns, but also expressed concretely in the dress and actions of the community. An example is the prophecy designating Joanna Ndlovu as the Morning Star and assigning the acrostic I.K.Y.I.Y.K.A. A subsequent prophecy says: "Y.-S.P.A.J.Z.J.F.B.T.M.J.A.L.T.S.K.-S.O.S. These are the names that were written on the glorious Morning Star.

This is how she has been the power of the Apostles that were written on her." These enigmatic letters of power, representing her status as Morning Star and representing the names of all the apostles given in prophecy, were stitched onto black stoles and worn by Joanna Ndlovu, as an expression and fulfillment of the prophecy, reinforcing the liturgical expression of what was spoken. The white stoles worn by both Ndlovu and Khambule were embroidered with the seven spirits of God, exactly as in this vision:

> There shall be white ones [stoles] marked with black or red. They are for the seven spirits of God. The one for the Judge [George Khambule] and the one for the Prosecutor [Joanna Ndlovu] shall be the same, together with the one for the Witness of the General of the Lord [Fakazi Mhlungu]. It shall be written in full "Witness of the General of the Lord." In each case the learner shall see for herself, says the Lord.[56]

A photograph of the group portrayed above shows that the prophecy is acted out to the letter in public performance, no doubt within the liturgies that record the prophecies. The prophecy fulfilling the seven spirits of Revelation is expanded with the text drawn from Isa 11:2, where seven spirits are to be written on the Messiah sprung from Jesse. The seven spirits of Isaiah can be seen embroidered on Khambule's stole in a photograph. The whole effect is characterized aptly by the prophecy, "The one who talks with angels should be dressed for heaven."

The same kind of relationship between vision and symbolic enactment can be seen in prophecies concerning the cross carried by Ndlovu and the staff with a snake on the top. This is the staff of Moses, which is carried by Khambule, the new Moses. The staff is understood to radiate power so that it can heal like the staff of Moses. For the people in the church and, indeed, for those in the surrounding community, the prophecies given to individual members become common property. As they are collected and performed, they often lose the mark of "authorship" and even time and place of reception. After all, the prophet is the medium and not the author. The dates of important events become embedded in the re-enacted liturgies and hymns, and the claim of the church to have angels present in its midst, to witness miracles, and to worship with heaven is fulfilled continually. The dates, events, and media of many other prophecies and songs are simply lost—or rather merged with the general pool of community consciousness and worship.

Continued after the Death of the Prophet

What most startled me, when I first read the texts of the Khambule church, was that the prophecies did not stop with the death of George Khambule in 1949. Indeed, they continued until 1953, carefully dated and with no sense of incongruity. George continues to visit the community: St. Nazar continues to be the medium of messages from Jehovah. The prophet "with the chin" (a distinctive feature of the prophet) visits again to warn, bless, and direct the community. In the case of iBandla Labancwele, the church ended with the death of Archbishop Mordekai Sikhakhane in 1970. However, in the case of other such prophets, like Isaiah Shembe in South Africa, where the church has continued, there are similar examples of the continuing voice of the dead prophet. After all, he continues as one of the living dead in communion with the living. In the case of Khambule's church, the living have already taken on the nature of angels, and the dead have conquered death and entered heaven. They now intervene in the life of the church using their "angelic" power on behalf of the living and continue to speak.

A Unity of Vision

This essay has examined the origin, growth, and development of a corpus of prophecy in a Zulu context. The questions arising within the early Christian movement, faced with the death of its messianic prophet, also arose within Khambule's church. Of course, there is no exact parallel from one historical and cultural context to another. However, the advantage of looking at the question of the early church via the Zulu context is that it prevents us from looking at the question unreflectingly and unconsciously from our own. In many ways, the rural, cross-cultural mix of colonial Zululand, isolated in some ways from the westernized cities and yet very aware of them—indeed constantly interacting with them in some cases—is closer to the situation of the early Christian community than our own.

What is interesting to observe is the way the weaving of prophecy into worship, song, and symbol constructs the social universe of the group. Not all of the prophecies, by a very long way, come from the messianic founder of the community, George Khambule. Perhaps even a minority of them do. Yet there is no doubt about the unity of vision and tone with which the texts speak. The prophecies construct the community and then in turn occasion further prophecies that build on the earlier ones. The constant repetition and internalizing of the messages guarantee a measure of homogeneity in the prophecies, so that they belong unmistakably to Khambule. The spirit speaks, and it is the spirit of Khambule, which, both the prophet and his community would claim, is the voice of Jesus himself. Many of the prophecies come from Khambule himself directly. Many manifestly do not come from him but from others who have no embarrassment in inserting themselves and their prophecies into a developing corpus of prophecy, even after the death of the founding prophet, all of which comes to be characterized as the prophecy of Khambule himself. The memory of exactly who was the mediator of the prophecy is less important than its significance for the life of the community. The ongoing oral performance in liturgy and song of what is written down and its re-encoding in new liturgies provides for a continuity and a homogeneity of the prophecy of the Khambule church.

Of course, these findings concerning the process of development of a written prophetic corpus in a small rural Zulu religious community cannot be directly applied to the development of a written corpus of prophecy in rural Galilee two thousand years ago. However, it does supply a possible analogy rooted in empirical data that can be tested. At least it shows that, even in a largely oral and largely illiterate community, there is a complex relationship between the oral events and written texts. The scribal process masks the process of formation of tradition and provides a deceptive appearance of unity in the corpus (which deceived even as perceptive a scholar as Bengt Sundkler). Yet the written text also provides clues to the geography of the earlier processes rhetorically encoded in the text.

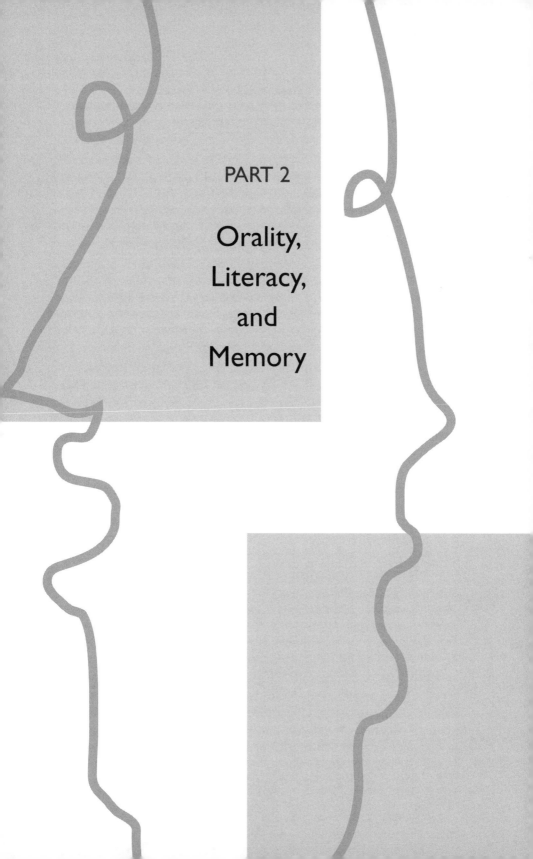

PART 2

Orality,
Literacy,
and
Memory

4

Form as a Mnemonic Device: Cultural Texts and Cultural Memory

Jan Assmann

B enedict Anderson defined nations as "imagined communities," im-
plying that there are communities that are not imagined but based
on some kind of "hard" essential reality such as family, clan, tribe,
and so forth.[1] On closer reflection, however, it becomes clear that all
communities or, to be more precise, all collective identities are imagined.
It is not "blood" or "descent" as such that keeps a group together but the
shared *consciousness* of it, the idea of common descent. The same applies
even to personal identity. Even the self-image of a person may be seen as
an imagined entity. Identity, on all its levels, from the individual person
to large groups such as nations and religious communities, is a product of
imagination and of mental representation.

The constitutive role of memory in this process of self-image making or identity formation was identified by the sociologist Maurice
Halbwachs in the 1920s[2] and is constantly confirmed and expanded by
modern psychology, psychotherapy, and brain research.[3] "We are what we
remember."[4] In the context of this discourse, memory is usually understood as a function of the human brain and as a matter of brain cells and
their connections. Halbwachs decisively expanded this narrow notion of
memory by showing its social dimension. Individual memory is a social
fact; it develops by socialization and communication. The same applies, as

George Herbert Mead has shown, to personal identity, to the category of selfhood that is formed by processes of mirroring or triangulation in relation to "significant others."[5] Thus, the slogan "we are what we remember" must be complemented by the phrase "we are what we belong to," since remembering and belonging are so closely interconnected. In this respect, a person may be defined as the juncture of two dimensions: the social dimension and the dimension of time. Our memory enables us to orient ourselves in both the temporal and the social dimension, to "belong" in the broadest sense, to form relations with others. Memory as a means of orientation has to be understood as a faculty of remembering and of forgetting. Those who remember everything are unable to orient themselves in time and society in the same way as those who notice everything are unable to orient themselves in space. Orientation requires selection. The function of memory is orientation, not the storage and reproduction of true and objective representations of the past.

For Halbwachs, the cement that keeps groups together, the principle of connectivity, from family to nation to religious communities, is emotion. He defined groups as *communautés affectives*. Emotion is certainly an important factor in the formation of collective self-images or imagination in the sense of Benedict Anderson. What seems much more important in this context and is being constantly undervalued, however, is the role of symbolization, of "symbolic forms" in the sense of Ernst Cassirer, whose work on the philosophy of symbolic forms[6] appeared simultaneously with Maurice Halbwachs's work on the social frames of memory. The human being as the *animal sociale*, the "*zōon politikon*" of Aristotle, is not so much the emotional but the symbol-using animal.

The notion of symbol forces us to transcend the frames of body and consciousness and to take into account the whole range of cultural expression, of texts, images, and actions, as carriers or representations of memory and identity expressive of time, selfhood, and belonging. It is not adequate to restrict the notion of memory to the individual psyche, as the psychologists do, or to the sphere of communication in the wake of Maurice Halbwachs and the social psychologists. My concern is to open up the sphere of culture—or at least a core domain comprising religion, art, history, and morality—to research into memory and to investigate what we call "cultural memory" in its forms and functions. In the following brief survey, I explain the memory function of cultural objects, which I divide into material objects, actions, and texts—or *deiknymena*, *drōmena*, and *legomena*, to use the terminology of the ancient mystery cults.

Material Objects

In the sphere of material objects, the memory function becomes manifest in a will to form or formative intention, which informs the productions of human activity so as to make them share a set of distinctive features or acquire a kind of family resemblance. The formal repertoire of tools, weapons, pottery, pictures, and buildings—in fact, all kinds of artifacts that, as traces of human existence, reach back over many millennia—is informed by a strict regularity that renders it accessible to morphological analysis, in the same way as the forms of nature. This regularity makes it possible to identify a singular object in terms of date, provenance, and function.[7]

The will to form leads to the formation of traditions and ensures cultural continuity and identity.[8] In this respect, we may speak of a *memory-function of culture*, even of material culture. This morphological tradition or memory is the basis of prehistory and archaeology and all other disciplines of cultural studies dealing with human artifacts. Art history, musicology, philology, literary studies, and so on reflect in their methodology the morphological features of cultural products that are expressive of the memory function of culture. There is a *will to form* that is a will of transmission, of transmitting a distinctive cultural identity to further generations. In its earliest stages, it must not necessarily have had a conscious purpose, and the formation of tradition among the first tribes of human beings was probably not very different from nature's ways of stabilizing traditions. Animals do things, such as building their homes, in forms that show a much more striking family resemblance, in fact, a complete identity. Seen this way, the principle of human ways of forming traditions seems to be variation rather than identity, in contrast to the animal world, where we see identical repetition and replication.

The principle of variation becomes more and more important with the advance of cultural evolution. We must not forget, however, that in the human world, family resemblance or distinctive features in artifacts do not stem from a natural, that is, instinctive disposition but from free choice among alternative solutions. Free choice requires orientation, and orientation is provided not by instinct, that is, biological memory, but by cultural memory. Thus we may say that, going back to a very early stage of the production of artifacts, a distinction between a functional, or primary, aspect and a symbolical, or secondary, aspect is possible, the primary being its function as a tool, the secondary consisting in its belonging to a tradition of tool making. An arrowhead, for example, shows in its primary aspect its function with regard to which it has been shaped by its maker, and it shows in its secondary aspect its stylistically distinctive features that tell us something about its date and provenance, its belonging to what prehistorians call a "specific culture." From its functionally distinctive features we learn that it is an arrowhead (and not a macehead), and from its stylistically distinctive features we learn that it belongs to a certain North American tribe of two thousand years ago.

From a certain time onward—which is usually connected with the invention of agriculture and pottery, that is, the "Neolithic revolution"— the distinction between the primary and the secondary level of shaping becomes even more obvious by the introduction of a new principle of form giving, *decoration*, which belongs exclusively to the second level. A knife and a jar do not fulfill their function any better by being decorated with ornaments or figures, but they gain immensely in morphological features, or pregnancy, permitting their identification with regard to provenance, date, and cultural context. At this stage, at the latest, we may confidently say that the distinction between the primary and the secondary was consciously made and practiced by the producers and users of cultural artifacts, for decorated artifacts do not carry these features just as symptoms that tell only the modern connoisseur about their contextual circumstances but display them as symbols conveying a certain message to the contemporary user and observer. These artifacts undergo a secondary formalization, enhancing not their functionality but their meaning, a meaning that aims at making visible certain elements of the semantic universe and the identity of the group. This is how the aesthetic makes its first appearance among the material productions of human culture.

The function of decoration is not to be described as "disinterested pleasure" (*interesseloses Wohlgefallen*, Kant's definition of the aesthetic experience) but as a kind of memorization technique by which the semantic universe is made not only visible but permanent and transmittable. Second-level formalization serves, within the sphere of objects of everyday life, as a principle of connectivity, stabilizing and transmitting cultural knowledge and symbolizing norms, values, and myths that constitute collective identity. In these early times, "before the era of art,"[9] the aesthetic seems inseparably linked to the mnemonic.

Action

The will to form imprints itself not only in artifacts belonging to the *entourage matériel* but also in actions, particularly in actions that were meant to be efficient beyond the moment of performance and thus to create and support memory. In the sphere of actions, the distinction between a primary and a second level of formalization becomes inevitable. This is the distinction between routines and rites, or "routinization" and "ritualization." In the case of routines, formalization is meant simply to relieve effort in the pursuit of a certain goal. This primary (functional) level of formalization already fulfills a mnemonic function. But there is also a possible secondary (symbolical) level of formalization in which the mnemonic function is much more prominent.

This secondary level of formalization may be called "ritualization." Rites are symbolic actions whose meaning exceeds the primary purpose of the action. The reaping of grain, for example, is an action that is usually heavily formalized in its technical performance without being, for this reason, a rite. Its only purpose is the fulfillment of an important step in the grain harvest. This is what we may call the "primary purpose," and the only function of routinization lies in paving the way to its easy achievement. In the ancient Egyptian festival of Min, on the other hand, the reaping of grain was celebrated with great solemnity in order to ensure not only the abundance of present and future harvesting but also the stability and legitimacy of the reign of the pharaoh as the guarantor of fertility and abundance. This goal exceeds by far the primary purpose of cutting grain. In this case, we are dealing not with a routine but with a rite. Routinization is just formalization and nothing more; in the case of ritualization, however, formalization fulfills the additional function of semiotization, of charging the action with meaning. Rites are "symbolic actions" referring to and acting upon the "semantic universe" (*Sinnwelt*) of human existence.

To give a more familiar example: eating and drinking are actions that on the primary level of routinization usually tend to undergo a certain formalization in family life. On the second level of ritualization, the eating of bread and the drinking of wine in Jewish families is celebrated on the eve of Shabbat as a "mnemonic mark," or *zikkaron*, both of the seventh day of creation and of the exodus from Egypt (*yitsi 'at mitsrayim*). In Christianity, the eating of bread and the drinking of wine is celebrated with greatest solemnity as the sacrament of the Eucharist. This rite was explicitly instituted with the words "*Do this in remembrance of me*" as a *zikkaron* in order to commemorate the death of Christ and to provide participation in its redemptory significance.[10] Even in cases in which the memory function is not made explicit, we are dealing with a form of memory. Every rite is a *zikkaron*, a commemorative symbol that refers either to a historical event, such as the exodus from Egypt and the crucifixion of Christ, or to a mythical event such as the seventh day of creation or the institution of pharaonic kingship.

Language

If we turn from objects and actions to speech and language, the distinction between a primary and a secondary level of formalization appears in a new light. *Language* is the generation of sounds with the purpose of denoting and expressing meanings. Here the semiotic function is already operative on the level of primary functioning. Speech is in itself already symbolic action[11] without, however, being ritual. Language, like any other kind of action and artifact, serves a certain function in everyday life—communication. This is its primary level, and the correspondent ways of primary formalization and routinization consist in the formation of traditions of articulation and formulation in everyday communication, in genres of speech or ways of saying things. In some cases, however, the second level of formalization becomes prominent, which has to do with the will of or need for transmission. In the sphere of language, the alliance between the aesthetic and the mnemonic becomes most obvious. If an utterance is designed to be preserved and to stay efficient beyond the moment of its pronunciation, that is, to serve the secondary purpose of becoming a mnemonic mark, it has to be submitted to a process of secondary formalization. Only by acquiring certain additional distinctive features of form and genre is an utterance capable of staying in memory and remaining accessible to later recourse, repetition, elaboration, and commentary. A formalized utterance is a carrier of memory, a mnemonic mark in being both an element of tradition (which is in itself a form of memory) and memorable for future recourse. It employs memory and creates memory.

Therefore, in speech and language, formalization acts as a means of stabilization. Its only purpose is to render meaning permanent. This is what Eric Havelock called "preserved communication." In my terminology, formalization is what turns an utterance into a text. "Text," in everyday use, means "formalized utterance," formalized, that is, in view of being remembered, transmitted, and repeatedly taken up. Text is speech in the status of a mnemonic mark. With the category of text, language passes, in my terminology, from the level of communication to the level of memory.

For this reason, the laws of morphology apply to language as well as to all of the other human artifacts. Also in the utterances designed for later use, which I propose to call "texts," there is manifest a will to form, which attempts to stabilize the word beyond its moment of pronunciation. Rhyme, assonance, parallelism, alliteration, meter, rhythm, and melody are devices of stabilization meant to render permanent the volatile words in the flow of time; in the same way as with material artifacts, these features render for the philologist a text definable in space and time in terms of style, genre, function, situational context, *Sitz im Leben*, and so forth.

In the following, I show that writing is just another kind of secondary formalization. Writing was invented and applied, in the first place, to linguistic units unfit for the usual poetical means of formalization. Writing was first invented for recording and preserving the prosaic and contingent data of economics and administration in the early states—that is, the data that could not possibly be memorized. No human memory and no memorization technique would be able to handle these data. Writing made it possible to turn lists of names, numbers, and objects into texts to preserve them for later reference and repetition without any further formalization.

What Is a "Text"?
Transmission and the "Extended Situation"

What is a text? The word *textus* is derived from *texo*, "to weave"; it indicates tissue, connection. Quintilian takes this metaphor to denote the connection of words, the structure and coherence of speech. There does not seem to exist any equivalent for this term in ancient languages outside Latin.[12] Quintilian refers to the rhetorical notion of "text." The rhetorical tradition distinguishes between information and message, subject matter and the act of speaking. This distinction is constantly blurred in oriental languages. Egyptian *mdt* and Hebrew *dabar* denote both speech and what speech is about. Whoever refers to something that has been said or written is unable to make clear whether he or she refers to the *form* or the *content* of speech. In the words of Werner Kelber,

> Writing is the technique of making words visible. This exteriorization of language tends to foster the impression of visible signs in separation from the actuality they refer to. In linguistic terms, writing forces the distinction between signs on surfaces, the signifiers, and the content with which they are being charged, the signified. It lies in the nature of written language that it can be abstracted from its signification. Spoken words are not visible

apart from their signifiers. In the absence of exterior manifesta-
tions, oral discourse appears to be more intimately allied with the
actuality to which it refers. When sounded words are thus known
to be effective in the act of speaking, it takes but one small step to
regard them "as being of the same order of reality as the matters
and events to which they refer."[13]

This is quite true: the non-distinction between signifier and signified is
typical of the oral situation. However, writing does not automatically bring
about an awareness of the distinction, nor is this awareness restricted to
writing. In the context of rhetoric, we are dealing with texts that are orally
delivered though often literally composed. What is decisive is the emergence of a level of meta-textual communication, in which it is the words
and the way of formulation that matter more than, or along with, but in
any case distinct from the subject matter.

Later, philology adopts the new notion and applies it to the object
of its own profession, opposing *textus* and *commentarius*. *Textus* is what a
commentarius refers to, and *commentarius* is the kind of discourse that has
a *textus* as its object. Philological work transforms a chain of words into
a *textus* in making it the object of its operations: text critique, establishing a text, comparison of variants, commenting, translating, exegesis. As
a rule, linguistic utterances as such are, at least originally, not meant as
texts. A poem, for instance, aims at being the object of any kind of enjoy-
ment—pleasure, reflection, learning—but not of philological treatment.
Philological treatment belongs to a level or horizon that is secondary and
posterior to the primary horizon of communication and reception. Within
this primary horizon, the notion of "text" has no natural evidence what-
soever. Therefore, it is unknown in most ancient languages. It arises only
in the context of rhetoric and philology, that is, of meta-textual reflection.
"Text," in other words, is a notion that belongs to meta-language, not to
object language. It is a meta-textual term.

In everyday language, "text" is mostly associated with writing. A linguistic unit becomes a text when it is written down. In linguistic terminology, however, the word "text" denotes the highest meaningful unit of
language—in opposition to "paragraph," "sentence," "phrase," "syntagma,"
"word," and finally "morpheme," the smallest meaningful unit—independently of whether or not this highest unit appears in oral or written form.
The linguistic definition of "text" is the complete inversion of its traditional and everyday meaning. While I asserted above that text has no
natural existence on the primary level of communication, it is, in the view
of modern linguistics, the only unit in which language naturally occurs in

communication, whereas all the other units are artificial subdivisions and analytical constructs. We communicate in texts and not in phrases, words, syllables, and morphemes. This notion of text, however, is much too general and indistinct to be useful to this chapter's argument. Texts may consist in just one word such as "hello" or in lengthy recitations such as *The Odyssey*, but they are the only natural communicational unit. However, in the present context we are interested not only in communication but also and above all in memorization and transmission. For these purposes, the everyday concept of "text," with its connotations of literacy, seems much more pertinent.

Konrad Ehlich, a scholar of Hebrew and of general linguistics, has formulated a linguistic concept of "text" that integrates some decisive semantic elements of the everyday concept.[14] Ehlich defines "text" as a message that is repeated, remembered, recovered, and referred to. The primal form of "text," not in the etymological but in the pragmatic sense, is the message that is delivered. The common denominator between the literary work that is commented upon and the message that is delivered is the act of reproduction. It is not the original speaker who generates the text, but the repeater—the messenger and the commentator. The decisive text-generating factor is the separation of the message from the situation of immediate communication, in other words, the creation of an "extended situation" (*zerdehnte Situation*) in which speaker and hearer, encoder and decoder are no longer co-present within the spatial and temporal limits of the human voice. In these cases, the original speech act has to be preserved beyond the limits of the original situation in order to be transported and repeated in a second situation. The messenger has to learn the message by heart in order to be able to deliver it at another time and another place to the addressee.

In this case, we may rightly speak of the "text" of the message. The written form of the message is not what is decisive, but the acts of storage, transmission, and reproduction are. The immediate situation is replaced with the extended situation unfolding in at least two and, in the case of literature, virtually infinite concrete situations that may stretch in time as long as the text is preserved and the conditions for its readability and understandability are assured. This notion of text replaces the narrow and technical correlation of *textus* and *commentarius* with the much more general correlation of text and transmission. Texts are speech acts in the context of extended communication situations. This concept has the great advantage of overcoming the all-too-close association of texts with written language; it allows for the idea of oral texts, but at the same time it retains a central semantic element of the philological and rhetorical tradition by connecting "text" with transmission and reproduction. Text is the unit of speech that, on the side of the speaker/encoder, is connected with a need for transmission beyond the boundaries of an immediate situation and, on the side of the receiver, with a need for retrieval and reactualization.

Institutionalizing the "Extended Situation": Cultural Texts and Cultural Coherence

"*Cultural* texts" are a sub-group of texts that are constantly taken up and reproduced by a whole society. The concept of "cultural texts" includes much more than just "texts" in the sense of a linguistic unit. It refers to every semantic unit that is encoded in symbolic forms such as images, gestures, dances, rites, festivals, customs, and even landscapes such as the Australian "song lines," the German Rhine valley, or the medieval pilgrimage routes to Santiago de Compostela, as long as they are to be understood as semantic and not just geographic units and as long as they are reproduced, that is, reenacted or reactualized in the life of the community.[15] Clifford Geertz introduced the term "cultural text" decades ago with respect to the Balinese cock fight, and I use it in this wide sense. In what follows, however, I will concentrate on verbal cultural texts. Cultural texts exert a binding energy on the community in a normative and a formative sense. Normative cultural texts codify the norms of behavior and range from simple proverbs to educational literature and books on manners and finally up to canonical and semi-canonical texts such as the Torah and the *Shulkhan Arukh* in the Jewish tradition. Formative texts formulate the self-image of the group and range from tribal myths and sagas of origin to literary works by Homer and Virgil, Dante and Shakespeare, Milton and Goethe. By the transmission of cultural texts, a society or culture reproduces itself in its "cultural identity" through the generations.

Extended situations do not occur naturally; they have to be culturally institutionalized. They cannot develop and persevere without institutional support and framing. This applies already to the institution of the messenger. It must be ensured that the messenger reaches his or her destination, that he or she is admitted to the addressee of the message, and that the addressee will recognize the messenger as representative of the sender: *hashaluah kasholeah 'oto* ("the messenger is like the one who sent him" as the Hebrew phrase goes).[16] The institute of the messenger is a kind of contract involving the sender, the transmitter, and the receiver of the message. The sender must trust the messenger that he or she will faithfully pass on the message, the messenger must totally identify with his or her role of transmitter and must stick to the wording and meaning of the message, and the receiver must treat the messenger as the representative of the sender. Every act of transmission and every kind of extended situation implies something of this contractual aspect. The fact that texts may be read over long temporal and cultural distances rests on institutional frames of this kind.

Time-Structure

"Culture" may be understood as the cover term for the sum total of extended situations or, rather, the extended hyper-situation including all other situations in which cultural texts are encoded, transmitted, and reenacted. To be sure, this is not meant as a definition of culture, but just as a way to highlight one specific aspect of culture. The extension of the situation of communication past the limits of direct interaction, as well as the creation of a hyper-situation extending over several millennia, is an achievement of memory; it is this temporal aspect of culture that highlights its memory function. Writing is just one form of transmission and reenactment, albeit a very decisive one. The use of writing in the transmission of cultural texts changes fundamentally the time-structure of cultural memory. All the other forms of institutionalizing an extended situation depend on time and place, on temporal recurrence and/or spatial translocation. You have to wait for a feast to return or a rite to be performed, and you have to go to an image, a monument, a sacred place in order to reconnect with its meaning.[17] To reconnect with the meaning of written cultural texts, you do not have to wait for the next performance, you just have to read them.

The difference may be illustrated by a quotation from Flavius Josephus, who opposed Jewish and Gentile forms of cultural participation:

> That high and sublime knowledge, which the Gentiles with difficulty attained unto, in the rare and temporary celebration of their Mysteries, was habitually taught to the Jews, at all times. . . . Where, in any place but in this, are the whole People, by the special diligence of the Priests, to whom the care of public instruction is committed, accurately taught the principles of true piety? So that the body-politic seems, as it were, one great Assembly,

> constantly kept together, for the celebration of some sacred Mysteries. For those things which the Gentiles keep up for a few days only, that is, during those solemnities they call "Mysteries" and "Initiations," we, with vast delight, and a plenitude of knowledge, which admits of no error, fully enjoy, and perpetually contemplate through the whole course of our lives.[18]

The Gentiles have to wait until the next celebration of their mysteries, but the Jews are in constant and continuous possession of their cultural texts, because they are "habitually taught" by "public instruction." Their "mysteries" are permanent. Their form of community or "body politic" coheres and reproduces itself not by way of ritual but by means of teaching and learning. When Josephus speaks of "teaching," he does not just think of teaching how to write and read, but of interpretation, or exegesis. To ensure the continuous readability of written cultural texts over a long stretch of time, which inevitably brings about changes of language and historical reality, the meaning of the texts must be kept alive by constant adaptation to changing circumstances. Otherwise the texts' meaning gets lost within three or four generations of social memory. In a literate culture such as the Jewish society Josephus describes, continuous exegesis fulfills the function of institutionalizing the extended situation of cultural coherence, which in the pagan world is fulfilled by ritual repetition.

This case may be generalized. Cultural texts form the cement or connective backbone of a society that ensures its identity and coherence through the sequence of generations. Leading the sphere of material objects aside, we may say that the dominant principle of coherence can be institutionally realized either in ritualistic or "textualistic" form. Ritual coherence is the predominant principle of cultural reproduction, in which the cultural texts are performed in the ways that Josephus ascribes to the Gentiles: feasts and rites. Textual coherence prevails when the cultural texts are reproduced by ways of teaching and learning, which do not require much ritualization and formalization. Textual coherence requires institutions of learning and interpretation. Oral societies need a memorization technique of transmission and a ritual or ceremonial organization of performance. Writing or notational systems of pre-writing such as knotted chords and pictography might play a subsidiary role for the specialists in helping them to remember long stories or lists in the right order. But memory remains always the main carrier of the central stock of cultural knowledge, and ritual performance remains the dominant form of reproducing the cultural texts. The more literate a society, the more continuous, de-ritualized, and individual is the form of participation in cultural texts. The greatest change in such participation has been brought about by the printing press.[19]

Text-Structure:
Mouvance and Exegesis

"Textual coherence" requires not only the use of writing but also a continuous long-term readability of the written texts. The language of the texts must not deviate too much from the spoken language, and the textual world must correspond to the actual world people are living in. Josephus, speaking of the Jewish case, refers to the "care of public instruction" and "accurate teaching" as devices the Jews employed in order not to lose contact with the meaning of their texts. The Jewish case, however, is extreme in that the cultural texts were not only written down but brought into the form of a canon, meaning that they must not be changed, neither in the stock of texts selected for canonization nor in the wording, the surface structure of the singular texts. If the texts themselves must not be changed, exegesis is the only solution to ensure textual coherence.

Before the canonization of texts and the rise of exegesis, however, the texts themselves were changed, that is, reformulated, amplified or substituted by other texts. Their "surface structure" was sacrificed in order to save at least part of their meaning. This is why even written texts tend to exist over a longer stretch of time in many different versions. In order to remain understandable, they are constantly rewritten, enlarged, continued. The continuous growth of the book of Isaiah, first into Deutero- then into Trito-Isaiah, is a typical case of how a cultural text changes in what the Assyriologist Leo Oppenheim called "the stream of tradition."[20] The epic of Gilgamesh developed in the course of its transmission and redaction from a cycle of sagas into the "twelve-tablet composition," as it appears in the Neoassyrian library of Assurbanipal at Niniveh. In a similar way, the Egyptian Book of the Dead developed from just a pool of unconnected spells out of which every individual funerary papyrus picked its own specific selection into a real book with a fixed selection of 167 spells in a particular order. Written texts, in this stream of tradition, share to a certain degree a sort of oral text. The medievalist Paul Zumthor, in his *Introduction à la poésie orale*, coined the term *mouvance*, by which he understands the flexibility even of written texts to adapt to changing audiences.[21]

This flexibility is categorically stopped and excluded by the process of canonization. A cultural text that becomes part of the canon shares the absolute fixation of its surface articulation with sacred texts. Sacred texts are not necessarily cultural texts; they can be magical spells only a few specialists know, whereas cultural texts are by definition the common property of the community or at least representative elite. Sacralization and canonization are different phenomena. They share the common principle of fixed wording but stem from different motives. The notion of "canonization" should be reserved for literate culture, concerning a specific form of the transmission of written texts, whereas sacralization occurs also in oral tradition. The borderline case of the Ṛgveda, which is an orally transmitted canon of sacred texts, must be explained separately and should not blur this necessary distinction. Sacred texts are verbal enshrinements of the holy. In sacred texts, not a syllable may be changed in order to ensure the magical power of the words to "presentify" the divine. In this context, it is not understanding that matters but the correctness of pronunciation, the ritual purity of the speaker, and other requirements concerning proper circumstances of performance. This principle of inflexibility and absolute fixation applies to sacred texts independently of their oral or literate form of transmission. Sacred texts, therefore, are exempt from the pressure to adapt to the hermeneutical conditions of a changing world.

In the process of canonization, the principle of sacred fixation is applied to cultural texts. They are treated like verbal temples that enshrine divine presence, but at the same time they require understanding and application in order to exert their formative and normative impulses and demands. The solution to this problem is exegesis. Exegesis, or hermeneutics, is the successor of *mouvance*. In the *mouvance* stage of literate transmission, the commentary is worked into the fabric of the text. This method has been shown by Michael Fishbane to be typical of the biblical texts in their formative phase.[22] They are full of glosses, pieces of commentary that later redactors have added to the received text. In Babylonia, the closure of the verbal surface structure of a text was applied not only to sacred but also to literary texts as early as the end of the second millennium BCE, when Mesopotamian scribes started inserting blessings and curses in their colophons of literary texts in order to prevent not only material damage of the tablet but also willful alteration of the text: "Neither add nor subtract!"[23] Once the text is closed by canonization, the commentary must stay outside and accompany the written text by separate ways of transmission, which are very often oral, as is still the case in a traditional Islamic *madrasa* or a Jewish *yeshiva*. Also in oral recitation, canonical texts are often set off from commentaries using a formalization of recitation typical of sacred texts. They are sung instead of spoken.[24] The difference between singing and speaking is as important for the performance of cultural texts as the difference between orality and literacy for their transmission.[25]

The "Cultic" and the "Classic"

To sum up: the main function of cultural texts may be defined as a connective principle working in both the social and the temporal dimensions, a kind of normative and formative cultural program that conveys and reproduces cultural identity from one generation to the next. This constitutes what may be called their "identity function." The original and traditional locus of cultural texts is memory (for storage and transmission) and ritual (for reproduction). Rituals provide the context for the ceremonial recitation, circulation, and communication of cultural texts. Although the evolution of literate culture and the invention of the printing press have led to a general accessibility of cultural texts, some traces of this original ritual framing are still preserved even in modern culture. In Germany you have to wait until Christmas for a public performance of the *Christmas Oratorio* and until Good Friday to listen to the *St. Matthew Passion* and *St. John Passion* by Johann Sebastian Bach; these rank among the cultural texts. This condition might be due to their religious meaning, but the same applies also to secular texts. *Die Fledermaus*, by Johann Strauss, is linked to New Year's Eve and *Parsifal*, by Richard Wagner, to Good Friday. But these are exceptional cases. Normally, our modern culture is characterized by the principle of ubiquitous and simultaneous accessibility of everything. Nevertheless, DVDs have not supplanted movies and plays, and CDs have not suppressed concerts. On the contrary, the concept of "live performance" has acquired a new importance in the age of technical reproduction and general accessibility. A performance receives its special status as "live performance" only through the existence of technological recordings, in much the same way as a linguistic unit receives its status as a text through the existence of its commentary or an "original" through the existence of copies.

Cultural texts partake of the cultic and the classic. With this I would like to come back to the point from which I started: the need for transmission and the will to form, both answering the specifically human condition of being in time, of existing in a temporal horizon extending the life span of an individual. In their cultic aspect, cultural texts (and I am again referring to "texts" in the broad sense of the term, including pictures, rites, dances, films) aim at participation, at shaping a community of participants; in their classic aspect cultural texts realize the will to form in an outstanding way and aim at imitation, variation, quotation, recycling. The cultic is related to the social dimension, the classic to the temporal dimension. A classic is an artifact that survives the changes of fashions, remaining a model of beauty and perfection because of its unsurpassable formal and symbolic pregnancy,[26] whereas the cultic binds a community of believers or simply lovers (and sometimes only a short-lived generation of fans, buffs, aficionados) under its spell because of the religious or otherwise compelling magnetism of its theme. In cultural texts, both principles combine, but in different proportions. Culture comprises much more than cultural texts, and however one defines the problematic concept of "culture," I am not arguing for its reduction to memory. By focusing on a section both of culture and of memory at which these notions intersect, we can see how cultural texts fulfill the memory function of culture, which is certainly not its only function but the one without which culture as a whole would not work.

5

Memory in Oral Tradition

John Miles Foley

Ej! Where we sit let us make merry:
Ej! May God make us merry,
Make us merry and give us conversation.
E! And may he assign us greater fortune
In this place and every other!
Now on this occasion, my dear brothers,
We wish to count out a song.
Ej! Sometime long ago it was in time,
Long ago it was, now we are remembering
In this place and every other.
In a certain epoch and in the olden time,
Sultan Selim declared war.[1]

With this prologue the South Slavic *guslar* ("bard") Salih Ugljanin began his performance of the oral epic later assigned the title *The Song of Baghdad*, and in the process he divulged a great deal about his concept of memory in oral tradition. It is with "insider" opinions and statements like his, conveyed as part of the story-performances themselves, that I will be concerned in this chapter. Rather than applying external frames of reference from contemporary western scholarship, in other words, I want to listen to what the practitioners themselves have to say about the role of memory. Fully aware that poetic description is in no way equivalent to the fruits of ethnographic investigation, I will provide samples of their remarks not from discursive dialogue but from within the special world and arena of the poem-performances themselves. It may prove useful for theorists of memory—necessarily working as "outsiders" to these oral traditions—to compare my findings with their analytical models, but for the present purpose my goal is to let the oral singers have the floor, to let them speak about memory in oral tradition using their own performance-specific idiom.

Before launching on an itinerary that will take us to early medieval England, twentieth-century Bosnia, and ancient Greece,[2] let me provide a methodological note and a telegraphic preview of the journey's conclusions. I am essentially "interviewing" oral epic poets from these three traditions and considering how their notions of memory compare with ours by concentrating on the relationship of performance to memorial re-creation. I have no expectation of absolutely uniform situations across various cultures and eras; the collapse of the Great Divide of orality versus literacy, as well as the growing realization that literacy must be understood as ideological rather than autonomous,[3] should disabuse us of such assumptions. What I propose, then, is to debrief the bards by looking at a few relevant passages from each tradition in order to deduce intracultural notions of what memory is and how it works. I should stress that the oral poets' "responses" are of course conveyed in their own words and indeed within a well-defined, narrow-spectrum register of language that is neither analytical nor academic.[4] For that reason the interviews won't necessarily dovetail with contemporary western research on memory; on the other hand, they may go straight to the heart of the matter in unusual ways.

To preview the conclusions—so that readers may follow the individual responses below more cogently—the oral singers tell us at least five things. First, memory in oral tradition is emphatically not a static retrieval mechanism for data. Second, it is very often a kinetic, emergent, creative activity. Third, in many cases it is linked to performance, without which it has no meaning. Fourth, memory typically entails an oral/aural communication requiring an auditor or audience. Fifth, and as a consequence of the first four qualities, memory in oral tradition is phenomenologically distinct from "our memory." And now to our interviews.

The Anglo-Saxon *Scop*

Within the approximately thirty thousand lines of oral-derived Old English (or Anglo-Saxon) poetry that survives in four major and several minor manuscripts dated to the last third of the tenth century, we find a curious 143-line poem, *Widsith*, that can most accurately be classified as an oral history. It amounts to a poetic travelogue recounting the experiences of its putative speaker, Widsith, meaning "Wide Journey" in Old English, as he plies his trade of itinerant poet across an enormous geographical area (the Celtic lands to Greece) and an equally impressive temporal expanse (the third through the sixth centuries). The poem's major editor, Kemp Malone, places the actual composition of *Widsith* in the seventh century,[5] with scholars leaving the riddle of precisely how it found its way into Bishop Leofric's Exeter Book manuscript some three hundred years later an open question.

Perhaps the best solution to these chronological and geographical illogicalities is to realize that the *Widsith* poet has constructed a fictive oral bard named Wide Journey who answers a number of purposes. Not only do his superhuman longevity and remarkable travelogue provide a vehicle for a larger-than-life portrayal of many courts and their regents in numerous lands over many years, but Widsith's legendary character serves as an anthropomorphization of the oral tradition itself. That is, the far-roaming, long-lived oral bard provides a vehicle for pan-European oral history over four centuries at the same time that he embodies the idea of oral tradition as a medium and presence in all of these cultures and venues. In this latter respect, Widsith the fictive persona functions as do many such parallel figures in South Slavic and Mongolian oral traditions and perhaps as does the legendary Homer himself.[6]

Here is how Widsith opens his performance (important phrases are italicized):

> Widsið *maðolade,*   *wordhord onleac,*
> se þe [monna] mæst   mægþa ofer eorþan,
> folca, geondferde.   Oft he [on] flette geþah
> mynelicum maþþum. . . .   4
>   Ongon þa worn *sprecan.*
> "Fela *ic* monna *gefrægn*   mægþum wealdan.   10
> Sceal þeoda gehwylc   þeawum lifgan,
> eorl' æfter oþrum   eðle rædan,
> se þe his þeodenstol   geþeon wile."

> Widsith *spoke, unlocked his word-hoard,*
> he who the greatest [of men], of tribes over the earth,
> of people, passed through. Often in the hall he received
> handsome treasures. . . .   4
>   Then he began *to speak* many things.
> "*I have learned* of the tribes of men.   10

Each of peoples must live according to its customs,
each of nobles must govern his native land after his forebear,
he who wishes his chieftain-throne to thrive."

What can we discern from the account of what this oral poet tells us he is doing? For one thing, the opening line alone provides a robust frame of reference for what is about to transpire. The formulaic phrase "[X] spoke" ("[X] *maðelade*") functions as a single, idiomatic unit of utterance that ritually introduces a speech, keying a fictive universe in which a character will directly address a real or imagined audience. Furthermore, the immediately following half line, "unlocked his word-hoard" (*word-hord onleac*), has deep traditional resonance as a cue for the onset of oral traditional performance.[7] In *Andreas* and *Beowulf*, two other poems from the Old English canon, the same phrase is used to describe the divulging of precious information via oral communication. Taken together, these two meta-narrative bytes—each of them most faithfully understood as a single "word"—indicate that Widsith will be delivering a remembered personal history as a speech-act of performance. Memory is here being portrayed as kinetic and linked with oral/aural exchange.

While we will not be surprised, then, when Widsith's historical account is characterized as "speaking" at line 9, we should pay close attention to what he means by saying "I have learned" (*ic gefrægn*) many things. The Old English verb *gefricgan* carries the specific sense of learning by asking through active inquiry—in other words, through oral/aural transmission. Widsith is telling us that he has learned about the "tribes of men," in particular the importance of the leader's respect for the individual customs of his people, via the medium of oral tradition. In the itinerary that follows, he will specify those courts he (supposedly) visited in person, but here he is also acknowledging his debt to other oral historians. And if we understand this larger-than-life bard as a personification of the oral tradition, then we can understand how history accrues to that tradition over time. Either way, the enterprise of oral history is understood as collective and transpersonal.

The *Beowulf* poet describes the process of remembering and transmitting cultural lore and identity in a similar fashion. His poem-performance takes the form of a different genre, the epic, and covers some 3,182 lines; nonetheless, he uses the same specialized storytelling language as does his colleague the *Widsith* poet.[8] *Beowulf* is, like all Old English poems, difficult or impossible to date with any precision because of its oral-derived nature, but the story itself goes back to a time before the Anglo-Saxon migration from Denmark and arrival in Britain (usually set at 449 CE), and the version that survives in a tenth-century manuscript probably stems from a composition no later than the eighth century. Most important for our purposes, the poem's texture of formulaic phrases, typical scenes, and narrative patterns locates it securely within the atemporal canon of manuscript works that derive from oral traditional performance.[9] During the interview the *Beowulf* poet will speak in the "large words" of oral tradition, very much within the register of poetic composition.[10]

One example of his poetic vocabulary is the brief but highly idiomatic unit that begins the epic, a prologue that, while different from the introductory segment in *Widsith*, has numerous parallels within surviving Old English poetry.[11] Here are the lines in question (with especially important elements italicized):

> *Hwæt, we* Gar-Dena   *in geardagum,*
> þeodcyninga   þrym *gefrunon,*
> hu ða æþelingas   ellen fremedon.   3

> *Lo, we* of the Spear-Danes *in days of yore,*
> of the chieftain-kings *have learned* the glory,
> how these nobles performed valor.   3

This small capsule packs a powerful traditional punch by idiomatically portraying the process of remembering as once again a kinetic and collective activity, a performance in which the poet will tell what he has learned from oral tradition. The element *Hwæt* ("Lo") is an interjection that signals the onset of performance in this and numerous other Old English poems, and the first person plural pronoun *we* ("we") describes the transmission of knowledge and lore between a performer and an audience (arguably between many poets and audiences over time and space). The mythic timeframe of the events to follow is cued by the formulaic phrase "in days of yore" (*in geardagum*), variants of which again occur throughout Anglo-Saxon verse. Moreover, just as in *Widsith*, the *Beowulf* poet identifies the source of his knowledge via the verb that entails "learning by asking" ("we have learned"; *gefrunon*), that is, that describes apprehending through oral tradition. What will follow, the *Beowulf* poet is affirming by a tried-and-true traditional mechanism, is now being remembered in kinetic, collective performance—that is, exactly as he learned it.

A second example from *Beowulf* describes the Danish court bard's activities in the wake of the hero Beowulf's triumph over the monster Grendel. In this part of the interview we glimpse an oral poet—the "king's thane," as he is called—both praising the recent event of the hero's victory and remembering a prior parallel event that amplifies the immediate action by reference to the traditional lore of the group (867b–74a):

> Hwilum cyninges þegn,
> guma *gilphlæden,   gidda gemyndig,*
> *se ðe ealfela   ealdgesegena*
> *worn gemunde,*   word oþer fand   870
> soðe gebunden;   secg eft ongan
> sið Beowulfes   snyttrum styrian,
> ond on sped *wrecan*   spel gerade,
> *wordum wrixlan.*

> At times the king's thane,
> a man *laden with glory, mindful of songs,*
> *he who of all of the old traditions (sayings)*
> *remembered a great many,* found another word [*singular*] 870
> bound in truth; the man in turn began
> to steer the tale of Beowulf wisely,
> and to successfully *drive out* a fitting story,
> *to exchange words.*

The singer, or *scop*, is characterized as a kind of human repository, someone who is "laden with glory" (*gilphlæden*, referring to the glories of heroic accomplishment that he knows and can tell about) and "mindful of songs" (*gidda gemyndig*). Moreover, he is specifically said to remember "a great many" of "the old traditions." In other words, the poet stores poem-songs about traditional events, poem-songs that were themselves circulated via oral performance, in his memory.

And what does he do with these riches? In this case, Hrothgar's unnamed court bard not only lauds the young hero for his defeat of Grendel but "finds another word / bound in truth"; that is, he reaches into his word-hoard and draws out the analogous tale (a single "word") of Sigemund the dragonslayer as a means of amplifying Beowulf's achievement by comparison. Aligning the new with a traditional precedent amounts to inculcating the new into the ongoing *ealdgesegena* ("old traditions," 869b), with the tale of Beowulf matched to the preexisting story. What he proceeds to narrate, then, is first the story of Sigemund, with its positive valence of bravery and a king's protection of his people, and then the obverse story of the evil king Heremod, an antitype who provides a model for all that Beowulf should not become. From main story to analogue, the singer is described as "exchanging words" (*wordum wrixlan*, 874a)—telling the story of Beowulf at one narrative remove, by indirection.

A few aspects of his remembering and his performance (and the two cannot be disentangled) should be emphasized. For one thing, this court poet performs with vigor by "driving out" (*wrecan*, 873b) his tale, a somatic trope that is both common to descriptions of Old English bardic activities and also a feature of performance situations in other oral traditions.[12] In a similarly cross-cultural fashion, the *Beowulf* poet uses the term "word" twice in this passage (870b, 874a) to indicate an entire segment of narrative, a story-byte, rather than the lexical or dictionary-enshrined atom of expression customarily defined by white spaces on either side of an unbroken sequence of letters. More generally, and as in *Widsith*, memory is being pictured as kinetic, emergent, and creative as well as linked indissolubly to performance. It must be enacted, not just passively retained. And in that regard memory involves an oral/aural communication that requires an audience of co-rememberers.

The South Slavic *Guslar*

The next stop on our itinerary is an interview with the performer of South Slavic oral epic, called a *guslar* in recognition of the accompanying instrument (the *gusle*) that both provides mnemonic support for his vocalization and cues narrative shifts in his stories.[13] I reproduce below a sample nine-line *pripjev*, or prologue, which happens to introduce Salih Ugljanin's November 22, 1934, performance of *The Song of Baghdad*. It is well to keep in mind that prologues are an optional and generic element in the South Slavic tradition, so that until at least the eleventh line this keynote passage could be affixed to any epic story within the taletelling tradition. Here, then, is the *pripjev* plus two lines of the main narrative, with significant features italicized:

> *Ej!* Dje sed*imo* da se veselj*imo*:
> *Ej!* da bi *nas* i Bog veseljijo,
> Veseljijo pa razgovorijo,
> *E!* pa ljepšu *nam* sreću dijeljijo
> *Na ovome mestu i svakome*!   5
> Sad po tome, *moja braćo draga*,
> Pa vel*imo* da pjesmu broj*imo*.
> Ej! Davno nekad u zemanu bilo,
> Davno bilo, sada *pominjemo*

Na ovome mestu i svakome.   10
Jednom vaktu a starom zemanu,
Sultan Seljim rata *jotvorijo. . . .*

Ej! Where *we* sit let *us* make merry:
Ej! May God make *us* merry,
Make [us] merry and give [us] conversation.
E! And may he assign *us* greater fortune
In this place and every other!   5
Now on this occasion, *my dear brothers*,
We wish that *we* may count out a song.
Ej! Sometime long ago it was in time,
Long ago it was, now *we are remembering*
In this place and every other.   10
In a certain epoch and in the olden time,
Sultan Selim declared war.

Several typical features help to represent this act of memory about to
be realized, a rite of remembering, as it were. The four instances of the
interjection *E(j)!* (1, 2, 4, and 8), parallel to the *Hwæt* that begins *Beowulf*
and other Old English poetic performances, key the performance arena
and ready the participants for the exchange by prescribing what sort of
event is about to ensue. The collective nature of the enterprise is absolutely transparent in the recurrent reference to "we" and "us," whether in
the first person plural endings of verbs (1, 7, and 9) or via correspondingly
inflected pronouns (2 and 4), and by the direct address to "my dear brothers" (6). Additionally, the speech-act of epic performance is portrayed as
transpersonal and transgeographic in the identification of the same event
as happening "in this place and every other" (5, 10); in other words, other
poets and audiences have conducted the ritual elsewhere and at different
times, and there is no reason to believe that it will not continue in various
forms and forums in the future.

Finally, in a powerful statement of how memory works in performance, the *guslar* Ugljanin speaks of the remembered story as being incar-
nated in an ongoing remembrance—not as a delimited, finite fact but as
a realization-in-progress. By using the imperfective form of the verb "to
remember" (*pominjemo*, "we are remembering"), he characterizes the singer's and audience's joint re-creation as, once again, a kinetic, emergent,
and creative act that takes the form of an oral/aural communication.

Another prologue from the South Slavic oral epic tradition may help
to emphasize some of these event-centered realities. The following *pripjev*, which was employed by the *guslar* Ibro Bašić in a performance of

Alagić Alija and Velagić Selim on June 7, 1935, presents the act of epic remembering as a highly natural, even inevitable, event:[14]

> *Aj!* Teško vuku ne jedući mesa,
> A junaku ne pijući piva,
> Mladu momku ne ljub*lj*eć' djevojku,
> A i nožu [u] nejakoj ruci,
> A i pušci u strašivoj ruci,   5
> I djevojci koja sama dodje—
> Prvo jutro prekorna je, *brate*;
> Da si kakva, ne bi sama došla.
> Pa po tome da pjesmu re*čemo*
> Od staroga vakta i zemana;   10
> Davno bilo, sad *se spominjalo.*

> *Ay*! It's hard for a wolf not to eat meat,
> And for a hero not to have a drink,
> For a young man not to kiss a girl,
> And for a knife in a weak hand,
> And for a rifle in a timid hand,   5
> And for a girl who comes alone—
> The first morning she's scolded, *brothers*;
> If you're such a one, you shouldn't come alone.
> Then in turn let *us* tell a song
> From that olden period and time;   10
> Long ago it was, now *it is being remembered.*

A few of the signals are familiar: the opening interjection *Aj!*, for example, or the collective address to the audience ("brothers," *brate*, 7) paired with the imperative construction indicating that the poet and audience are jointly conducting the ritual ("let us tell," *rečemo*, 9). The ending affirmation of a continuous and continuing process of memorial re-creation ("it is being remembered," *se spominjalo*, 11) takes a slightly different shape from "we are remembering" in the prior example, appearing here as an impersonal, but similarly transpersonal, attribution. And there is also another emphasis: in Bašić's *pripjev*, the power of the rite is explicitly foregrounded in the series of proverbs that constitute the first eight lines of the eleven-line unit. Each of the first three compared scenarios—a wolf's need for meat, a hero's predilection for (alcoholic) drink, and a young man's desire to kiss a girl—document familiar and universally expected processes in nature. The next two, involving the knife and rifle, are heroic inevitabilities; weapons are useless in the hands of those who can't wield them, we're being told. The last proverb speaks to the equally natural difficulties a new bride experiences in the home of her husband's family, a much-lamented plight in various song genres within this patriarchal and patrilocal culture.

To summarize this interview with the South Slavic *guslar*, these two prologues clearly illustrate several of the conclusions previewed above. The model of memory described and implied by Salih Ugljanin and Ibro Bašić is the furthest thing from a retrieval mechanism whose function it is to recall static data. Both singers present memory as a kinetic, emergent, and creative activity that occurs and recurs in a ritualistic fashion, "in this place and every other," as Ugljanin puts it. Their recall process is also not an analytical act of individual achievement but rather a collective and contextualized re-creation undertaken by "us," the *guslar* and the audience together, in what amounts to co-performance. This oral/aural communication takes place in the virtual arena of performance and is characterized by both of these singers as an ongoing process ("now we are remembering," "now it is being remembered"). The goal of memory is not retrieving data but rather re-creating and re-living an experience.

Homer and the *Aoidoi*

My interview with Homer will consist of examining three passages from *The Odyssey* in which we are given an insight into how he and his tradition conceive of memory. The first of these is the celebrated prologue to the poem, with its address to the Muse (Book 1.1–10):

> Ἄνδρα μοι ἔννεπε, Μοῦσα, πολύτροπον, ὃς μάλα πολλὰ
> πλάγχθη, ἐπεὶ Τροίης ἱερὸν πτολίεθρον ἔπερσε.
> πολλῶν δ' ἀνθρώπων ἴδεν ἄστεα καὶ νόον ἔγνω,
> πολλὰ δ' ὅ γ' ἐν πόντῳ πάθεν ἄλγεα ὃν κατὰ θυμόν,
> ἀρνύμενος ἥν τε ψυχὴν καὶ νόστον ἑταίρων.
> ἀλλ' οὐδ' ὣς ἑτάρους ἐρρύσατο, ἱέμενός περ.
> αὐτῶν γὰρ σφετέρῃσιν ἀτασθαλίῃσιν ὄλοντο,
> νήπιοι, οἳ κατὰ βοῦς Ὑπερίονος Ἠελίοιο
> ἤσθιον. αὐτὰρ ὁ τοῖσιν ἀφείλετο νόστιμον ἦμαρ.
> τῶν ἁμόθεν γε, θεά, θύγατερ Διός, εἰπὲ καὶ ἡμῖν.

O Muse, *say* many-turning man *in me*, who very many times
Was beaten back, after he sacked the sacred city of Troy.
He saw many men's cities and came to know their minds,

And he suffered many woes in his heart on the sea,
Striving to win his soul and his comrades' return.
But even so he did not save his comrades, though desiring to.
For they perished by their own recklessness,
Foolish ones, whom the cattle of Hyperion's son Helios
Utterly consumed. And so their return-day was lost.
Of these events, *from somewhere*, O goddess, daughter of
    Zeus, *speak also to us.*

Homer is asking for his memory and performance to be stimulated by the Muse assigned to epic poetry, Calliope, specifically imploring her to "say . . . in me" (*moi. . . ennepe*) the tale of Odysseus the many-turning man. The re-creation of the story, which, as Plato's *Ion* tells us, amounts to a divinely inspired embodiment of the dramatis personae (and thus of the narrative action) by the singer and audience, will occur within the cooperative synergy of performance. Homer acknowledges this collective environment by asking the Muse, located "somewhere" else (*hamothen*), to "speak also to us" (*eipe kai hēmin*)—not just to the poet himself, in other words, and not only to this group; the pronoun "us" and the adverb "also" bring the present audience and other poets and audiences integrally into the picture. Once again we have a portrayal of a rite of performance, a recurring and participatory experience shared by poet(s) and audience(s) as they re-create the events in question. The Olympian Muse serves as priestess for that temporal rite of memorial performance.

The Odyssey also presents two portraits of practicing bards (*aoidoi*) that offer complementary perspectives and help us to understand the indigenous idea of memory in ancient Greek oral tradition. The first of these occurs in Book 8 and involves Demodokos, court poet in the land of the Phaeacians; Odysseus is instructing the herald to bring an offering of food to honor the singer (8.477–81):

"Κῆρυξ, τῇ δή, τοῦτο πόρε κρέας, ὄφρα φάγῃσι,
Δημοδόκῳ, καί μιν προσπτύξομαι, ἀχνύμενός περ.
πᾶσι γὰρ ἀνθρώποισιν ἐπιχθονίοισιν ἀοιδοὶ
τιμῆς ἔμμοροί εἰσι καὶ αἰδοῦς, οὕνεκ᾽ ἄρα σφέας
οἴμας Μοῦσ᾽ ἐδίδαξε, φίλησε δὲ φῦλον ἀοιδῶν."

"Herald, come now and take this slice of meat, so that he may eat,
To Demodokos, for I would greet him even though he is grieving.
For among all peoples on the earth the singers
Are due a share of honor and respect, since to them
The Muse taught the *pathways*, for she loves the singers' tribe."

In addition to boosting the social prominence of the singer Demodokos and (at one remove) asserting the prominence of his own identity and
profession as well, Homer is revealing something vital about memory in
oral tradition through his description of what the Muse provides to *aoidoi*.
While we might expect her bequest to consist of a fine voice, a large repertoire of songs, or perhaps the ability to retrieve large blocks of myth-data,
Homer instead characterizes her gift as instruction in how to navigate
pathways (*oimas*, 8.481). According to his perspective, the *aoidoi* exercise
not a rote, text-like memory but a plastic, generative process of recall, not
a static knowledge of a preexisting inventory but rather an ability to nego-
tiate networks with multiple possibilities. This negotiation, undertaken as
we have learned in the company of the co-creating audience(s), is a process that leads to the products we call "performances." Each performance
will take shape as both a singular, time- and space-bound experience and
concurrently a version of a larger, inexpressibly plural set of potentials.
Successful performance means remembering how to travel the pathways.

The same underlying concept informs Homer's portrait of the bard
Phemios, the court poet at the palace of Odysseus and Penelope on Ithaca.
In this brief passage from Book 22, during the aftermath of the slaughter
of the suitors, the *aoidos* Phemios pleads for his life with his master Odysseus (22.344–49):

> "γουνοῦμαί σ᾽, Ὀδυσεῦ. σὺ δέ μ᾽ αἴδεο καί μ᾽ ἐλέησον.
> αὐτῷ τοι μετόπισθ᾽ ἄχος ἔσσεται, εἴ κεν ἀοιδὸν
> πέφνῃς, ὅς τε θεοῖσι καὶ ἀνθρώποισιν ἀείδω.
> αὐτοδίδακτος δ᾽εἰμί, θεὸς δέ μοι ἐν φρεσὶν οἴμας
> παντοίας ἐνέφυσεν. ἔοικα δέ τοι παραείδειν
> ὥς τε θεῷ· τῷ μή με λιλαίεο δειροτομῆσαι."

> "I entreat you, Odysseus. Respect me and have pity on me.
> There will be woe for you yourself afterwards if you kill
> The singer, I who sing for gods and humans alike.
> I am self-taught, but the god implanted in my mind
> *Pathways* of all kinds. I am worthy to sing before you
> As before a god. So do not be eager to cut my throat."

Not illogically, considering that Odysseus has just destroyed the suitors and unfaithful servants and left the hall littered and bloody, Phemios's
primary motive is to save his own skin. But his argument for being spared
goes beyond a call for respecting his profession and reveals a good deal

about his conception of the bardic craft. Arguing that he is "self-taught" (*autodidaktos*), Phemios affirms that he realizes songs in his own way; that is, he puts a personal and idiolectal stamp on his traditional inheritance. And how does he proceed? Once again we hear an *aoidos* speak of navigating "pathways of all kinds," in this instance networks that the god (ostensibly the Muse) *implanted* in his mind (*enephysen*; literally, "caused to grow"). As he pleads for his life, the singer characterizes his value to his master and to Ithacan society as most fundamentally an ability to harness the structural and idiomatic potentials that constitute his tradition.

Postscript:
Oral Tradition and the Internet

Homer's three responses reveal a concept of memorial performance that sounds a great deal like a familiar modern activity: navigation on the Internet. Although the two media might seem strange bedfellows—in many instances flanking a long and highly developed age of print—in fact they both operate via negotiation of multifaceted networks. Like oral performance, surfing the Web is an interactive, emergent process that contrasts dramatically with the experience of reading a book.

Consider for a moment the phenomenon of the Web site address, as it exists in the electronic commonplace of the URL. While that designated string of alphanumeric characters has a certain composite logic, stemming from the prefix "www" plus a name for a Web site plus a domain designator such as ".com" or ".org," it is only in its idiomatic entirety that the URL makes any real sense. Like the Homeric phrase "swift-footed Achilles," whose mission as a composite "word" is to conjure the character of the great Greek hero for emergent deployment in the narrative, so the URL's purpose is to take you to a particular node in the network where further activities are possible. Change one "syllable" of either "word," and the process aborts: either you are sent to the wrong character/site, or your pathway abruptly comes to an end.[15]

For Homer and his bardic compatriots from medieval England and twentieth-century Bosnia, then, memorial performance amounts essentially to surfing their oral traditions. Navigating through the system of pathways, where options present themselves at every narrative juncture, is a far different kind of involvement than that demanded by a text, which, however variously it may be received, still remains an item, an objective reality. From Widsith's speech-act to the *guslar*'s continuous remembering to Homer's pathways, these oral poets present themselves not as text-analysts but as entrepreneurs of reawakened experience.

Thus, oral tradition and the Internet share some core characteristics. Neither medium is a static retrieval mechanism for data; each is ever-evolving and brought into being by the performer or computer user. Both are demonstrably kinetic, emergent, creative activities, and both are linked to actual performance (as opposed to being predetermined and fossilized within the covers of a book). Finally, and because of these shared features, oral tradition and the Internet are phenomenologically distinct from our default, prosthetic (because text-modeled) concept of memory. To put it aphoristically, oral tradition and the Internet mimic the way we think.[16]

6

Tradition in the Mouth of the Hero: Jesus as an Interpreter of Scripture

Ellen Bradshaw Aitken

"Every hero is a performer." Thus writes Richard P. Martin in his discussion of heroic speech in the archaic Greek poetic tradition, *The Language of Heroes*.[1] Or, to put it another way, heroes in poems such as *The Iliad* and *The Odyssey* utter authoritative speech acts (designated as μῦθοι in the poems themselves) in a traditional medium; each hero is represented as composing in performance so as "to project his individual voice."[2] Martin argues further that this display of heroic performance provides ways of understanding the poetics of the tradition itself, not least of which is the status of the traditional poet or "singer" as a hero, a phenomenon that we can observe in relation to the figure of Homer in ancient Greek culture, as also with traditional poets in many other cultures.[3]

Taking its cue from Martin's work, this chapter examines two early Christian portrayals of Jesus as a performer, specifically as a "performer" of scripture. These various portrayals can offer clues to the "poetics" of traditions about Jesus, that is, indications of the process of the formation in community of ways of speaking about Jesus. A consideration of heroes as performers of particular kinds of speech—within the conceptualization of Greek hero cult—provides both perspective on the portrayals of Jesus and also a possible matrix of practices that informed the ways of remembering Jesus within early Christianity. This work is part of a larger ongoing project investigating the role of hero cult in early Christianity. This project does not so much focus on the story-pattern of the hero as a model for stories about Jesus and others[4] but rather emphasizes the dynamics of cult practice, namely, the means by which worshippers engaged with heroes through consultation, veneration, initiation, and remembrance—among other practices.[5] As I look at the intersection of hero cult and traditions about Jesus, I therefore attend particularly to the practices of remembrance as portrayed in the mouth of Jesus.

At the outset, however, a few words of orientation are necessary. By "remembrance" and "the poetics of remembrance" I mean the practices in community for shaping, telling, and retelling a tradition (narrative, hymnic, or otherwise) centering around a specific figure or event and being uttered through the medium of an existing treasury of words, motifs, and authoritative ways of speaking. "Remembrance" is thus grounded in performance, in the conventions of marked speech (speech acts) within a tradition, and in previous acts of remembrance.[6] It is also intrinsic to cult practice as one of the means of activating the presence of the cult hero and of engaging with that hero.[7] In defining remembrance in this way, I am particularly indebted to the stream of Homeric scholarship beginning with Milman Parry and Albert Lord[8] and developing through the work of Gregory Nagy,[9] Leonard Muellner,[10] Nicole Loraux,[11] Richard P. Martin,[12] Corinne Pache,[13] Casey Dué,[14] and others.

It is also my working assumption that hero cult was alive and well in the Hellenistic world of early Christianity and that it was ubiquitous in the environments in which traditions about Jesus were developing in the first through third centuries CE and beyond.[15] This is confirmed not only in relation to material culture but also in the writers of the Second Sophistic. Philostratus, for example, composing his *Heroikos*, drew upon the practices of hero cult not as nostalgia but as living traditions in his own time; he is by no means alone in using this strategy.[16]

The *Heroikos* is thus one of the three texts that I employ here, drawing upon the extensive recent study of this text[17] and specifically upon the work Jennifer Maclean and I have done on the dynamics of interpretation and authoritative speech in the mouth of the hero at the center of the *Heroikos*, Protesilaos.[18] For the portrayal of Jesus as an interpreter of scriptures, I shall investigate how this dynamic works within the Gospel of Luke, particularly with the Emmaus story in Luke 24, and in the Letter to the Hebrews—texts that are deeply indebted to the conceptualization of cult practice in their constructions of Christian communal identity.

Flavius Philostratus, better known as the author of the *Life of Apollonius of Tyana*, composed the *Heroikos* in the early years of the reign of the emperor Alexander Severus, that is, between 222 and 235 CE.[19] The work is formulated as a dialogue between a skeptical yet curious Phoenician merchant who lands on the tip of the Thracian Chersonesus and a vine-dresser who tends the vineyards there around the grave of the hero Pro-tesilaos, the first Hellene to die in the Trojan War. Within the cult site of the hero's grave, the vinedresser has direct encounter with the hero "who has come back to life" (ἀναβιόω) and who appears to this devoted fol-lower. Over the course of these encounters, the hero transmits his knowl-edge to the vinedresser; specifically he tells the way "it really happened" in the Trojan War, thus exhibiting superhuman consciousness of events that happened even after his death.[20] The vinedresser describes Protesilaos's knowledge:

> To be cleansed of the body is the beginning of life for divine and thus blessed souls. For the gods, whose attendants they are, they then know, not by worshipping statues and conjectures, but by gaining visible association with them. And free from the body and its diseases, souls observe the affairs of mortals, both when souls are filled with prophetic skill and when the oracular power sends Bacchic frenzy upon them.
>
> At any, among those who critically examine, who will you say reads and has insight into them as Protesilaos does? Indeed, my guest, before Priam and Troy there was no epic recitation, nor had anyone sung of events that had not yet taken place. . . . Nev-ertheless, *Protesilaos knows everything of Homer and sings of many Trojan events that took place after his own lifetime,* and also of many Hellenic and Median events. (Philostratus, *Heroikos* 7.3-6, my emphasis)

This narrative framework provides a medium for the critique of Homer. Although the hero Protesilaos expresses high praise for Homer's talents as an epic singer, he repeatedly corrects Homer's account and descriptions. One of the most significant points of critique concerns Homer's emphasis on the hero Odysseus to the extent of omitting any mention of Odysseus's rival, Palamedes (Philostratus, *Heroikos* 24.2; 43.13-16). The stories of this bitter rivalry are known in other parts of the epic and dramatic tradition, as well as in art, but are absent from *The Iliad* and *The Odyssey*. By omitting events concerning Palamedes, the hero alleges, Homer distorts key mat-ters such as the cause of Odysseus's wandering and the reason for Achilles' wrath (Philostratus, *Heroikos* 25.13-17). In this way, Protesilaos reshapes the motives underlying the plots of both *The Iliad* and *The Odyssey*.

Correction of Homer is, of course, common in antiquity. Other Second Sophistic writers juxtapose alternative epic (often epichoric, local) traditions to the panhellenic "canon" of Homer.[21] What is distinctive about the *Heroikos*, however, is that Philostratus places this critique in the mouth of the hero (in contrast, for example, to finding the "right version" in an ancient inscription or from an Egyptian priest—two of the strategies employed by Dio Chrysostom[22]). The hero who has come back to life (ἀναβίοω) becomes the repository and source of the "truth" and the "right way of telling the story." As the Phoenician merchant says to the vinedresser, "I do not think it amazing that Protesilaos knows these things, since he is now a daimon" (τὸν μὲν γὰρ Πρωτεσίλεων δαίμονα ἤδη ὄντα οὐδὲν οἶμαι θαυμαστὸν εἰδέναι ταῦτα; *Heroikos* 43.3). In the conceptualization of the dialogue, the hero has superior knowledge to that of the received text (Homer) and thus supplies a more authoritative version of the corpus that defines Hellenic identity. In addition, by identifying the tendencies in Homer's version and the underlying reasons for them, he provides the audience with the interpretive tools for reading Homer. The hero, as Nagy has pointed out, "has a totalizing control of epic narrative" and provides "a model of poetic inspiration that centers on the superhuman consciousness of the oracular hero."[23]

The authoritative knowledge of the hero is not limited to the poetic, epic tradition but extends to matters of agriculture, lifestyle, and correct worship. It is manifested as well in his availability for healing and for oracular consultation. The hero's "wisdom" (σοφία) is accessible through cult (see, for example, Philostratus, *Heroikos* 14.1–17.6). In other words, the *Heroikos* conceptualizes the hero as a performer of the tradition (of epic remembrance) in the context of cultic relationship.[24] In this respect, moreover, the *Heroikos* is in continuity with notions, stretching back into the archaic period, that recognize the authoritative speech of the hero activated through hero cult.

Turning now to the Gospel of Luke, we find a portrayal of Jesus as an interpreter of scripture, that is, as a performer of the authoritative text. Moreover, in these performances, Jesus provides the "special knowledge" that permits the "correct" interpretation ("correct" from the vantage point of the Gospel) of the authoritative text. Luke signals this dynamic at the outset of Jesus' public ministry in chapter 4, in which he depicts Jesus reading from Isaiah in the synagogue in Nazareth (v. 16) and then sitting down to interpret the reading, "Today this scripture is fulfilled in your hearing" (v. 21). This enigmatic utterance is widely taken by commentators as self-referential; that is, Luke pictures Jesus as indicating that the words of Isaiah are fulfilled in his own person.[25] As such, the performance as a whole includes both the authoritative text (Isaiah) and the authoritative interpretive principle—Jesus himself.

Matching this opening scene is the episode near the end of the Gospel, in Luke 24, in which Luke depicts Jesus after his death appearing to two disciples on the road to Emmaus. What I would emphasize here is, first, that Jesus "beginning with Moses and all the prophets interpreted [διερμήνευσεν] to them the things concerning himself in all the scriptures" (v. 27). Second, the two disciples only recognize the stranger as Jesus through the experience of cult, namely, through the shared meal, which Luke depicts in the same terms that he used for Jesus' Last Supper, that is, in terms of the eucharistic practice familiar to his audience.[26]

Using the terms of hero cult discussed above, I would describe Jesus as appearing in this scene as an enigmatic presence not initially recognized but nonetheless a performer of the entire tradition: he interprets "all the scriptures" "beginning from Moses and all the prophets." Jesus is thus depicted as having totalizing control of the tradition. Second, this performer is again the "term" of the interpretation: he interprets the scriptural tradition as "concerning himself" (Luke 24:27). As was the case with Protesilaos in the *Heroikos*, the "right" means of understanding the tradition derives from the performer himself, as one who has returned from the dead. We may call this a clear instance of tradition in the mouth of the hero. Moreover, Luke's narrative portrays this knowledge as accessible through cult; recognition (ἐπιγνῶσις) both of the person and of the experience of performed tradition happens as a result of eating together. The cult practice of the ritual meal prompts recognition of the experience of intimacy with the hero. As a result of the recognition of Jesus at the meal, the disciples recount something like the frisson of the earlier encounter when they ask, "Did not our hearts burn within us as he spoke to us on the way, as he opened the scriptures to us?" (v. 32).

Luke's highly developed literary work refracts the cultic practices of its context. This aspect has been recognized particularly in regard to Luke's account of the Last Supper (22:14-21).[27] It is thus reasonable to argue that in the Gospel of Luke is embedded a conceptualization of performance of scripture in which "correct" interpretation is available through cult practices that activate the presence of Jesus. I would further propose that the poetics of performance embedded in the portrayal of Jesus as a performer of the scriptural tradition are those of the producers and performers of authoritative interpretation of scripture in the immediate culture of Luke's Gospel. In other words, Luke embeds a cult practice in which the voice of the hero (Jesus) and the voice of the poet (the one who tells the story about Jesus) merge.

A similar dynamic is reflected in the Epistle to the Hebrews, a discourse that quotes the scriptures of Israel extensively. A marked feature of Hebrews is the fact that it nearly always places these quotations in the mouth of a divine speaker, "God," "Jesus," or "the spirit"; see, for example, the instances of divine speech in Heb 1:5-14, quoting a catena of psalms. This technique stands in contrast to quotation techniques in other non-narrative texts, in which "as it is written" or "as the scripture says" are more common. Harold Attridge has referred to this technique as "divine ventriloquism" and has argued that it matches the opening verses of Hebrews: "In many and various ways, God, having spoken to the ancestors in the prophets, at the end of these days spoke to us in a Son, whom he appointed heir of all, through whom he also made the aeons" (Heb 1:1-2).[28] Most of the quotations in Hebrews, moreover, are drawn from the realm of cult practice, namely, from the psalms and texts referring to the remaking of the covenant (e.g., Jeremiah 21). I have argued elsewhere that Hebrews is indebted to the ritual practices of its community, particularly in its shaping of Jesus' suffering and in its argument about how the Passion changes the situation of the audience with relation to the covenant.[29] Throughout Hebrews, furthermore, it is clear that "looking to Jesus" (Heb 12:2) provides the interpretive lens whereby the audience is to interpret both the words of scripture and the experiences of their lives.[30] Repeatedly, the portrayal of Jesus in Hebrews is as one who interprets scripture as referring to himself, as is the case with the quotation of Psalm 40 in Hebrews 10, "Therefore when he comes into the world he says, 'Sacrifice and offering you have not desired, but a body you have arranged for me'" (Heb 10:5).

Bringing the strands together we may say that Hebrews portrays Jesus—a cosmic figure now seated in heaven (Heb 1:3)—as one who performs the authoritative text in a way that makes himself and his experience the authoritative principle of interpretation. Jesus' performance here has a totalizing control provided by his cosmic perspective: "heir of all, through whom the aeons were made." The indications of cult practice as the means of access to this performance are less explicit than in the Gospel of Luke or the *Heroikos*, yet the close proximity of this arguably homiletical discourse[31] to cult practice on a number of fronts suggests that Hebrews refracts the poetics of cultic remembrance. Here again the voice of the hero as performer of authoritative texts merges with that of the "poet," if you will, of Hebrews.

To sum up briefly, in the Gospel of Luke and the Letter to the Hebrews, to remember Jesus as a performer—an interpreter of scripture—locates the poetics of tradition in the mouth of Jesus. This creates, moreover, a dynamic of reciprocity and merging of identity between poet and hero, typical of the poetics of hero cult, as was seen through the role of the hero as a transmitter of tradition in the *Heroikos* of Philostratus. The special knowledge of the hero, finally, becomes available through the media of cultic practice to those who cultivate affiliation, devotion, and intimacy with the hero. This preliminary exploration of the poetics of performance in these two New Testament texts suggests an avenue for investigating other ancient portrayals of Jesus in terms of hero cult.[32] Such an investigation may then illumine our understanding of the processes and occasions of "remembering" that were necessary for the composition and transmission of stories about Jesus.[33]

7

Jesus and the Canon: The Early Jesus Traditions in the Context of the Origins of the New Testament Canon

Jens Schröter

The Meanings of "Canon"

This chapter considers the early Jesus traditions in the context of the beginnings of a collection of writings that the church would come to regard as authoritative. Recent discussion of the canonical and extra-canonical Jesus traditions will be treated in connection with research on the origins of the New Testament canon. In the broader horizon, what is at issue is the question of the relationship between the witness to Jesus Christ found in the New Testament and the activity of the earthly Jesus. I also discuss the question of the relationship between oral Jesus traditions and their being committed to writing. I will begin with a look at the current state of the discussion.[1]

Research on the New Testament canon has shown that it developed over a fairly long period of time, that its development proceeded in different ways in the various regions of the Roman Empire, and that it did not represent a document defining the unity of Christianity but rather collected the writings in which the early church found the contents of Christian faith to be expressed.[2] It is also clear that the concept of a "canon" (κανών, *regula*) can only contribute in a limited fashion to illuminating the process in question, inasmuch as it was first applied to the acknowledged writings in the fourth century, whereas before that time it described the standards of Christian faith and teaching.[3] For example, the canon could characterize repentance (μετάνοια) as the basis for the Christian way of life,[4] serve as a summary description of the fundamentals of faith laid down in the New Testament writings,[5] or be applied to service in the community[6] or to the correct date of Easter.[7] The essential content of the Christian creed could also be summarized in this concept,[8] even in the first and second centuries, when a fixed creedal text or the connection between creed and baptism cannot yet be assumed.[9] Later, conciliar decrees were also called "canons," because they established binding rules for the form of the Christian faith. This understanding of the expression as a summary of the bases of Christian belief appears in other, more defined phrases such as "canon of faith" (κανὼν τῆς πίστεως/*regula fidei*), "canon of truth" (κανὼν τῆς ἀληθείας/*regula veritatis*), and "canon of the church" (κανὼν τῆς ἐκκλησίας or ἐκκλησιαστικὸς κανών).[10]

The case of "apocryphon" and "apocrypha" (ἀπόκρυφος, ἀπόκρυφοι) is different insofar as we find these terms as early as the second century in the titles of works or as designation of certain writings.[11] The words refer to special, secret revelations accessible only to a few chosen ones. FIn the works of ancient church authors like Irenaeus, Tertullian, and Origen, in contrast, the expression "apocryphal" has a negative meaning and is equated with "rejected" or "counterfeit" (νόθος/*falsa*). From this developed the contrast between "canonical" and "apocryphal" writings.[12]

Against the background of this understanding of "canon," the Council of Laodicea (circa 363) distinguished between the "non-canonized books" (ἀκανόνιστα βιβλία) and the "canonical [books] of the new and old covenant" (τὰ κανονικὰ τῆς καινῆς καὶ παλαιᾶς διαθήκης). Similarly, not long afterward, in his thirty-ninth Easter Letter of 367, Athanasius differentiated the "canonized writings that have been handed down and attested as divine" (τὰ κανονιζόμενα καὶ παραδοθέντα πιστευθέντα τε θεῖα εἶναι βιβλία) from the "so-called apocrypha" (οἱ λεγόμενοι ἀπόκρυφοι).[13]

It follows from this that the distinction between acknowledged and rejected writings needs to be seen within the context of the developments through which early Christianity secured its own identity. There is thus a dialectical relationship between the developing norms of Christian faith and the collecting of authoritative writings, to the extent that these norms are founded on the testimony of writings regarded as binding and are considered to be in substantial agreement with them, while the norms in turn affirm and support these writings. Thus the early church was not simply founded on a collection of authoritative writings; rather, the collection was created in close association with the apostolic tradition, which was regarded as foundational.[14]

A second consequence can be developed from the starting point of Ernst Käsemann's much-quoted dictum that the New Testament canon does not furnish the foundation for the church's unity.[15] Käsemann based this judgment on the diversity of theological positions found in the New Testament, some of them irreconcilable, and on this basis he distinguished between letter and spirit—concretely, between canon and gospel. Thus he resolved the problem of the multiplicity and partial self-contradictoriness within the canon by introducing a normative content criterion, with the aid of which he separated the merely external (literal) canon of twenty-seven writings from the internal (spiritual) canon, the latter inaccessible to the historian and able to be comprehended only through faith.[16]

While we can agree unreservedly with his exposition of the diversity within the New Testament canon, the problem with Käsemann's suggestion—which, like those of Marcion and Luther, can be classified within the model of a "canon within the canon"[17]—is that he wants to found the New Testament canon on a provisional, changeable theological standard. But in fact this undermines its function as the basis and expression of the binding convictions of early Christianity. That is, if the New Testament canon is measured against a norm that serves to distinguish more and less "important" writings, the principle that underlies its origin fades away. That principle was by no means to define a theological norm against which the writings could be judged, but instead, by collecting the apostolic faith-witness and separating it from later "counterfeits," to preserve the tie between Christian faith and its origins.

An excellent example of this is a passage in which Irenaeus, at the end of the second century, summarizes the content of Christian preaching and Christian faith:

> Now the Church, although scattered over the whole civilized world . . . received from the apostles and their disciples its faith in one God, the Father Almighty, who made the heaven, and the earth, and the seas, and all that is in them, and in one Christ Jesus, the Son of God, who was made flesh for our salvation, and in the Holy Spirit, who through the prophets proclaimed the dispensations of God (οἰκονομίαι). . . . Having received this preaching (κήρυγμα) and this faith (πίστις) . . . the Church . . . carefully

preserves it . . . and preaches them harmoniously, teaches them, and hands them down.[18]

Therefore in what follows I will take a different path from Käsemann's in approaching the meaning of the canon. If I restrict myself to the Jesus traditions, it is not only for reasons of clarity but also because recent discussions of the so-called apocrypha have emphatically brought to our attention that the Gospels that have become canonical[19] represent only a small fragment of the early Jesus traditions. Quite recently, in the context of the question of the historical Jesus, especially in North American research, there have been repeated calls for abandoning the ancient church's distinction between "orthodox" canonical and "heretical" apocryphal tradition. From a historical point of view I can agree with that call unreservedly, since, naturally, there is no excluding the possibility that writings condemned as heretical may contain historically valuable information.[20] But it would be a distortion of the results to conclude from this historical stance that the early Jesus traditions are all equal and were divided for dogmatic reasons into those that were accepted and those that were rejected only at the end of the second century. This needs to be explored in more detail.

First I should note that I do not agree with the dating of apocryphal writings to the first century,[21] often asserted without further evidence, especially in the case of the *Gospel of Thomas*. Independently of the question of the older traditions that the *Gospel of Thomas* may contain, a date of origin for the document itself in the second century seems likely.[22] The same applies, *mutatis mutandis*, to the other apocryphal Gospels. The value of the extracanonical Jesus tradition thus does not lie in its ability to alter an image of Jesus derived from the first-century writings. Rather, it illustrates constellations and controversies of the second and third centuries in which different ways of relating to Jesus were being separated from one another.

When, in what follows, I discuss the genesis of the distinction between authoritative and "apocryphal" Jesus traditions, my primary intention is to illuminate how the early Christians dealt with a variety of Jesus traditions, as well as their development of criteria for acceptance or rejection.

One aspect that should be noted but is for the most part overlooked is found in the textual history of the New Testament writings.[23] A very important development in this regard has taken place recently within the field of New Testament textual criticism. While for a long time it unquestioningly regarded the reconstruction of the oldest accessible reading as its task,[24] that premise has now, at last, been called into question.[25] The New Testament manuscripts from the early (first) centuries suggest, rather, that the traditioning process was from the very beginning characterized by a variety of versions (and translations) of the New Testament writings and that these existed with equal validity alongside each other. The text printed in the Novum Testamentum Graece (Greek New Testament) is not attested by any single manuscript, but represents another, modern variant of the New Testament that probably never existed before in this form. This finding leads to a fundamentally different picture of the New Testament than the one that underlies the notion that the goal of studying the history of the text is to arrive at an "original" text of the New Testament,[26] which will furnish the basis for interpretation. The search for one form of the text that approaches as nearly as possible the origin of the writing itself may, instead, in light of the textual history of New Testament manuscripts from the first centuries, appear as inappropriate and therefore in need of revision. I will need to return to this later.

The Authority of the Lord

The authority of Jesus' teaching was an important impetus to the creation of the New Testament canon—perhaps even "the starting point of 'canonical' development" overall.[27] However, from the beginning this teaching was understood as a tradition that was to be interpreted in terms of different situations, consequently expandable, and variable in its wording. The earliest indications of this are in Paul, who from time to time refers explicitly to the authority of the Lord.[28] Characteristically, in these references Paul integrates the words of the Lord he is citing into his argument, both in their wording and in their meaning, and adapts them to the current situation.

Thus, for example, there is no quotation either in 1 Cor 7:10-11 or 1 Cor 9:14; instead, Paul himself formulates the advice that he identifies as having the Lord's authority. It is further characteristic of both passages that Paul weaves the words of the Lord into his remarks on divorce and on the apostle's right to support in such a way that they constitute one argument among others. In 1 Cor 7:8-12 he gives advice to the unmarried and widows, as well as "the rest," on his own authority and explicitly differentiates this teaching from that of the Lord. In 7:25 he contrasts the "command of the Lord" (ἐπιταγὴ κυρίου) with his own opinion (γνώμη) in introducing the teaching about virgins. At the end of the whole section he grounds the assertion that his own opinion also has a claim to authority by saying that he, too, has the Holy Spirit.

In chapter 9, Paul founds his right to support from the Corinthian community on a word of the Lord (ὁ κύριος διέταξεν), but he regards his own decision not to claim such support as a valid stance in terms of his service to the gospel.

In 1 Thess 4:15 Paul uses "a word of the Lord" to formulate his teaching about the living and the dead at the Lord's parousia. Here again he is quite obviously not citing the earthly Jesus; rather, Paul places his own teaching under the Lord's authority.

Paul introduces the account of the institution of the Lord's Supper cited in 1 Cor 11:23-25 with the remark that he received it from the Lord and was handing it on to the Corinthians. It is quite obvious that he is referring not to words of the earthly Jesus but to a Christian tradition and is thus placing it within a traditional context. This is apparent from the very fact that the quoted tradition is introduced by the characteristic terms for handing on tradition, "received" (παραλαμβάνειν) and "handed on" (παραδιδόναι), showing that Paul is here quoting an early Christian tradition about the Lord's Supper (see also 1 Cor 15:3). The same is evident also from the fact that, shortly before this, Paul had introduced a different interpretation of the early Christian meal (1 Cor 10:16).

When Paul, in these passages, always refers to the Lord (κύριος) but never speaks of a "word of Jesus," it shows that he understands the "words of the Lord" to be a teaching legitimated by the Risen and Exalted One that is made concrete in various situations through the apostles and prophets. His intention is thus not to hand on, word for word, what was spoken by the earthly Jesus but to connect to a tradition grounded in the authority of the Lord as the basis of early Christian teaching. In instances involving words that originated with the earthly Jesus, Paul is interested in the fact they are Jesus' words only insofar as the earthly Jesus is also the one raised and exalted by God. This is underscored by the fact that, beyond the explicit references to the Lord, we find an abundance of analogies to traditions in other early Christian writings, including the Synoptic Gospels, that nonetheless are not described by Paul or other writings as words of the Lord.

The saying about the thief in the night in 1 Thess 5:2 appears also in 2 Pet 3:10 and has analogies in Rev 3:3 and 16:15. In Luke 12:39//Matt 24:43 and in Gos. Thom. 21:5-7, the metaphor of the thief is transformed into an image used by Jesus. In every case the context is an urging to alertness because the time when Jesus will come for judgment is unknown.

The call to be peaceful in 1 Thess 5:13 (cf. Rom 12:18) is introduced in Mark 9:50 (cf. Matt 5:9) as a command of Jesus.

Analogies to the appeal in 1 Thess 5:15 // Rom 12:17 not to repay evil with evil as well as to the related admonition in Rom 12:14 to bless persecutors and not to curse them appear in the Sermon on the Plain and the Sermon on the Mount (Luke 6:28 // Matt 5:44) and also in 1 Pet 3:9. This is a *topos* of early Christian paraenesis that was received both in the Synoptic Gospels and in the epistolary literature.

The saying about kindness to enemies in Rom 12:20, which Paul cites from Prov 25:21, appears in the Synoptic tradition as Jesus' commandment of love of enemies (Luke 6:27, 35 // Matt 5:44).

Compare the *topos* in Rom 14:14, that nothing is of itself unclean, with Jesus' words in Mark 7:15 // Matt 15:11: "there is nothing outside a person that by going in can defile."

The saying about the faith that moves mountains in 1 Cor 13:2 has analogies in Mark 11:22-23 // Matt 17:20 (cf. Luke 17:6; *Gos. Thom.* 48 and 106).

These findings show that even before the origins of the Gospels there was a sphere of tradition made up of words of Jesus, early Christian teaching authorized by the Lord, *topoi* from Jewish-Hellenistic ethics, and citations from scripture. Within this sphere, out of which primitive Christianity created its own tradition and associated it historically with the phenomenon called "the teaching of the apostles" (Acts 2:42), the distinction between "genuine" words of Jesus and other traditions played no part at all. What was decisive, rather, was that early Christian teaching as a whole was regarded as resting on the authority of the Lord.

The Authority of the Gospels

The creation in the last decades of the first century of written narratives about the work and the fate of Jesus represented a new phenomenon. The explicit attribution of the whole tradition to Jesus and its incorporation within his earthly activity constituted a historicizing of the primitive Christian tradition. The intention behind it can be described as a phenomenon of memory: a few decades after Jesus' activity, the memory of his earthly work was to be recorded in writing, and at the same time the early Christian tradition was to be secured, in its enduring validity, by attribution to Jesus. The specific combination of a historical-biographical interest in Jesus—evident, for example, in the description of his relationship to

John the Baptizer, his activity in Galilee and Jerusalem, the people around him, the content of his preaching, and the story of his Passion—with the orientation to his enduring significance as God's exclusive representative finds explanation against this background. As with Paul, so here also it is true that the authority of the earthly Jesus is founded on his identity as the Risen and Exalted One.[29] Of course, what is different is that now the recollection of his earthly work forms the literary frame within which the early Christian teaching, formerly found in different contexts and with different kinds of authority, has been handed on.[30] In what follows I will focus especially on two aspects of this development: (1) the expansion of the meaning of the term "gospel" and (2) the use of apostolic preaching to enhance the authority of the Jesus tradition.

(1) The creation of narratives about Jesus resulted in a semantic expansion of the concept of "gospel," which now could be applied also to words of the Lord and later became the literary designation of the Jesus narratives. This process is discernible within the early Jesus narratives in the Gospel of Mark, where the word "gospel" was first applied to a depiction of the story of Jesus.[31] With this, the story of Jesus' life and work is declared to be a part of the Christian proclamation. It is true that Matthew and Luke do not follow this practice, and the Gospel of John does not use the word "gospel," either. But in the years that followed there was frequent reference to "the gospel," sometimes with a quotation. This presupposes the existence of written stories of Jesus, evident not least in the fact that now words of the Lord could also be quoted as "scripture." For the most part these were not literal references, but free recollections now placed within new contexts. Thus the writing down of the Jesus traditions contributed to their authorization as binding traditions of early Christianity, but that authority by no means rested on one particular form of these traditions.

Thus, for example, the *Didache* introduces the Lord's Prayer with an injunction that one should pray "as the Lord commanded in his gospel."[32] In *Did.* 11:3 the instructions for the treatment of apostles and prophets are traced to a gospel injunction (δόγμα τοῦ εὐαγγελίου). In 15:3-4, in the admonition to mutual peace, as well as to prayer, almsgiving, and "all your acts," it is pointed out that this is what the addressees "find in the gospel" (ὡς ἔχετε ἐν τῷ εὐαγγελίῳ).

Also instructive is what we find in *2 Clement*. In *2 Clem.* 8:5 a word of the Lord is introduced with "The Lord says in the gospel." The first part of what is quoted is not in the Gospels, but the second part agrees word for word with Luke 16:10 ("If you have not kept the little things, who will give you the great things? For I say to you: Whoever is faithful in a very little is faithful also in much."). In 2:4, following an Old Testament citation (Isa 54:1), a word of the Lord is introduced with "and another Scripture says." What follows has a word-for-word parallel in Mark 2:17, and analogies in Matt 9:13 and Luke 5:32. At other places in *2 Clement* words of the Lord are introduced with "Jesus said" (4:5) or "the Lord says" (5:2; 6:1; 9:11; 13:2; 15:4; cf. 3:2) and in one place even with "God says" (13:4). Some of these are sayings that have very close parallels in the Synoptic Gospels, but others are only thematically related.[33] In 13:2 an Old Testament quotation (Isa 52:5b) is introduced with "For the Lord says." Finally, in 12:2 there is a saying that has analogies in *Gos. Thom.* 22 and in the Gospel of the Egyptians (found in Clement of Alexandria, *Stromata* 3.2.2–93.1) but is not attested in the Gospels that have been included in the canon: "For when someone asked the Lord when his Kingdom was going to come, he said, 'When the two shall be one, and the outside like the inside, and the male with the female, neither male nor female.'"

Clearly, the author could refer to words of the Lord, just as to Old Testament passages, as "scripture." There is an analogous phenomenon in 1 Timothy.[34] Here, in 5:18, a proverb is cited as "scripture" that we find in the Q tradition (Matt 10:10 // Luke 10:7) as a saying of Jesus. Another such occurrence, likewise without attribution to Jesus, is in *Did.* 13:2.[35] What is interesting in this passage is that the saying in 1 Timothy is cited, together with the scriptural reference from Deut 25:4 that is also used by Paul in 1 Cor 9:9, as γραφή, and the free formulation of the Lord's words Paul uses in 1 Cor 9:14 ("In the same way, the Lord commanded that those who proclaim the gospel should get their living by the gospel") is replaced by a quotation from the Synoptic tradition.[36]

As these results show, the word "gospel" was always used in the singular in writings up to about the middle of the second century. The reference was not always necessarily to a particular writing, although we ought to reckon with knowledge of a particular narrative about Jesus—as, for example, in the case of the *Didache*, which appears to know the Gospel of Matthew.[37] However, the word "gospel" is still primarily descriptive of content and indicates the Christian proclamation—which also includes the teaching of Jesus himself. As the quotations from *2 Clement* show, Jesus traditions were still being quoted freely, even when we may assume knowledge of a written Gospel. This is a phenomenon to which recent scholarship has come to apply the term "secondary orality." This expresses the idea that the Jesus traditions committed to writing influenced the further process of traditioning—not by being quoted as the authoritative form of the tradition but by the imprinting of their language, which then influenced later reception.

This can also be seen in the traditions included in *1 Clem.* 13:1-2 and 46:7-8 as "words of the Lord Jesus" (λόγοι τοῦ κυρίου Ἰησοῦ).[38] The first passage contains a list of seven appeals to mercy and forgiveness that have analogies in the words of the Sermon on the Mount and Sermon on the Plain, although neither of those seems to represent a concrete literary model. In 46:8 the saying about the millstone, which is analogous to Matt 26:24b and 18:6 (Mark 9:42), is introduced, but again no direct literary derivation can be established.

In addition—for example in *2 Clement* 12, in the *Gospel of Thomas*, or in the *Gospel of the Hebrews*—words from the written narratives about Jesus appear alongside others that are not found there but are indebted to later development of the Jesus traditions. An analogous phenomenon can be perceived within the textual tradition of the Gospels. This is a clear indication that the boundaries between "canonical" and "apocryphal" Jesus traditions were fluid for a long time.

Thus, for example, Codex Bezae (D, early fifth century), after the story of plucking grain on the Sabbath in Luke 6:1-4, inserts a saying that is neither in other Luke manuscripts nor in the parallels in Mark and Matthew: "On the same day he [Jesus] saw someone working on the Sabbath and said to him: 'Man, if you know what you are doing, blessed are you; but if you do not know, you are cursed and a violator of the Law.'" But the saying that is found here in other manuscripts, and also in Mark and Matthew, "The Son of Man is lord of the Sabbath" (Luke 6:5), appears in D instead after the subsequent episode about a healing on the Sabbath (between Luke 6:10 and 11).[39] It is no longer possible to determine when the apothegm transmitted by Codex Bezae entered the Jesus tradition, but it is clear that the scribe of Codex Bezae regarded it as an appropriate component of the Sabbath controversy presented in Luke 6. It is also clear how unproductive a distinction between "canonical" and "apocryphal" would be here. If we follow Codex Bezae, one of the oldest biblical codices, the apothegm undoubtedly belongs to the "canonical" Jesus tradition!

The story of Jesus and the woman taken in adultery is part of the older—perhaps Latin—Jesus tradition and was later inserted into the Gospel of John at different places (though usually after John 7:52). The oldest Greek version could be represented by the translation from the Old Latin tradition made for the (bilingual) Codex Bezae. A possibly independent variant of the episode is found in Didymus the Blind (fourth century).[40]

Here again, close examination reveals a gray zone between "canonical" and "apocryphal" Jesus tradition. Whether the episode in question is counted as part of the authoritative Jesus tradition depends on which textual tradition is followed. As in the previous example, it is evident that a search for the oldest form of the text would not be of further help because the text that was ultimately accepted by the church contains the episode, though it is not found in numerous old manuscripts.[41]

In the tradition of the Lord's Prayer many manuscripts contain a doxology that is not yet present in the early codices Sinaiticus (ℵ) and Vaticanus (B), both fourth century, Bezae, and Dublinensis (Z, early sixth century). Most common is the form that is still in use today, "For thine is the kingdom, and the power, and the glory for ever. Amen." Alongside this are other variants in which either one element (kingdom, power, glory) is lacking, or there is the addition, after "glory," of "of the Father and the Son and the Holy Spirit." Thus, the prayer, in liturgical use from an early period, existed in several versions that have been recorded in the textual tradition. It would make neither methodological nor historical sense to try to trace an original form of the prayer lying behind these and then attempt to trace it farther back, perhaps even to Jesus himself.[42] Instead, this very example shows that the notion of an "original form" of the tradition is deficient, and the task of textual as well as of tradition criticism has to be formulated differently.[43]

Finally, a further characteristic of the tradition appears to be that words of the Lord were handed on in small, dialogue-type scenes, apparently secondary to the already-existing Gospels. Examples of this are found in *2 Clem.* 5:2-4; *Gos. Thom.* 13; 21; 22; 60; and the *Dialogue of the Savior.*[44]

Hence it is characteristic of the period in question that, even after the creation of the first written narratives, we cannot establish either the extent or the wording of the Jesus tradition. What could be presented as the words of the Lord or as belonging to the Gospel was not yet defined, which is why the Jesus tradition could still, in principle, be expanded. This explains the multiple traditions that arose in the second century; these include variants on the Synoptic traditions, but frequently they also expand the scope of the Jesus tradition.

Let us consider some examples of reception of the Jesus tradition in second-century writings.

Papyrus Egerton 2,[45] in both of its identifiable fragments, contains different episodes that appear close, in part, to the written Jesus traditions but vary them and go beyond them. As shown especially by the expansion in *Papyrus Köln 255*, discovered later, it is probable that we have a combination of Jesus traditions from the Synoptic and Johannine spheres of tradition.[46] We need not consider a process of literary transmission here.

The *Gospel of Peter*,[47] of which we have a portion in Greek discovered in 1886–87 to which two fragments were later added,[48] contains a version of the Passion and Easter narrative. Numerous features indicate that this was a version belonging to a later stage of tradition history than the accounts handed on in the Synoptics and John. These include especially the attribution of the guilt for Jesus' death to the Jews as well as the elaboration of the resurrection scene: the stone that rolls away by itself, the motif of a cross that follows Jesus and speaks, and a voice from heaven.

The *Gospel of Thomas*,[49] which is retained in Greek fragments from the beginning of the third century and an almost complete Coptic copy from the fourth century,[50] represents a collection of Jesus sayings and parables that are presented as "secret words of the living Jesus." These include sayings that are part of the oldest level of Jesus tradition and have parallels in the Synoptic Gospels, but also some sayings of subsequent date that already reflect a later historical situation.

The *Gospel of Mary*,[51] a long section of which has been retained in Coptic in a codex that is part of the Berlin papyrus collection, the so-called *Berolinensis Gnosticus* (*BG* 8502), plus two Greek fragments from the third century,[52] contains, on the remaining pages (pp. 1–6 and 11–14 of the original eighteen pages are missing), a dialogue of the "Savior" with his disciples before his departure, and after that a dialogue between Mary and the disciples. Within this latter dialogue, Mary reports special revelations given to her in a vision, apparently also including a heavenly journey. At the end there is an argument about Mary's authority, which is disputed by Peter and Andrew but defended by Levi. The *Gospel of Mary* presupposes the narratives of the appearances of the Risen One in the Gospel of Matthew, and probably also those in the Gospel of John, and therefore presents a post-Easter dialogue situation.[53]

Thus the writings originating in the second century presuppose already-existing stories about Jesus but are not bound to them, either in their language or in the interpretation of their content. Rather, it is characteristic of them that they choose different literary genres for their treatment of the Jesus traditions—such as the revelatory dialogue or the sayings collection—and thus also attach different accents to the content. For example, the Jesus tradition is here associated with philosophical *topoi*, but more often there is an appeal to secret revelations. Quite often this is accompanied by a detachment of these traditions from their Jewish context.[54]

The fact that some of the writings deliberately claim the title of "Gospel"[55] shows that the word was also used as a designation for literary works and placed the newly created writings in competition with those already in existence. Probably this title had already been attached to the Jesus narratives that later became canonical. This is indicated by the unusual form "Gospel according to . . . ," which expresses the idea that this is the *one* Gospel, transmitted in a variety of narratives. This form of the title is then imitated, for example, by the *Gospel of Peter* and the *Gospel of Thomas*. The earliest external attestation of the literary designation of these writings is found in Justin, who calls them both "Memoirs of the Apostles" (ἀπομνημονεύματα τῶν ἀποστόλων) and "Gospels" (εὐαγγέλια), thus using the word in the plural.[56] Around the middle of the second century, the word thus acquired a second meaning, alongside that of characterizing the content of the Christian proclamation, namely, the literary designation of writings that contain traditions about Jesus.

Thus, we may conclude that the Jesus tradition, from its earliest attestation, was not oriented toward the preservation of original sayings of Jesus and the recording of their wording. Rather, from the very beginning the teaching of Jesus is found in a variety of receptions, variable in language and elastic in extent. The Jesus tradition is thus, from the time of its earliest attestation, a free and living tradition,[57] and therefore the idea of a fixed, authoritative form of that tradition must be abandoned.

(2) A second tendency in the development of the Jesus tradition in early Christianity, in some ways contrary to the findings just presented, appears in the efforts to give authority to the Jesus tradition by tying it to the apostolic preaching. This is especially evident in the Prologue to the Gospel of Luke. There Luke, in the ancient tradition of introductions to literary works, describes his presentation as one that is superior to its predecessors in completeness, accuracy, and composition.[58] In addition, he emphasizes the link to the eyewitnesses of the beginning, who handed on these things and later became "servants of the word."[59]

Comparable to the interest of the Lukan Prologue is what Papias is reported as saying about Mark and Matthew.[60] Papias, too, emphasizes the reliability of Mark's account (ἀκριβῶς ἔγραψεν) and criticizes its lack of order (οὐ μέντοι τάξει). In addition, the attribution of the two Gospels to Mark and Matthew secures their link to the apostolic tradition: Mark is said to have been the "interpreter" (ἑρμηνευτής) of Peter, while "Matthew" of course means the disciple of Jesus with the same name. In this same category is the remark, also said to be by Papias, about the superiority of oral to written tradition.[61] If the note in Eusebius[62] about the fourfold writing of the gospel by Matthew, Mark, Luke, and John, after its having originally been preached orally, also goes back to Papias,[63] it would be a further indication of the tendency, evident in the case of Papias at the beginning of the second century, to give authority to the written Gospels by linking them to the apostolic preaching. The attribution of the written Jesus narratives to apostles or disciples of apostles is probably explained precisely against this background. Thus Papias acknowledges the written Jesus traditions known to him but feels himself in no way bound by their compass or form—something that could be indicated by the title of his lost writing, "The Sayings of the Lord Explained" (Λογίων κυριακῶν ἐξήγησις). Instead, he legitimates them by tying them back to the oral witness of the apostles.

Accordingly, while for Luke and Papias the linking of the Jesus traditions to their apostolic origin is still more important than repelling false teaching—though the latter is not entirely absent[64]—the question of distinguishing orthodox from heretical interpretation of the early witnesses to the faith moves, under the pressure of the controversies that arose in the second century, more and more to the fore. We cannot trace the details of these controversies here; the most important were the clashes with Marcion, the Gnostic groups, and the Montanists. It suffices to note that these controversies served to refine the criteria for judging which writings were to be accepted and which were to be rejected.

Guidance was taken from the criterion already mentioned, that a writing must be in harmony with the apostolic witness; that is, it must preserve the tie to the beginnings of Christian tradition. The apostolic authorship of a writing could thus—as in the case of the Gospels of Mark and Luke—be mediated, as the Letter to the Hebrews also shows: in that case Origen recommended its acceptance because he found Pauline thought expressed there.[65] By contrast, the *Gospel of Peter*, although it also claims apostolic origin, was regarded as counterfeit and was therefore rejected, as were the *Gospel of Thomas* and the *Gospel of Matthias*, of which Clement of Alexandria quotes three (or four) passages.

It should be noted that the distinction between accepted, disputed, and rejected writings in the ancient church never led to a formal decision to adopt the authoritative writings.[66] Rather, the question of accepting or rejecting a writing always arose when it was already in use in some community or other. The criterion of apostolicity in the sense of agreement with primitive Christian tradition thus led to the establishing of a four-Gospel collection, the beginnings of which probably lie in the mid-second century; soon afterward it was probably also attested by codices.[67] Irenaeus presumes the number four when he speaks of the "fourfold gospel" (εὐαγγέλιον τετράμορφον) around the year 180, and he defends it against either reduction or expansion.[68] Origen also distinguishes between the four Gospels of the church and the "many" of the heretics.[69]

Certainly, these statements by theologians of the ancient church should not give the impression that the fourfold Gospel was universally accepted by the Christian communities at the end of the second century. That would be an inadmissible and unreliable projection into the second and third centuries of the results of the historical development that only came to a relative conclusion in the second half of the fourth century. The polemical statements of Irenaeus and Origen in fact point in the opposite direction, as does the letter of Serapion regarding the *Gospel of Peter*.[70] And we should again mention the free treatment of the oral and written Jesus traditions discussed above. Finally, we have to suppose that the collection of writings available in any one place—and therefore accessible and at hand to be read in worship—differed from congregation to congregation. The authoritative Jesus tradition was therefore secured not by a general acceptance of the four Gospels, and certainly not by a normative compass and wording of those writings, but by the "canon of faith" (κανὼν τῆς πίστεως), the *regula fidei*, which was expressed in the fourfold Gospel.

The Canonization of the Gospels

Finally, I need to augment these findings with some observations on the textual tradition of the New Testament Gospels and the process of their canonization. Here we should again recall what has already been said about the flexibility of the tradition, which did not halt the process that must be presumed to have occurred in the phase of oral tradition, but rather continued it and even reinforced it, since now a variety of written versions of the same Gospel appeared alongside the oral transmission of those traditions. This applies not only to the expansions, mentioned above, which the Gospels underwent as additional words or episodes were included, but also to the wording of the already existing text.

The textual tradition of the Gospels reveals a truly astonishing freedom in dealing with these texts, reflected in the variability of the wording.[71] In the process, the form of the text could even change the understanding of the respective content. Bart D. Ehrman has investigated this phenomenon with regard to the early Christian christological controversies and developed a variety of tendencies toward an "orthodox" alteration of the text (anti-adoptionist, anti-separationist, anti-docetic, and anti-patripassianist). His conclusion: "It is not only thinkable that scribes would make such changes, it is manifest that they did. Scribes altered their sacred texts to make them 'say' what they were already known to 'mean.'"[72]

Thus, for example, Luke 2:33, which speaks of Jesus' father and mother, is changed in many manuscripts to "Joseph and his mother" in order to avoid a statement about an earthly father that could compete with Jesus' divine sonship. There is a similar change in Luke 2:48, where Mary's exclamation, "Look, your father and I have been searching for you in great anxiety!" is altered to "We have . . . searched." In the baptism story in Luke 3:22 many ancient manuscripts have the scriptural quotation "You are my son; this day have I begotten you" (see also Acts 13:33). This, too, was changed to the mixed quotation in Mark and Matthew, "This is my beloved Son, in whom I am well pleased," in order to correct a statement that could sound adoptionist. In Luke 22:43-44 a passage that describes Jesus' agony on the Mount of Olives ("his sweat became like great drops of blood falling on the ground") was probably inserted later (it is lacking in many ancient manuscripts) to fend off docetic tendencies.

It can also be observed that texts such as the Lord's Prayer, the words of institution at the Last Supper, or Jesus' saying about divorce were handed on in a number of different versions that cannot be understood according to the pattern of an original version and secondary versions derived from it. The different versions are, rather, the expression of different understandings that have been expressed in the several forms of the text and could have existed as equals alongside one another.

Kurt Aland still maintained that the edition prepared by the Institut für neutestamentliche Textforschung in Münster and the United Bible Society could be regarded as having achieved the goal of establishing the original Greek text of the New Testament.[73] The analogy to the search for the one "historical Jesus" behind the multitude of receptions of his work and life is obvious.[74] But during most of its existence the church has lived without a fixed form of the New Testament text[75]—and, naturally, without a "historical Jesus." The effort to uncover the *one* text or the *one* Jesus behind the multitude of traditions appears therefore more and more clearly as an inappropriate attempt to discover a unified starting point for the tradition. This is not an adequate approach to the tradition because there never was such a starting point. Early Christianity was not oriented toward the preservation of a single origin; it held fast to its relationship to its own beginnings in the form of a free, living tradition.

There are consequences from this finding with regard to the New Testament canon. As stated at the beginning of this essay, the idea of a canon in earliest Christianity referred to the central content of the faith and on that basis was then applied to writings that were compatible with that content. The idea of the "New Testament" as a book in which these writings were collected in an authoritative form, reproducible as often as possible in identical fashion, only arose with the invention of printing. In the first centuries of Christianity there was no codex containing some collection such as the four Gospels and the letters of Paul or the catholic letters. Even the four codices from the fourth and fifth centuries that contain nearly all the biblical writings were not produced as one book but in multiple volumes. Thus, there was no "New Testament" in the modern sense in ancient Christianity. Rather, there were various manuscripts that contained individual or sometimes many writings; their familiarity and accessibility differed from congregation to congregation.[76] The Jesus of early Christianity was thus the Jesus remembered in a living tradition, a tradition that gained sharper contours in the course of the controversies of the second century with other ways of relating to him.

A Free, Living Tradition

Early Christianity and the early church understood the Jesus tradition from the beginning to be a free and living tradition. It could, therefore, be combined with primitive Christian teaching, ethical instructions from Hellenistic Judaism, and quotations from scripture transmitted as "the teaching of the apostles." This did not change when, with the creation of the Gospels, the process of giving authority to this teaching through its attribution to the earthly Jesus and its link to historical-biographical memories began. As the reception of the Jesus tradition in the second century shows, neither the compass nor the wording of the traditions traced to Jesus or to "the gospel" was firmly fixed. The manuscripts surviving from the first centuries of Christianity confirm this finding, for they continue the process of tradition in the way described and augment it through the ongoing creation of written versions of the individual Gospels.

We may conclude from this that there was no fundamental difference in the first centuries of Christianity between oral and written tradition. Instead, in both spheres we observe the analogous process of a free, living tradition that adapted its concrete form to the understanding of the content in each case. It is no accident, then, that the distinction between "orthodox" and "heretical" Jesus traditions was also grounded in the continuity of the tradition and thus connected to the rule of faith. Nor is it an accident that this changed only in the modern period, when the invention of printing gave rise to the idea of a New Testament, and with it a new development leading to the idea of one fixed compass and wording behind the free, living tradition.

This finding, then, also has consequences for the question of the "historical Jesus." That question, too, is typically modern in its search for the one Jesus who can be discovered by historical research behind the multiple traditions, which are thereby markedly reduced. I am not arguing that such an approach to the Jesus tradition is unjustified. But it should be asked whether, in light of the way in which the Jesus tradition originated and was transmitted in the first centuries, the question should not be transformed. One might proceed from the insight that the "historical Jesus" represents a product of historical-critical approaches to the texts that, first of all, are reduced to *one* textual form out of which then *one* person is constructed. What is in question is not the correctness, in principle, of such an undertaking, but the claim that such images of Jesus would come closer to the person of Jesus than the early texts themselves. Historical pictures of Jesus do not take us back *behind* the texts; they move, as abstractions from the multifacetedness of the tradition, always *in front of* them. They are therefore to be regarded as hypotheses, grounded in historical criticism, that mediate between the person of Jesus and one's own present.

As for the connection between Jesus and the New Testament canon, it follows from these observations that the tradition associated with the actions of Jesus was, from the beginning, interpreted in light of the early Christians' faith-convictions. What was determinative for the church as it constituted itself, long before the extent of the accepted writings was established, was agreement with the rule of faith as the "canon" of early Christianity, which secured continuity with the apostolic witness of the earliest time. The rejection of other Gospels, which therefore came to be seen as apocryphal, happened because they contradicted this canon and represented, for example, a docetic or Gnostic interpretation of Jesus' actions. Therefore, what is crucial in regard to the connection between Jesus and the canon is that the early Christian reception of Jesus' teaching took place within a spectrum of interpretation that demanded a distinction between accepted and rejected interpretations. That the rule of faith did not thereby lead to a standardization of the accepted Jesus traditions, but instead made possible a broad spectrum of interpretations, is evident especially from the fact that within the Christian canon, four Gospels, very different in their theological uniqueness, found acceptance.

PART 3

Orality,
Literacy,
Memory,
and
Mark

8

Interfaces of Orality and Literature in the Gospel of Mark

Vernon K. Robbins

Werner Kelber's work on orality and literacy in Mark inaugurated a new discussion of orality in New Testament scholarship.[1] The discussion about orality and the New Testament has changed considerably since the appearance of his 1983 book, *The Oral and the Written Gospel*.[2] One of the major changes is a result of the publications by John Miles Foley in the intervening years,[3] including the application of many of Foley's insights by Jonathan Draper and Richard Horsley.[4] Another has been the use of the *Progymnasmata*, with special focus on the *chreia*, in analysis of New Testament texts.[5] The changes call for a return to the Gospel of Mark with different eyes. In 1994 Kelber himself reformulated the position he had presented in his 1983 book, articulating a more nuanced view concerning the relation of the oral and the written during first-century Christianity than his previous work had asserted.[6] Careful study of Aelius Theon of Alexandria's *Progymnasmata*, a rhetorical manual most likely written during the time of the writing of the New Testament Gospels, shows that writing and speaking were closely intertwined in the act of performing a composition like the Gospel of Mark. As I stated in 1993,

> A presupposition that culture-transmitting traditions invite, in fact require, continual reformulation, just like speaking does, guides

> the [progymnastic compositional] exercises. . . . Performing oral
> and scribal traditions in this way creates a rhetorical culture—one
> in which speech is influenced by writing and writing is influenced
> by speaking. Recitation, then, is the base of a rhetorical culture.
> People know that certain traditions exist in writing. They also
> know that all traditions, oral and written, need to be composed
> anew to meet the needs of the day. Each day as they spoke, they
> were interacting with written traditions; whenever they wrote,
> they were interacting with oral traditions. This interaction char-
> acterized their thinking, their speaking, and their writing.[7]

The Synoptic Gospels, in particular, show how first-century Christian
writers composed in a *progymnastic* manner, rather than in a mode of
scribal copying or oral transcribing. The amount of verbatim similarity,
in a context of substantive variations, shows that they composed without
returning either their eyes or their ears to a manuscript source as they
composed. They had learned, as the first exercise in Aelius Theon's *Pro-*
gymnasmata instructs, that it was appropriate to compose both orally and
in writing either "in the same words or in others as well."[8]

Whitney Shiner's *Proclaiming the Gospel*, appearing exactly twenty
years after Kelber's book, exists as a rich resource into the nature of reading and writing performances in Mediterranean antiquity and the nature
of the Gospel of Mark in the context of those performances.[9] He has
helped to establish the case that while it is true, in one sense, that a written text "is but the dead, fossilized remains of my living voice,"[10] oral
tradition also lies "dead" in an oral storyteller until he or she gives voice to
the tradition. A reader gives voice to a written text, much as a storyteller
gives voice to an oral text. The difference, as Quintilian said, is that "we
can reread a passage again and again if we are in doubt about it or wish to
fix it in the memory."[11] But both oral tradition and written tradition are
dead until they are given voice in performance. Speed reading in twentieth-century American culture often set a goal to move people away from
creating an inner voice that vocalized the words. The reader was supposed
to learn from the pages by sighting quickly through them. The data from
antiquity make it virtually certain that there was no reading based on
sighting quickly through the pages in antiquity. There would be sighting
for location, but reading would then be a matter of voicing the text, even
if it was a matter of voicing it to oneself.

One of the problems that still haunts the investigation of orality in
early Christian literature is an imprecise use of the terms "orality" and
"oral culture" in analysis of New Testament writings. As Foley states,

"Orality alone is a 'distinction' badly in need of deconstruction, a typology that unfairly homogenizes much more that it can hope to distinguish; it is by itself a false and misleading category."[12] A major problem is a failure to distinguish the kinds of orality that exist on a spectrum from cultures in which people are unaware of writing and written texts to those in which written texts are immediately accessible both in their hands and in their minds. It is helpful, as a heuristic starting point, to distinguish between seven different kinds of speaking, reading, and writing cultures: (1) oral culture, (2) scribal culture, (3) rhetorical culture, (4) reading culture, (5) literary culture, (6) print culture, and (7) hypertext culture.[13] Among these alternatives, the most accurate definition of the early Christian "tradition biosphere"[14] is rhetorical culture rather than oral culture. "*Rhetorical culture* features comprehensive interaction between spoken and written statement. . . . In practice this means that writing in a rhetorical culture imitates both speech and writing, and speech in a rhetorical culture imitates both speech and writing."[15] Virtually all early Christians were aware, in the dynamics of their discourse, of the existence somewhere of tradition they referred to as "the writings" (*hai graphai*), which most modern-English Bibles translate either as "scripture" or "the scriptures." Early Christians who spoke, who read aloud to groups, and who wrote were continually working with an interplay between speaking and "things that were written."

In this essay I will focus on two portions of the Gospel of Mark that refer in some way to "the writings." In certain ways, this is a sequel to my 1997 study of orality in the context of rhetorical composition in the *Gospel of Thomas*,[16] in which I described the inner principle of the *Gospel of Thomas* as a two-step process: (1) If there is something about Jesus you do not understand, find a saying of Jesus. (2) If there is something about a saying of Jesus you do not understand, find another saying of Jesus that will shed light on the first saying you found. In the language of Foley, using the work of Dell Hymes, M. A. K. Halliday, and others, this inner principle of the *Gospel of Thomas* is a register.[17] Tradition exists in culture in registers. Foley, using Hymes, first defines "registers" as "major speech styles associated with recurrent types of situations."[18] Then he introduces Halliday's definition:

> A register can be defined as the configuration of semantic resources that the member of a culture typically associates with a situation type. . . . Since these [semantic] options are realized in the form of grammar and vocabulary, the register is recognizable

as a particular selection of words and structures. But *it is defined in terms of meanings*; it is not an aggregate of conventional forms of expression superposed on some underlying content by "social factors" of one kind or another. It is the selection of meanings that constitutes the variety to which a text belongs.[19]

The tradition register of the *Gospel of Thomas* is a wisdom register. In contrast to the registers functioning in the New Testament Gospels, there is no appeal to "the writings" (scripture) in the wisdom register operative in the *Gospel of Thomas*. One of the dynamics of the register in the *Gospel of Thomas* is a startling saying in logion 52:

> 52.1: His disciples said to him, "Twenty-four prophets have spoken in Israel, and they all spoke of you." 2: He said to them, "You have disregarded the living one who is in your presence, and have spoken of the dead."[20]

The sayings of the twenty-four prophets in Israel who spoke of Jesus are present in "the writings" to which all the New Testament Gospels refer. Here in the *Gospel of Thomas* is the view of a written text that Kelber presented in his 1983 book. From the perspective of the register in the *Gospel of Thomas*, the voices of the "scribed" prophets are dead. The "living one" is the Jesus who is speaking directly to them. The irony, of course, is that a primary medium in the *Gospel of Thomas* for the voice of "the living one" is a list of sayings of Jesus that are present in writing! Even in the oral environment from which the *Gospel of Thomas* emerged, written versions of Jesus' sayings played a dynamic role.

In other words, early Christianity was a rhetorical culture, with interplays between writing and orality present in virtually every sector of its activity. In contrast to cultures in which people have never seen, or even heard of, language in written form, early Christians knew and saw various kinds of writings. They both heard and made reference to writings, even if they themselves were unable to read any of them. In this rhetorical context, there were significantly different interfaces of orality and literature in different environments of communication. A significantly wide variety of interfaces are present among the Synoptic Gospels themselves, and even more interfaces are present in the relation of the New Testament Gospels to the *Gospel of Thomas*.

In contrast to the *Gospel of Thomas*, the registers operative in the New Testament Gospels function in relation to the following principle: If you do not understand a saying or action of Jesus, find some verses in the writings that can help you understand it. This means that the major registers of tradition operative in the New Testament Gospels are present in the tradition of the Hebrew Bible. Since there are many ways the registers of the writings function in the New Testament Gospels, I focus here on two instances in the Gospel of Mark and their parallels in Matthew and Luke.

In the first instance the narrator of Mark begins the story by reciting from "the writings" (1:2-4). After this initial recitation by the narrator, Jesus steps into the role of reciting from the writings in various places in the story. One example of Jesus' recitation from the writings is after the parable of the vineyard owner who sent servants and his son to get the produce from the vineyard. This is only one example of a special aspect of the Gospel of Mark: after the introduction in Mark 1:1-8, only Jesus and his interlocutors recite from the writings. The Markan narrator does not recite from the writings to support assertions in the narration of the story. In contrast, both Matthew and Luke at various points recite from the writings to explain to the reader "what was fulfilled" in the words and deeds of Jesus. Matthew and Luke sometimes expand on the internal function of the writings as they are present in Mark. At other times, they recite from the writings in a manner that makes the writings external to the narration of the story itself. Thus, there is an array of interfaces between orality and literature among the Synoptic Gospels. The Gospel of Mark is singular, however, in keeping references to the writings internal to the narration of the story of Jesus after Mark 1:1-8 launches the story of Jesus from inside the writings of "Isaiah."

I will limit my focus to the initial recitation of "what is written in the prophet Isaiah" by the narrator in Mark 1:2-4 and one instance in Mark in which Jesus recites from the writings. I will not attempt to analyze the manner in which recitation from writings is embedded at many points in Markan narration itself.[21]

John the Baptizer as "the Voice" in the Gospels

Mark 1:1-8 as Narration with Internal Literary Voice

In *Proclaiming the Gospel* Shiner discusses the beginning of the Gospel of Mark in a section on "vocal effects" and a chapter on "including the audience."[22] I would like to revisit those opening verses of the Gospel of

Mark in the context of excellent observations Shiner makes about how they might function in an oral performance. My approach is guided in particular by information from Aelius Theon's *Progymnasmata*, which emphasizes the deep relationship between speaking and writing in the context of composing written instances of *chreiai*, narratives, and fables.

One of the most noticeable features of the opening verses of Mark (1:1-8) is their nature as "run-on" statements. Oral performance regularly continues on and on, with very long sentences containing short clauses and statements. Once the sentence at the opening of Mark starts, either with "Beginning" (*archē*) or with "Just as" (*kathōs*), it continues paratactically with "and" (*kai*) through John's statement that ends in 1:7-8. This produces the following run-on string containing four sets of five statements as follows:

Beginning of the Gospel of Jesus Christ Son of God, (1:1)

(A1) as it is written in Isaiah the prophet,
(A2) "Behold I send my messenger before your face,
(A3) who will prepare your way, (1:2)
(A4) a voice of one crying in the desert
(A5) prepare the way of the Lord,
(A6) make straight his paths," (1:3)

(B1) came John baptizing in the desert,
(B2) and preaching a baptism of repentance for forgiveness of
      sins, (1:4)
(B3) and all the Judean country came out to him
(B4) and all the Jerusalemites,
(B5) and they were baptized by him in the Jordan river,
(B6) confessing their sins, (1:5)

(C1) and John was clothed with camel hair
(C2) and a leather girdle around his waist
(C3) and was eating locusts
(C4) and wild honey (1:6)

(D1) and he preached saying,
(D2) "He who is stronger than me is coming after me,
(D3) of whom I am not worthy
(D4) stooping down to loosen the thongs of his sandals. (1:7)
(D5) I baptized you with water;
(D6) but he himself will baptize you with holy spirit." (1:8)

It is noticeable that Shiner stops this recitation at the end of what is "written" in Isaiah the prophet, even though there is no conjunction to indicate any kind of "stop" at the end of it.[23] Nestle–Aland punctuates the Greek text quite well here, placing only a comma after the *autou* at the end of the recitation. For the narrator, the recitation of "what is written" flows immediately, without any break, into the recitation of the narration.

Here we see the first interface of orality and literature in the Gospel of Mark. For the composer, that which is written outside the text has an internal relation to that which is being recited in the text. In other words, that which is outside the text is inside the text through recitation of it in a continuous string with recitation of the narration in the text. This is a manifestation, I propose, of a particular aspect of the early Christian prophetic register in the Gospel of Mark. The precedents for this internal function of that which is written lie especially in the writings that are called in the Christian Bible the "major and minor prophets." These writings contain, on the one hand, words of God from outside the text that are now inside the text. Words of God flow into words of the prophet in a manner that makes it almost impossible at certain points, in a book like Isaiah, for example, to determine exactly what voice is speaking. In addition, narrative that presents the story of the prophet merges with words of God and words of the prophet in an ongoing flow of narration. This is the register that is operative at the beginning of the Gospel of Mark. The narrator presents Isaiah the prophet telling the story of "the beginning of the Gospel" by showing God speaking to Jesus, telling Jesus how John is coming "before his face, preparing his way" (Mark 1:2).[24] From the perspective of Markan narration, Isaiah continues with a description of the messenger as "a voice" of a person crying in the desert (Mark 1:3). This prophetic narration then continues with a description of John preparing the way by baptizing people and preaching (1:4-6), which ends with a recitation of what "a voice" said (1:7-8). There is no break between what is written and what is oral in the Markan narration in these verses. The narrator's narration, the narrator's recitation of a blend of Exod 23:20 and Mal 3:1, the narrator's recitation of Isa 40:3, the narrator's description of John and of how people came to him, and the narrator's recitation of what John preached flow continuously forward into one another. The narration ends with a recitation (1:7-8) of the content of "a voice" to which Isaiah referred (1:3). Markan narration reaches its first "stop," then, when "the voice of John the baptizer" ends in Mark 1:7-8.

Matthew 3:1-6 as Narration Supported by External Literary Voice

There is a great contrast here between Mark and both Matthew and Luke. The other two Synoptic Gospels show a conscious relation to writings outside their narration that produce a manner of setting off the writings from the recitation of the story itself. For example, Matthew has many "formula quotations" while Luke reflects on other writings that recite the story of "the things that have happened among us" (Luke 1:1-4). This difference shows itself in the way Matthew and Luke incorporate the information in Mark 1:1-8 in their Gospels.

Matthew starts by referring to the narration that follows as a "book" of the genealogy of Jesus Christ, Son of David, Son of Abraham (1:1). This book orientation also exhibits itself when Matthew recites information about John in 3:1-6. Matthean narration unfolds in the following manner:

Now in those days came John the Baptist

(A1) preaching in the desert of Judea (3:1)
       saying,
       "Repent;
       for the kingdom of God has come near," (3:2)

(A2) for this is what was spoken through Isaiah the prophet
       saying,
       "A voice of one crying in the desert,
       prepare the way of the Lord,
       make straight his paths." (3:3)

(B1) Now John himself had his garment from camel hair
       and animal skin around his waist,
       and his food was locusts and wild honey. (3:4)

(B2) Then Jerusalem went out to him,
       and all Judea
       and all the surrounding country of Jordan, (3:5)
       and they were baptized in the Jordan river by him
       confessing their sins. (3:6)

Matthew makes the recitation of the writings a narrational argument that presents the reason why John spoke in the manner in which he did.

The first thing Matthean narration presents is "John speaking." The second thing it presents is "the reason" the voice spoke, namely a recitation from Isaiah that asserts that a voice was coming. After narrating what the voice said and presenting the reason why the voice came and said what it did, the Gospel of Matthew narrates things that happened around John. Instead of having the narration about John flow directly out of the recitation of what Isaiah said, as Mark does, Matthew creates an argumentative unit: Because God said[25] "through Isaiah" that a voice cries in the desert preparing the way of the Lord, John came "speaking," rather than "baptizing and preaching" (Mark 1:4). Once the narrator has told the reader why John came speaking, then the narrator can continue with narration that describes how John looked, who came out to him, and what John did when they came out. This narration continues, then, with a long presentation of "the voice" in Matt 3:7-12. In this way, Matthean narration begins with "a voice" (3:2) and ends with "the voice" (3:7-12). Once Matthean narration has presented the voice of John the Baptist, it can introduce Jesus, namely, "he who is coming after me," to the reader (3:13-17). This sequence creates, of course, a strange content for John's speech at the beginning of the unit: John speaks what Jesus speaks later in Matt 4:17! Matthew needed content for John's voice to open the unit, followed by the rationale for the voice from the writings. The result was the creation of a new content for John's voice, namely, the same content conventionally given to Jesus' voice in early tradition.

In Matthew, then, the early Christian prophetic register has a different interface between orality and literature than the manifestation of the prophetic register in Mark. At this point in Matthean narration, recitation from the writings is external to narration of the story, serving as outside authoritative support for the importance of the story the narration is telling. In contrast to Mark, the writings in Matthean narration are not internal to the orality of the narration of the story. Rather, the orality refers to writings that lie outside the text and recites words from the writings as authoritative commentary on the story itself.

Luke 3:1-6 as Narration Supported by Literature

Luke 3:1-6 has a significant relation to Matt 3:1-6, since Lukan narration also recites "what is written" in a manner that places it outside the narration of the story. The difference is that Luke presents what is written as literature rather than as the voice of God through Isaiah. Instead of actually reciting what the voice said, Lukan narration simply asserts that John came "preaching" (3:3). Luke focuses on John's voice at the beginning, rather than on John's "baptizing and preaching," —the emphasis of Mark 1:4, as the narration flows out of the recitation of what is written in Isaiah the prophet. The Lukan narration (3:3-6) unfolds as follows:

> And he came into all the region around the Jordan,
>
> (A1) preaching a baptism of repentance for forgiveness of sins, (3:3)
> (A2) as it is written in the book of words of Isaiah the prophet,
> "A voice of one crying out in the desert:
> 'Prepare the way of the Lord,
> make his paths straight. (3:4)
> Every valley shall be filled,
> and every mountain and hill shall be made low,
> and the crooked shall be made straight,
> and the rough ways made smooth; (3:5)
> and all flesh shall see the salvation of God.'" (3:6)

After this eight-line recitation of Isa 40:3-5, Lukan narration continues with the statement of the voice to the multitudes in Luke 3:7-9. In Luke, in contrast to Matthew, the aggressive statement by John that "they should not begin to say to themselves" that they have Abraham as their father (3:8) calls forth questions from the multitudes (3:10), from tax collectors (3:12), and from soldiers (3:14). In Luke, then, the voice engages in dialogue with various groups of people, setting the stage for Jesus' confrontation of multiple groups of people throughout the story. This leads to a summary statement by the voice in 3:15-17, followed by the narrator's summary and transitional narration in 3:18-20 that subtly introduces Jesus in 3:21-22 "among those who were baptized." In the Lukan sequence, "a voice from heaven" has the final word as it tells Jesus he is the beloved Son, in whom God is well pleased (3:22).

In summary, Markan narration that introduces John the Baptizer to the reader shows the manner in which the story that is narrated flows naturally out of that which is written. In contrast, that which is written lies outside of Matthean and Lukan narration of the story. In their Gospels, that which is written provides argumentative support for the story that is being narrated. Therefore, recitation from the writings regularly interrupts the narration of the story to provide special explanations to the reader. In the Gospel of Mark the interface of written and oral in the prophetic register is internal to the narration of the story itself. In other words, the narrative voice contains within itself an interface between oral and written. In contrast, in Matthew and Luke there is an interface in the prophetic register between two levels of narration: (1) narration of the story and (2) narration of written texts that lie outside the story.[26]

Reading about "the Stone" in the Gospels

The next passage in my analysis features Jesus confronting others in a manner that implies that Jesus himself had read a certain portion of the writings. This takes us to another interface between orality and literature in Mark, namely, oral statements by Jesus in which he implies that he has first-hand knowledge of certain portions of the writings by reading them himself.

"Have You Not Read about the Stone?": Mark 11:27—12:12

In the Gospel of Mark, Ps 118:22-23 occurs in the speech of Jesus in a manner that displays Jesus' knowledge of the writings in the presence of chief priests, scribes, and elders. These Temple hierarchies, among whom specifically are "writers," come to Jesus while he is walking in the Jerusalem Temple and ask him a question about his authority to do what he is doing (11:27). As the story unfolds, Jesus' speech in Mark highlights Jesus' knowledge of "writings he has read" by featuring a rhetorical question that flows directly out of Jesus' presentation of the parable about the vineyard owner. The unit begins in Mark 11:27 and moves directly into Jesus' teaching in parables as a way to respond to the question by the Temple hierarchies about his authority (12:1). When Jesus completes the parable (12:9), he continues directly with a question to the chief priests, scribes, and elders that is designed to answer their question about his authority to do the things he is doing. Here I will quote only the last part of the unit.

> (A1) "What then will the owner of the vineyard do?
> (A2) He will come
> (A3) and destroy the tenants
> (A4) and give the vineyard to others. (12:9)
>
> (B1) Have you not read this writing,
> (B2) 'The stone that the builders rejected,
> (B3) this has become the cornerstone; (12:10)
> (B4) this came from the Lord,
> (B5) and it is amazing in our eyes'?" (12:11)

(C1) and they wanted to seize him,
(C2) and they feared the crowd,
(C3) because they knew
(C4) that he had told the parable against them,
(C5) and leaving them he went away, (12:12)

(D1) and they sent to him some of the Pharisees
(D2) and some of the Herodians,
(D3) to entrap him in his talk. (12:13)

In this unit in Mark, the issue in relation to the parable is what the owner of the vineyard will do when his servants are rejected and his son is killed. The issue, therefore, concerns action. Toward this end, Jesus asks a rhetorical question and answers it himself (12:9), then presents an authoritative recitation from the writings in the form of a rhetorical question that insinuates that the chief priests, scribes, and elders have never read a certain portion of scripture that judges their actions as shameful. In this context, the Gospel of Mark includes not only Ps 118:22 about the stone, but also v. 23 in Jesus' speech: "this came from the Lord, and it is amazing in our eyes" (12:11). The additional lines from Psalm 118 focus the attention on the Lord in relation to actions through which people reject and actions through which things that are rejected are reclaimed for very special roles, namely, to function as a cornerstone or keystone. In Mark 11:28 the chief priests, scribes, and elders ask Jesus by what authority he is doing the things he is doing. Jesus' authoritative recitation from the writings is an answer to them. What he is doing comes from the Lord, and it is an amazing thing!

Much of the scholarly debate about the recitation of Ps 118:22-23 in Mark 12:10-11 has centered around the possibility or implausibility of its authenticity in speech of the historical Jesus.[27] Here I wish to focus on the manner in which something from the writings is presented as an internal part of the orality of Jesus' speech. Jesus' rhetorical question leads to an answer he himself gives, in which he embeds a recitation from the writings that contains in itself a reference to the Lord who authorizes marvelous things. The polemical nature of Jesus' speech is evident in his insinuation that "they have evidently never read the passage"! The speech of Jesus is designed to give the impression that Jesus regularly reads the writings, and on some occasion in the past he has read Ps 118:22-23.

It is informative, in light of the internal interface of orality and literature in the speech of Jesus in the Gospel of Mark, that scholarly commentary on this passage regularly has focused on recitation of scripture and personal embodiment of scriptural verses, in the historical Jesus' speech and action. Even though "the quotation of Ps 118:22-23 clearly comes from the LXX,"[28] scholars have created an extensive scenario of the presence of an Aramaic interplay on "son" (*benē*) and "stone" (*'eben*) that creates "a remarkably consistent, but very subtle, exegetical thread running throughout Jesus' entrance into and activity within the temple precincts."[29] The internal interface between orality and literature in Markan narration has beautifully produced the effect the narration is meant to imply! In contrast to the *Gospel of Thomas*, in which the implication of the narration is that the writings have no potential for helping the hearer to understand the nature of Jesus, the Gospel of Mark implies from the very beginning that the gospel must be understood as a story that flows naturally, as it were, out of the writings (1:1-8). Interpreters of Mark naturally perceive an interplay between "son" and "stone" that is operative from the moment Jesus enters the Temple until he leaves it.

In the Gospel of Mark, then, it is not only the case that the writings have an internal relation to the narration of the story of Jesus. Rather, it is also the case that the writings, which Jesus either claims or implies that he has read, have an internal relation to the speech of Jesus.[30] Both the narration of the overall story and Jesus' speech have an oral flow that presents an internal interface of orality with written literature. Mark 12:9-11 presents a forward-flowing orality from which emerges a rhetorical question that Jesus himself answers (12:9), followed by a second rhetorical question in which Jesus embeds a recitation of four lines from the writings: "Have you not read this writing, 'a stone which the builders rejected, this has become the chief cornerstone [or keystone],[31] this has come from the Lord and is a marvel in our eyes'?" (12:10-11). In Mark, Jesus' speech flows directly from the parable to rhetorical questions that contain his own authoritative assertions alongside authoritative assertions in the writings.

After Jesus' recitation from the writings, the narration continues with a description of how the chief priests, elders, and scribes tried to seize him while he was in the Temple, because they knew he told the parable against them. They were afraid to do so, however, since they feared the crowd (12:12). When he went away, therefore, they sent some Pharisees and Herodians to trap him "in his talk" (*logōi*; 12:13). In Mark, therefore, Jesus' statement about a stone the builders rejected indicts Temple authorities with shameful actions, insinuating that even though there are scribes among them, they have never read the writings that explain what is happening in the story of Jesus. In response, the Temple hierarchies inaugurate new actions against Jesus, enlisting some Pharisees and some Herodians to help them gain evidence from his talking that can help them develop a case to arrest him.

Psalm 118:22 as a Saying of Jesus in *Gospel of Thomas* 66

Gospel of Thomas 66 presents Ps 118:22 without giving any clue that these words exist somewhere in the writings. Without v. 23, Jesus' speech also makes no assertion about the Lord. Rather than launching an attack on Temple authorities, who include writers, *Gos. Thom.* 65–70 invites deep thinking about what people know and do not know in a context of rejection and persecution. Thus, the issue is knowledge rather than action. In the process, the interface of orality and literature in Jesus' speech is very different from the Gospel of Mark.

Gospel of Thomas 66 makes the initial couplet of Ps 118:22 into a *chreia* saying of Jesus: "Jesus said, 'Show me the stone that the builders rejected: that is the cornerstone.'" Introduced with "Jesus said," the two assertions become a saying of Jesus about builders who tossed a stone away because they did not recognize it had the qualities to be a cornerstone for a building, or perhaps a keystone for an archway.[32] They threw the stone away, not realizing that it could function as the primary stone for their entire building project.

There is no suggestion in *Gos. Thom.* 66 that the words in Jesus' saying are also present in the writings. This saying of Jesus stands in a sequence of *logia* about: (1) a vineyard owner whose servants were almost killed, then whose son was killed, when he sent them to collect his share of the produce from the vineyard (65); (2) a stone that builders rejected, which was the cornerstone or keystone (66); (3) the one who knows all but is lacking in oneself is utterly lacking; (4) blessed are you when you are hated and persecuted and no place will be found, wherever you have been persecuted; (5) blessed are those who have been persecuted in their hearts, because they are the ones who have truly come to know the Father (69:1); (6) blessed are those who go hungry, so the stomach of the one in want may be filled (69:2); and (7) if you bring forth what is in you, what you have will save you, but if you do not have that within you, what you do not have within you will kill you (70).

In the midst of this sequence of sayings of Jesus, *Gos. Thom.* 66 is a saying about a stone that builders rejected. It continues the topic of rejection that is present in the preceding parable about the vineyard owner (65) and provides a bridge to the sayings after it that explore the relation of knowledge to deficiency within oneself (67), the relation of being hated and persecuted to being able to find the place where the persecution occurred (68), the relation of knowing the Father to being persecuted "in the heart" (69:1), the relation of individual hunger to making food available to others in need (69:2), and the relation of "that within you" to being saved or being killed (70). This is not the place to interpret more fully the relation of these sayings to one another.[33] The goal here is to observe that Jesus' orality has no interface with the writings. Rather, words that scholars know are in the writings are simply words of Jesus that function alongside other words of Jesus in a sequence of sayings that explore various aspects of being rejected, having knowledge, having certain kinds of things in oneself, and bringing certain kinds of things forth from within oneself.

The contrast between *Gos. Thom.* 65–70 and Mark 11:27—12:12 calls attention to a significantly different register in early Christian rhetorical culture. In the *Gospel of Thomas* the prophetic register functioning in the Synoptic Gospels is absent. In its place is a wisdom register that presupposes the dynamics of a personage who possesses knowledge from the sphere of the divine. This personage leads hearers into ever more reflective and inquiring exploration of sayings that are vehicles of insight into divine wisdom. Introducing a series of sayings in a sequence creates a context in which it is asserted that knowing certain kinds of things can be helpful in contexts of rejection and persecution. The literature at work in the orality of the sayings of Jesus in the *Gospel of Thomas* is literature that contains more sayings of Jesus. In other words, for the *Gospel of Thomas* there is no interface between orality and the writings from which the Gospel story flows, as in Mark, or that function as external support for the narration of the story, as in Matthew and Luke (and John).

Matthew 21:23-46 as Jesus' Elaboration of What Is Written

An interpreter begins to see the many interfaces of orality and literature in the Gospel tradition by seeing how Matt 21:40-46 expands the internal interface of orality and literature in the Markan presentation of Jesus' speech. The Matthean version of Jesus' speech unfolds as follows:

> (A1) "When therefore the owner of the vineyard comes,
>   what will he do to those tenants?" (21:40)
> (A2) They said to him,
>   "He will put those wretches to a miserable death,
>   and let out the vineyard to other tenants
>   who will give him the fruits in their seasons." (21:41)

(B1)   Jesus says to them,
       "Have you never read in the writings:
       'The stone that the builders rejected,
       this has become the cornerstone;
       this was from the Lord,
       and it is amazing in our eyes'? (21:42)
       Therefore I tell you,
       the kingdom of God will be taken away from you
       and given to a nation that produces the fruits of
       it." (21:43)
       And when the chief priests and the Pharisees heard his
       parables,
       they knew that he was speaking about them, (21:45)
       and wanting to seize him they feared the crowds,
       because they regarded him as a prophet. (21:46)

(C1)   And again Jesus answered and spoke to them in parables,
       saying . . . (22:1)

Instead of presenting Jesus' recitation of the writing as a direct continuation of the presentation of the parable, Matthew precedes the recitation with: "Jesus says to them, 'Have you never read in the writings?'" (21:42). The Matthean version, then, merges the *chreia* approach to the speech of Jesus evident in *Gos. Thom.* 66 with the "recitation of writing" approach in the Gospel of Mark. Matthew introduces a new unit of speech for Jesus with the assertion that "Jesus says to them" and the use of the plural form, "the writings," rather than the singular, which would refer simply to the text he recites.

    In Matthew the introduction of a new unit of speech with "Jesus says to them" is part of a dialogue that starts with the chief priests and elders in the Temple when they ask Jesus who gave him authority to do the things he is doing (21:23). Jesus' first response is to ask them a question (21:24-25), to which they respond, "We do not know" (21:27). Jesus tells them in return that he will not tell them the authority behind what he is doing, but he has a question for them about a son who said he would go to the vineyard to work but did not, while the other son said he would not go but did (21:28-30). When they respond to Jesus that the son who said he would not go but did had done the will of his father, Jesus responds that the tax collectors and prostitutes will go into the kingdom of God before they do (21:31). After providing a rationale for this assertion (21:32), Jesus tells them to "Listen to another parable" (21:33). At the end of the parable, Jesus asks the chief priests and the elders another question: "Now when the owner of the vineyard comes, what will he do to those tenants?" (21:41). When they respond that the owner will "put those wretches to a miserable death" (21:41), Jesus says to them, "Have you not read in the writings . . . ?" (21:42). Then he presents a conclusion to the dialogue: "Therefore I tell you, the kingdom of God will be taken away from you and given to a people that produces the fruits of the kingdom" (21:43). After narration that tells the hearer that chief priests and Pharisees heard the parables of Jesus, that they perceived that Jesus was telling the parables "against them," and that they wanted to arrest him but couldn't (21:45-46), Jesus continues to answer them by speaking to them in parables (22:1).

In Matthew's presentation, Jesus' recitation of Ps 118:22-23 functions as an authoritative thesis and rationale gleaned from the writings (21:42) that produces the conclusion: "Therefore I tell you, the kingdom of God will be taken away from you and given to a nation producing the fruits of it" (21:43). The thesis is that "the stone the builders rejected has become the cornerstone [or keystone]." The rationale is that "this is the Lord's doing and it is a marvelous thing." From the writings, then, Jesus has gleaned a thesis and rationale that are the first and second part of a syllogistic argument. The third part is a conclusion that Jesus "authoritatively" generates in his own speech. Jesus begins the conclusion with, "Therefore I tell you" and asserts that God is taking the kingdom of God away from the people with authority over the Jerusalem Temple and giving it to "another nation" that will produce the fruits of the kingdom. The presence of the divine passive in "will be taken away" and "will be given" carries "the Lord's doing" from the rationale to the conclusion.

In summary, Matt 21:23-43 is a continuous dialogue that ends with a special unit that contains Jesus' recitation from the authoritative writings that presents a thesis and a rationale from the writings (21:42), the presentation of a conclusion to both the syllogistic argument and the dialogue (21:43),[34] and a narrational conclusion to the dialogue (21:45-46) that leads into Jesus' continuation of his teaching in parables. The narrational conclusion refers back to the two parables Jesus told the chief priests and elders (21:28-30, 33-39), and it extends the awareness of the chief priests and elders that the crowd regarded John as a prophet (21:26) to an awareness that the crowds also regarded Jesus as a prophet (21:46). Instead of following the Markan approach, in which Jesus simply embeds an oral recitation of a written text in a rhetorical question to the Temple authorities (Mark 12:10-11), Matthew builds Jesus' recitation from the writings into an authoritative response at the end of an extended dialogue that began with a question about his authority to do the things he was doing (Matt 21:23-24).

Matthew, then, builds the internal interface of orality and literature present in Mark into a syllogistic conclusion by Jesus containing a thesis and rationale from the writings that leads to a conclusion about what God will do to them. The Matthean presentation of Jesus' speech leaves nothing in the domain of subtle with regard to Jesus' telling of the parable. Jesus not only speaks the parable "against them"; he asserts that God will take the kingdom of God away from them and give it to another group of people (12:43). The third line in the recitation of Ps 118:22-23 functions not only as the first statement in the rationale ("this was the Lord's doing") but also as an answer to the question by the chief priests and elders at the beginning of the overall unit: "By what authority are you doing these things, and who gave you this authority?" (21:23). Jesus would not tell them who gave him the authority, but he would let the authoritative writings tell them! In turn, Jesus' conclusion that the kingdom of God will be taken away from them and given to a people that produces the fruits of the kingdom (21:43) is a reformulation of the rationale he gave in 21:32: "For John came to you in the way of righteousness and you did not believe him, but the tax collectors and the prostitutes believed him; and even after you saw it, you did not change your minds and believe him" (21:32).

Another interface of orality and literature among the Synoptic Gospels occurs where another Gospel, like Matthew or Luke, builds the internal interface of orality and literature in Jesus' speech into an argumentative sequence in which the recitation from the writings functions as a thesis, a rationale, or a conclusion. In Matt 21:42 the recitation provides the thesis and rationale, and an additional saying by Jesus provides the conclusion (21:43).[35]

Luke 20:16-19 as Explanation of a Literary Text

The Gospel of Luke presents the sequence in the Jerusalem Temple in a way that relates both to the Markan and to the Matthean version of the scene.

> ". . . What then will the owner of the vineyard do to them? (20:15)
> He will come and destroy those tenants and give the vineyard to others."
> (A1) When they heard this, they said, "Heaven forbid!" (20:16)

(B1)   But he looked at them and said,
       "What then does this text mean:
       'The stone that the builders rejected has become the cor-
       nerstone'? (20:17)
       Everyone who falls on that stone will be broken to pieces;
       and it will crush anyone on whom it falls." (20:18)

(C1)   When the scribes and chief priests realized that he had told
       this parable against them,
       they wanted to lay hands on him at that very hour,
       but they feared the people; for they perceived that he had
       told this parable against them. (20:19)

(D1)   And they watched him and sent spies who pretended to
       be sincere, that they might take hold of what he said, so as
       to deliver him up to the authority and jurisdiction of the
       governor. (20:20)

On the one hand, Luke, similar to Matthew, presents Jesus' recitation from the writings as a separate unit introduced by "But he looked
around at them and said" (20:17). On the other hand, the Lukan version does two things the Matthean version does not do: (1) it refers to
the words from the writings as "this that is written" (*to gegrammenon
touto*), and (2) it presents a conclusion to the recitation of scripture in
another recitation of scripture that is not identified as coming from the
writings.
   Lukan narration, in contrast to Mark and Matthew, features Jesus
teaching the people in the Temple, with chief priests, scribes, and elders
listening in. When Jesus is teaching the people (20:1), chief priests,
scribes, and elders ask him by what authority he is doing what he does
(20:2). When Jesus asks them to tell him if the baptism of John came
from heaven or was of human origin (20:4), a major concern is that if
they say, "Of human origin," "all the people will stone us, because they are
convinced that John was a prophet" (20:6). The reference by the Temple
hierarchy to the fear of being stoned by the people keeps a focus on the
people and sets the stage for the special comments about the stone that
occurs in 20:17-18. After Jesus refuses to tell the Temple hierarchies by
what authority he is doing what he does (20:8), he begins to tell the
people about the man with a vineyard who sent servants and finally his
"beloved son" to get its produce (20:9-15). When Jesus ends the parable with his own rhetorical question and answer that the vineyard owner

will "destroy the tenants and give the vineyard to others" (20:15-16) the people respond aghast with, "Heaven forbid" (*mē genoito*). At this point, Jesus looks around at the people and says, "What then does this which is written mean?" (20:17). The focus on the singular written text creates an image of Jesus with a text in front of him, pointing to a specific line in the text.

After reciting only the first two lines about the stone, without the comment about "the Lord" and the marvelous things the Lord is doing (Mark 12:11 // Matt 21:42), Jesus continues with a recitation of Isa 8:14-15, "Everyone who falls on that stone will be broken to pieces; and it will crush anyone on whom it falls" (Luke 20:18). In this instance, Jesus interprets the written text about the stone that is rejected with another written text, without indicating that the interpretation also comes from the writings. Here one sees an even deeper interface with literature in the orality of Jesus in Luke. In a manner related to Jesus' reading from "the place where it was written," "The Spirit of the Lord is upon me" (Isa 61:1-2 // Luke 4:17-19), where words from a specific written place become Jesus' own words, so Jesus interprets Ps 118:22 with Isa 8:14-15 as though they were his own words.

Lukan narration, then, comes full circle through the use of written words to interpret events, like the coming of John the Baptist (3:4-6), to a use of written words in the speech of Jesus much like *Gos. Thom.* 66. In other words, even Lukan narration nurtures a dynamic interface between orality and literature in the speech of Jesus. Rather than bypassing literature as an external support for both the narration of the story and the speech of Jesus, however, it uses the writings both for external support and for internal orality. This special feature in Luke was so effective that many manuscripts add Luke 20:18 at Matt 21:44. With this addition to Matthew, not only does Jesus end the discussion with the syllogistic argument about the stone and the Lord's doing in 21:42 followed by the conclusion in 21:43, but Jesus adds yet another authoritative judgment that convinces the chief priests and scribes that they must find a way to arrest him.

In Luke, then, the prophetic register of the interface between orality and literature comes full circle through the speech of Jesus. Not only does Jesus recite from the writings, as he does in Mark (and also Matthew), but he also recites from the writings in a dynamic, oral manner, like the *Gospel of Thomas*, that acknowledges no indebtedness to the writings.

A Multitude of Voices

I would argue from the evidence I presented above that all of the recitation of the writings in the Gospel of Mark are internal either to the narration of the story itself, to speech of Jesus, or to an interlocutor. There is no instance in Mark in which the narrator appeals to the writings for external support for an event or for an assertion in the narration. This is an important part of the orality of the Gospel of Mark. It means that the interface between orality and literature in Mark is internal to the narrational voices in the text. This is a phenomenon close to the dynamics of oral speech in a rhetorical culture, when an oral speaker does not, himself or herself, regularly read substantive portions of other literature. Rather than authoritatively presenting recitations from the writings on the basis of his or her own authority as a narrator, like Matthew or Luke (or John), the narrator of the Gospel of Mark attributes "the authority" for recitations to a personage like Isaiah (1:2-4), to Jesus, or to an interlocutor like "the Pharisees" (10:4).

A major characteristic of the interface between orality and literature in the Gospel of Mark is the presence of assertions that, from a scholarly point of view, are "errors." It is not accurate to say that the wording of Mark 2–4 is "written in Isaiah," but the interface between orality and literature in the prophetic register in the Gospel of Mark manifests itself in this kind of assertion. There are other assertions like this in Mark that are, from a scholarly point of view, either inaccurate or highly uncertain.[36] Scholars regularly insist that there must be a lost written source somewhere that is the basis for the assertion. This position, I suggest, is based on a misunderstanding of the interface of orality and literature in the Gospel of Mark. When orality is in a dominant position, literary "errors" are a natural feature of the discourse.

Moreover, the written nature of the Gospel of Mark in no way destroys the orality of its narration. Both Matthew and Luke participate in the oral effect of Markan narration in dynamic ways. They may expand the orality in argumentation, proceeding in ways that are highly characteristic of speech making during the first century. Or they may rework the narrational voice to include a recitation from writings that supports either a narrational assertion or a narrative account of an entire event with a prophetic rationale. In addition, it is possible, as we have seen in Luke 20:18, that the interface of orality and literature in the speech of Jesus comes full circle. Starting with orality in the speech of Jesus that flaunts

Jesus' knowledge of the writings in the context of well-established writers (scribes), the Gospel writers feature Jesus reciting authoritatively from the writings in his own speech, without indicating that the words are from the writings.

Does only orality give life, then, while writing kills? Not at all. The question is precisely what kind of interface between orality and literature exists at certain points in a written or oral composition. When the early Christian prophetic register is present, an intermingling of multiple voices of authority that feature a dynamic interplay of orality and literature is, as one might say, the order of the day. One should expect exactly this dynamic interplay of voices to be present, since it is precisely the manner in which meanings are evoked in traditional cultures.

9

Memory Technology and the Composition of Mark

Whitney Shiner

On the basis of orality studies by Walter Ong, Eric Havelock, and others, Werner Kelber emphasized in *The Oral and the Written Gospel* the profound effect that a written Gospel had upon the early church.[1] Discussions since that time have generally confirmed that position. Writing in the ancient world was often related to issues of power and authority, and whether or not it was the author's intention, a written life of Jesus would tend, at least over time, to be invested with a different type of authority than that of oral sources. This was at least in part because those in the church who could lay no claim to familiarity with the fast-disappearing authorities of the earliest period of the church could wield authority on the basis of such written records and could use the authority of a fixed text to challenge the different understandings of representatives of oral tradition. Those who made such claims were successful in spite of the often-stated preference of writers in the Roman world for the living oral word over the dead written letter and the freedom with which both speakers and writers adapted such oral authorities.[2]

While Kelber had stressed the differences between oral and written media, his later writings have explored the complex interrelationship between the two in rhetorical cultures such as that found in the Roman Empire during New Testament times.[3] Oral delivery was still the norm in a rhetorical culture, but the nature of the compositions and the method of composition were very different from those found in purely oral cultures. While there were certainly works that could only exist in writing, such as extended histories and encyclopedias such as Pliny's *Natural History*, to cite some very obvious examples, in the complex mix of orality and writing found in rhetorical cultures, there was a grey area of composition types that could be produced for either medium. Kelber concluded that the Gospel of Mark was definitively a written work; however, it appears to me, given the complexity of composition in both media, that the Mark falls into that grey area of uncertainty.

The Epic Model of Oral Performance

The model of oral composition and performance presented in *The Oral and the Written Gospel* is largely derived directly or indirectly from the work of Milman Parry and Albert Lord on the oral performance of epic poetry in the Balkans and its relationship to the works of Homer.[4] Their model of oral composition/performance describes one form of memory technology found in oral cultures. According to this model, an oral performer is able to perform extended narratives in verse by weaving together various types of narrative material that he or she has retained in his or her memory. On one level there is the overall plot structure of the epic and the more extended narrative of which the epic may be a part. The plot structure is filled out with various themes, which are fairly stereotyped episodes that may be used at the appropriate places in a number of different epics. On a smaller scale, the epic singer had at his or her command a great number of fixed verbal formulas that could be used in the description of these elements, such phrases as Homer's "wine-dark sea" or "rosy-fingered dawn." These formulas were particularly useful for the performance of epics, in which the singer had to maintain a certain metrical structure. Rather than memorize an epic word for word, the singer recomposed the epic for each performance based on these elements stored in his or her memory.[5]

When applied to Gospel material, this model suggests that in its oral phase this material was recomposed for each performance and did not maintain a fixed verbal form. In his analysis of the Gospel of Mark, Kelber showed that the individual episodes of Mark exhibited significant oral features, but he argued that while individual episodes exhibit characteristics of oral communication, the Gospel as a whole does not. The Gospel only existed as a written document and had not existed as a whole in an oral stage in which it would have been recomposed from memory for performance.[6]

A significant challenge to Kelber's understanding of the written genesis of Mark has been presented by Pieter J. J. Botha, who also drew on the model of epic composition described by Parry and Lord.[7] Botha argued that the Gospel of Mark appeared to be constructed in the same manner as the oral epics, given appropriate adjustment to the theory for prose narrative, and concluded that "it is quite possible that the Gospel of Mark is a casual transcription of what has been performed orally."[8]

He argued that formulaic composition could be detected in stylized expressions such as ἤρχατο διδάσκειν, καὶ ἔλεγεν αὐτοῖς, ἀποκριθεὶς . . . λέγει, προσκαλεσάμενος . . . λέγε / ἔλεγεν, εὐθύς, Πέτρος καὶ Ἰάκωβος καὶ Ἰωάννης, and the repetition of prepositions with compound verbs.[9] The use of formulas in composition would also explain the anomalous use of ἀποκριθεὶς . . . λέγει in situations where the speaker is not replying to a question (9:5, 10:24). It should be noted, however, that the Markan use of formulas is not a reliable indicator of oral composition according to Lord's account of the composition process. Lord states that it is the density of formulaic expressions that indicates oral composition, while written works may make use of a smaller number of formulaic expressions.[10] By that standard Botha's list of formulas is not very impressive. But the use of formulas in oral epic is largely a result of the singer's need to fit the composition into a regular metrical structure, so one would assume that there would be much less frequent use of formulas in orally composed prose narratives.

Botha argued that composition by theme can be detected in the repetition of similar episodes and the use of episodes similar to typical narrative units found in the surrounding culture.[11] Much of the work of the form critics has been devoted to cataloging and analyzing these typical units, and Kelber himself has also pointed out oral features of the individual Markan units. While Kelber and the form critics saw these oral features in Mark as the fossil remains of their earlier oral life, however, Botha suggests that they represent the way that Mark himself composed his narrative. As Botha points out, there are several cases in which Mark repeats much verbatim material, as if he is remembering a common story and making appropriate changes as he goes. Botha's examples of thematic composition include confrontations with an unclean spirit (1:23-26; 3:11-12; 9:25-26), calling disciples (1:13-14, 16-18, 19-20), bread miracles (6:34-44; 8:1-9), and preparations (11:1-7; 14:12-16). The examples vary in terms of the amount of similar material and similar verbal expression.[12]

A careful analysis of the verbal similarities in the two feeding stories may be found in Robert Fowler's *Loaves and Fishes*.[13] Fowler concluded from the number of similarities that Mark had himself constructed one of the feeding stories on the model of the other, but Botha's theory of oral composition, in which the stories would be variations on a common theme, fits the evidence just as well. Thematic composition would also explain the anomaly found in Mark 5:43, where Jesus commands those present that no one should know about the healing of Jairus's daughter, even though the whole town knows she is dead and the next room is full of mourners. The simplest explanation for the anomalous command to silence is that it is part of the Markan version of the theme of healing, and even when it did not fit a particular variation on the theme, the habits of thematic construction outweighed the importance of internal consistency.

Botha raises important points about the oral-like nature of the Markan narrative, and additional material could be cited in support of his points. Because of the complexity of the oral-written mix in the first century, however, his argument does not seem to me to be conclusive.

The Impact of Writing
on Composition Techniques

The epic singers described by Parry and Lord generally sang traditional songs and occasionally composed new songs making use of traditional material. Originality in itself was not considered an important aspect of the performance. Instead, the emphasis was on the artistic performance of traditional material. Singers claimed to be repeating exactly the song they had heard no matter how much they may have changed or improved it. In the rhetorical culture of the first-century Roman world, however, originality was more highly valued, and most pieces were intentionally composed for a specific situation or range of situations. Most oral cultures also value skill in presenting speeches or songs addressing specific issues or situations, but in the rhetorical culture of the Roman world the delivery of previously composed speeches became the norm, at least among the elite. Thus, oral performances based on (more or less) fixed texts would be familiar, at least to those who lived in cities and towns. This new category of oral performance embodied features that Ong and Havelock associate with writing, for example, in their approach to logical argumentation. While there is little evidence for performances among the nonliterate part of Roman society, the performances of trained rhetoricians were popular on all social levels, and the more polished pieces of these performers may well have influenced expectations for performance among those whose compositions were constructed without the benefit of formal training or the use of writing.

Prefabricated speeches did not completely supplant spontaneous composition even among the elite. In debate one often found that the prefabricated speech did not address unforeseen arguments from an opponent, and show speeches were often composed *ex tempore* because the ability to compose as one spoke was highly admired. Nevertheless, the norm one learned in rhetorical schools was the carefully crafted prepared speech. The result was a different sort of composition in which the use of memory as a tool for composition and delivery was more intentionally developed.

The epic singers studied by Parry and Lord appear to be more or less unconscious of the memory system they actually employed in reproducing traditional epics. Parry and Lord discovered this memory system through an analysis of the epics. The singers received no instruction in this method of reproducing traditional songs. On the contrary, the method of reproducing such songs appeared to rely on the innate abilities of human beings or at least a certain number of human beings with superior memory skills, and it parallels the unconscious acquisition of a language.[14]

By the first century CE, however, a number of more self-conscious memory techniques had been developed. Some of these techniques facilitated the fabrication of *ex tempore* speeches, but others allowed for the more or less verbatim performance of previously composed speeches. They also made possible a third category of oral performance, the repeated performances of previously composed material, which, while not identical as verbatim repetitions, were more nearly the same than the performances of the epic singers. This tended to blur the distinction between written material and oral performance.

Our best sources for understanding memory technologies in the ancient Roman world are the rhetorical handbooks.[15] Memory was one of the five topics considered in most discussions of rhetoric, since the ability to remember vast amounts of material was imperative if one were to become a successful orator. In the rhetorical handbooks we can discern three distinct forms of memory technology. Two of these were presented as specific memory techniques to be employed by rhetoricians. The third is implicit in the process of rhetorical education.

The implicit program of memory development closely approximates the memory technology of the epic singers, but the process has become more self-conscious. The various unconscious processes of the epic singers were transformed into a deliberate educational program through which a proficient student could learn to produce effective rhetorical performances.

Quintilian clearly understands that a significant part of the rhetorician's art is acquired unconsciously through a student's exposure to good models of rhetoric. So he prescribes for his students a wide reading not only in the great rhetorical performances of the past, but also in the historians, whose style and method may be adapted to rhetorical performance. Compared to the learning process of the epic singers, this process has been greatly formalized. Students are expected to be able in various ways to consciously mimic these performances from the past. Nevertheless, much of what a student learns through this exposure to past models happens through unconscious processes.

The teachers of rhetoric, however, did not rely on these unconscious processes alone. This unconscious learning process is supplemented with a very stringent program of conscious education in the art of rhetoric. When one examines this program of education, however, it is readily apparent that it parallels in many ways the unconscious memory system of the epic singers. Students are taught to discern various forms of rhetoric, corresponding to the ability of people in oral cultures to discern the rules and techniques of various genres performed in that culture. They are taught the standard outlines for speeches in those genres, corresponding to an epic singer's grasp of the narrative frame for a particular epic. They are taught standard forms of argument and specific commonplaces that can be used in specific situations, corresponding more or less to the type scenes of the epic singers. Students were also expected to develop in their memory a storehouse of quotations from the classic writings and speeches that could be inserted at appropriate times into their own speeches, rather like the formulas of the epic singers. A student who learned well all these aspects of rhetoric would be able to construct speeches for future delivery as well as *ex tempore* speeches when necessary.

Technology of Memorization

In addition to teaching students to construct speeches from these basic building blocks, the rhetorical handbooks describe two techniques for the memorization of speeches once they had been constructed. There are three major sources for our understanding of these techniques: the *Rhetorica ad Herennium*, Cicero's *De oratore*, and Quintilian's *Institutes*.

Though they differ somewhat in their attitudes toward memorization and memorization technique, they present a rather consistent view of the general practice in the ancient world. There were two approaches to the memorization of speeches. Some speakers learned their speeches verbatim, while others were content to memorize the order and essence of their speeches. Quintilian prefers the former method, although he allows those with weak memories to adopt the latter.[16]

The method preferred by Quintilian for the memorization of speeches requires that the speech be written out before delivery. One then memorizes the speech by repeatedly listening to one's own reading of it or, since all students in his school were upper class, having a slave read it.[17] This procedure obviously requires literacy.

There was another system for memorization, however, that did not require literacy. This system was based on the use of images associated with the material to be memorized.[18] Before using the system, one had to memorize a building or landscape as a background for future memory tasks. Then, when one wanted to memorize any body of material, one developed images representing the material and mentally placed the images at set points in the previously memorized background. This allowed one to remember one's material in order by progressing through the background image. Some rhetoricians used the system for verbatim memorization, placing an image of each word into a place on the background. It could also, with much less effort, be used to memorize the outline of a speech.

The system was so well known that Cicero simply alludes to it and expects his audience to understand, and none of the extant handbooks give a complete description of it.[19] It may be that the system was learned early in children's education to facilitate the oral recitation that was so important both in the lower level of school and in the pre-rhetorical studies of secondary school. Since the early stages of Greek and Roman education were based on rote memory,[20] it may even have been taught prior to the students' learning of letters. Because the system did not rely on the skills of literacy, it may well have been used by people with no schooling at all.

Memory Technology and Composition

Memory technology is pertinent to the issue of composition because memory was an important tool for composition, whether the composition was intended for oral or written media.[21] Most writing was done by dictation, and authors generally worked out their material in their memory before dictating it to a scribe. The more fastidious authors would then work over the written composition to perfect the wording. A description of this process is furnished by Pliny the Younger:

> If I have anything on hand I work it out in my head, choosing and correcting the wording, and the amount I achieve depends on the ease or difficulty with which my thoughts can be marshalled and kept in my head. Then I call my secretary, the shutters are opened, and I dictate what I have put into shape; he goes out, is recalled, and again dismissed. Three or four hours after I first wake . . . [I] work out the rest of my subject, and dictate it.[22]

In this case Pliny works out relatively short pieces of his composition before dictation, as he repeatedly recalls his scribe. Virgil composed in a similar manner, dictating a portion of a poem to his scribe in the morning and later working over the wording. The method could also be extended to the composition of complete works, as shown by Quintilian:

> For there are places and occasions where writing is impossible, while both are available in abundance for premeditation. . . . This practice will not merely secure the proper arrangement of our matter without any recourse to writing . . . but will also set the words which we are going to use in their proper order, and bring the general texture of our speech to such a stage of completion that nothing further is required beyond the finishing touches.[23]

If one were willing to forgo the finishing touches, one could entirely skip the stage of writing, and it is clear that this was the practice of many rhetoricians. It was not at all infrequent for rhetorician's speeches to equal or exceed the length of the Gospel of Mark, so it would seem that the Gospel could well have been composed in this manner, and it could have been fully composed in the author's head before being committed to writing.

The ancient evidence suggests it would be possible for Mark to have composed the Gospel in his head, but is there any way to tell whether or not Mark did such a thing? Would it not be equally possible for Mark to operate like Pliny and to have composed the Gospel section by section?

The most important evidence bearing on that issue is the method of composition that is evident in many ancient authors. When using existing sources, ancient authors seem for the most part to have followed a single source for a particular portion of their work. They may have switched sources several times, but they generally produced a serial patchwork of sources rather than, as modern authors try to do, reconfigure isolated events or incidents from all the sources into a new coherent whole. Various scholars have noted this method in Livy, Plutarch, and Apollonius Sophista.[24] The same method is apparent in Iamblichus's *Pythagorean Life* and Philostratus's *Life of Apollonius of Tyana*, since those writers left blatant seams evident in their works. Many of the *Lives* of Diogenes Laertius display little if any attempt to pull diverse material into a coherent whole. When using a variety of sources, even the most sophisticated ancient writers had difficulty pulling them all into a seamless whole.

This procedure is quite different from what Quintilian was contemplating in the quotation above. Why could a rhetorician drawing largely on existing material create a brand new coherent whole while historians, biographers, and philosophers often created serial paste jobs? T. J. Luce suggests that Livy would not dissect his sources into bits and then fashion the bits into a new whole because that would have seemed irresponsible and willful.[25] Both Pelling and Small, on the other hand, believe the serial patchwork to be more the result of the difficulty of using written material of the time and the reliance of the authors on their memory as the vehicle of their compositions.[26]

It appears to me that the answer lies in the way the two groups used their memory in composition. The rhetoricians' method of composition, as shown above, was much more similar to that of the epic singers. The preexisting material was broken down into various quotations, figures of speech, arguments, and speech outlines so that, like the epic singer, they could weave the new composition out of existing parts. Unlike the epic singers, however, they had the memory technology to hold their compositions in their memory in relatively fixed form. The patchwork authors, on the other hand, either relied more directly on written sources or had not deconstructed their sources into their individual parts.

It is interesting to note that Luke, generally considered the most sophisticated of the Synoptic writers, follows the pattern of other historians using multiple sources and tends to use material from Mark and Q in blocks, while Matthew integrates the material much more thoroughly, for example, melding material from different sources into coherent speeches to make Matthean points. Like the epic singers and the rhetoricians, he disintegrated his material into individual blocks with which he could compose more freely than Luke, and he almost certainly carried much if not all of the material in his mind so that he could combine material into new compositions without referring to written sources at all. In sections where he follows Mark more closely, he may be reading sections of Mark and then rewriting them from memory, but it is equally possible that he had memorized Mark, either from a written copy or repeated oral performances, and he could refer to his memorized Mark and follow it along in his head as a guide for the more Markan sections of the Gospel. Since Matthew shows little concern for word-for-word fidelity to the written Mark in his Gospel, it seems reasonable to assume that he would be equally free in his memorized version.

Composition of Mark

We have been able to say this much about the composition styles of Matthew and Luke because we possess one of their sources in written form, the Gospel of Mark, and can make, at least in the majority opinion of scholars, a more or less reasonable restoration of the content of another, Q. With Mark, on the other hand, we do not have any of his sources, and while there have been proposals for quite a few written sources for various portions of Mark, there is no general consensus on any of the proposals. Therefore, if we are to say anything about Mark's method of composition, we would have to rely on a different type of evidence.

I believe there is evidence for his method of composition in the structure of the Gospel. There is certainly no consensus on the structure of Mark, so it might seem fruitless to argue from structure to composition technique, but there are certain aspects of the structure for which there is general agreement, such as the basic plot development, the importance of repetitions in parts of the Gospel, and the lack of strictly linear development. There is also general consensus that Mark used the three Passion predictions to structure the portion of the Gospel between Peter's confession and the Jerusalem section (8:31—10:52).

In spite of that lack of consensus, I argue that Mark's composition technique can be seen from the structure of Mark I suggested in *Proclaiming the Gospel*.[27] In that book I argued that the structure itself served to facilitate its memorization. Here I would like to argue that the structure suggests the use of a simplified version of the architectural image memory technology for the composition of the Gospel. It appears that a great deal of the structure of the Gospel can be explained through the repeated use of a very basic architectural structure that allows for the inclusion of a very limited number of elements. This would be the sort of structure that students beginning to read might have used for modest memory tasks.

One very simple and ubiquitous architectural structure is the typical temple front, and I will use that as the basis for showing how the Gospel could be composed by means of this memory technology. The image I am using was adapted from the Parthenon, but most other temple fronts would function just as well. Since everyone was familiar with temple structures, most people could probably envision such a structure without having to consciously commit it to memory.

There are only two parts of the structure that need to be remembered. The first is the pediment. One can easily organize material for memorization along the pediment of the temple a number of different ways, in general by setting up a number of fixed positions along it. One might remember the placement of these fixed positions by associating them with figures in the frieze below them, but for five, seven, or even nine positions, one could probably simply place images associated with the material to be remembered at equal intervals, and the number of positions would probably be memorable enough. Two such possible sets of positions are indicated in figures 1 and 2.

For memorization tasks involving a larger number of items, one might learn the figures in the metopes (the sculptured panels in the band between the columns and the pediment) and remember the order of material by associating an image for each section with the image of a

Fig. 1.

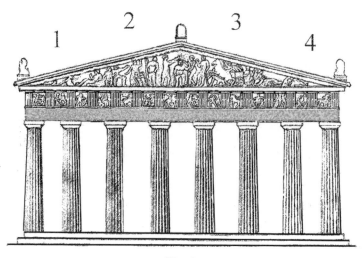

Fig. 2.

particular metope. In many cases, these figures reproduced a well-known mythological story, so that the order of the metope figures would already be known from the story.

Most of Mark can be structured by using the pediment, so I will concentrate on that as a memory structure. It should of course be remembered that one did not have to slavishly follow the structure, since a certain number of deviations could be easily remembered. It is likely that such deviations might stick in the memory especially well as being deviations from the general pattern.

Here for reference is the structure of Mark as presented in *Proclaiming the Gospel*:[28]

> Preface (1:1-13 or 15)
>   I. First triplet: calling and commissioning the disciples
>   A. Call one (1:16-20), marking the beginning
>   of section one (1:16—2:12)
>   B. Call two (2:13-14), marking the beginning
>   of section two (2:13—3:12)
>   C. Commissioning (3:13-19), marking the beginning
>   of section three (3:13-35)
>   II. Major discourse one: The parables (4:1-34)
>   III. Second triplet: boat stories
>   A. Stilling of the storm (4:35-41), marking the transition to section one (4:35—6:44)

    B. Walking on the water (6:45-52), marking the
       transition to section two (6:45—8:26)
    C. Discussion in the boat (8:14-21), marking the end
       of section two
IV. Third triplet: Passion predictions
    A. Preface: Peter's confession (8:22-30)
    B. First Passion prediction (8:31), marking the
       beginning of section one (8:31—9:29)
    C. Second Passion prediction (9:30-32), marking the
       beginning of section two (9:30—10:31)
    D. Third Passion prediction (10:32-34), marking the
       beginning of section three (10:32-52)
 V. Fourth triplet: entries into Jerusalem
    A. The triumphal entry (11:1-10), marking the
       beginning of the first section (11:1-11)
    B. Second entry; cursing the fig tree, part one (11:12-
       15a), marking the beginning of section two (11:12-
       18)
    C. Third entry; cursing the fig tree, part two (11:20-
       27a), marking the beginning of section three
       (11:20—12:44)
VI. Second major discourse (13:1-36)
VII. Passion narrative (14:1—16:8).

The basic structure consists of a preface, four sections structured in various ways around triplets of similar episodes, two major discourses, and the Passion narrative. It should also be apparent that each of the triplet structures is organized in a slightly different way.

Markan Structure and Memory Technology

Let us look at how the basic structure of this outline correlates with the memory technology of an image on an architectural background. We will start with the major sections (see figure 3, which shows the use of images to remember the basic structure). I suggest that the prologue, being much shorter than the other sections, would be treated as an introduction and would not be included in the memory structure. The first section, structured by the call and commissioning stories, is represented with a picture of Jesus on shore calling fishermen in a boat. The second section, the parable discourse, is represented with an image of Jesus teaching from the boat. The third section, structured around the boat crossings, is represented by an image of Jesus and the disciples in the boat. The next section, which in my division of the Gospel is the central section, is structured around the Passion predictions. This is represented by Jesus on the cross. The next three sections are represented by images of Jesus and Jerusalem. An image of the Temple represents Jerusalem. The fifth, sixth, and seventh sections of the Gospel are represented by Jesus entering Jerusalem on a donkey, Jesus on a mountain, and Jesus on the cross outside of the Temple, which has been torn in two.

Fig. 3.

The fact that the basic structure of Mark can be represented by means of such an image is certainly not evidence for the use of the image memory system for the composition of Mark. Any structure with a limited number of segments could be represented by such an image. It is the nature of the subsections that suggests that image technology was used in composition. The triplet structure divides each of the sections (apart from the discourses and the Passion narrative) into subsections short enough to be represented on the simple pediment structure. There are very few written works in the ancient world that can be represented so easily on a simple structure such as this. Most written narrative is much more linear than this without clearly divided subsections. To memorize such a linear narrative with the image memory system, one would have to employ an elaborate and extensive background such as those used by the rhetoricians. In that case the image system does not facilitate composition. In fact it restricts the reworking of the material, since every time one added or took out a section, one would have to rememorize the entire narrative. It is much like the difference between writing with a typewriter, which requires a retyping of the whole in order to accommodate changes, and writing with a word processor, which allows one to freely insert and delete material without retyping the whole.

Here are a few examples of how the subsections can be represented on the pediment image. Rather than construct images for each of these subsections, I will simply indicate through typography how the material would fit the pediment image.

Subsection IA
Section marker: call story by the sea (1:16-20)
A. Teaching in Capernaum (1:21-28)
    B. Healings at Simon's house (1:29-34)
        C. Jesus' fame and the reason for his coming (1:35-39)
    D. Cleaning the leper (1:40-45)
E. Healing the paralytic (2:1-12)

Subsection IB
Section marker: call story by the sea (2:13-14)
A. At dinner with Levi (2:15-17)
    B. Fasting (2:18-20)
        C. Double parables of new and old (2:21-22)
    D. Plucking grain on the Sabbath (2:23-27)
E. Man with the withered hand (3:1-6)

Subsection IC
Section marker: By the sea and commissioning the twelve
    (3:7-19a)
A. Jesus' family (3:19b-21)
    B. Scribes say Jesus has Beelzubul (3:22)
        C. Triple parables in rebuttal (3:23-27)
    D. Unforgivable sin (3:28-30)
E. Jesus' family (3:31-35)

The simplicity and clarity of the structure of each of these subsections suggest that the triplet of by the sea and call or commissioning stories is actually being used as a structuring mechanism. Each of the subsections builds toward a narrative climax: the scribes' attack on Jesus, the Pharisees' plotting with the Herodians to kill Jesus, and Jesus' redefinition of his family. Each contains in the middle some kind of member material commenting on the action in the subsection. In IA and IC the outer members deal with similar issues (authority and identity of Jesus; family of Jesus). The repeated use of symmetrical structuring suggests that some composition technique is being used that facilitates symmetrical structures.

While not all of the subsections in the proposed structure of Mark display such a simple structure, they do all appear to be variations on the single symmetrical structure or the types of deviations that one might introduce if one were using the simplified memory technology as a tool for composition. While the triplet structure does provide for the repetition of important points, it is not clear to me why anyone would structure a narrative that way (rather than in a more linear fashion) unless the triplet structure were an outcome of the composition method.

Memory Technology
and the Composition of Mark

How might the structure develop through the use of the image memory system? Mark appears to have started with a considerable amount of formerly unstructured material that had been given no structure. He needed to structure it into a coherent whole by showing interrelations and creating some sort of linear plot. The material seems to divide into a number of subplots, and it would be impossible to include all of it in a simple plot outline. So Mark selects a limited amount of material to construct a basic plot. This is the material that forms the triplets. The triplets indicate a basic plot: (1) Jesus calls the disciples, (2) the disciples misunderstand Jesus, (3) Jesus instructs the disciples about the Passion, (4) Jesus enters Jerusalem and interacts with the Temple, and (5) the Passion (which was not developed as a triplet). The two discourses provide interpretive commentary on the plot. That is certainly one of the important plot lines in the Gospel. But it does not include all of the plot lines, which concern Jesus' identity and authority, the antagonism of the authorities, and Jesus' miracles and the various reactions to them. All this material has to be woven around the triplet plot structure.

So after constructing a basic plot outline by means of the simplified image system, Mark could turn to developing each of those sections in a way that made use of his material to develop certain plot lines. There is no particular reason that Mark would have started off thinking of the triplets as triplets. There is no particular reason that he would have to include three call or commissioning stories. In fact, since the first is actually two call stories, he could just as easily have created four subsections. Mark does have a penchant for repeating things three times, but I expect that the triplets may have developed as he worked on fitting his other material into and around the basic plot structure.

The pediment image works quite well for organizing the smaller sections. One can place the key episodes on the pediment first and then decide on other episodes to fill out the section. One would generally place these important key episodes at the important places in the pediment—the corners and the peak. This would define what the section is about. So, for example, in the first subsection, Mark might want to introduce to his audience the question of Jesus' identity and to induce them to think about how that relates to Jesus' healings. So he places on the left corner of the pediment a story in which people ask about Jesus' identity based on an exorcism, and he places on the right corner of the pediment a story in which Jesus declares that his healing is a sign of his authority. He might also want to introduce at the beginning of the narrative a contrast between the reaction of the people and the reaction of the authorities in order to set up the Passion narrative later in the Gospel; foreshadowing the Passion narrative might be called for because it was considered the most important part of the Gospel. So he shows the positive reaction of the people in the first episode and has the authorities start talking about Jesus' blasphemy in the last episode.

If he wants to show Jesus as reluctant to have people know who he is, Mark needs to explain why Jesus is running around healing everyone. So he shows in the first story that Jesus is forced into healing in order to keep his identity secret. Mark can develop that idea by having Jesus state that his purpose is to teach, not to heal. So an episode indicating that purpose is placed at an important place, the center of the pediment. As he develops the Gospel, he may decide that he wants to introduce the idea of the misunderstanding of the disciples early on, so he makes the central episode in this section include Peter searching out Jesus to have Jesus respond to his fame and correct Peter. Once the central episodes are set, Mark can fill in the sides of the pediment with any healing stories in order to show that Jesus is a great healer, but the particular details are not that important.

I believe this is why we find so many chiastic structures in New Testament writings. If an author is using a simple symmetrical building in his or her memory on which the sections of narrative are placed, those sections will tend to turn out as chiasms. The structure suggests balancing similar pieces on the opposite sides. If similar material is placed on each side, the order is much easier to remember. It is not clear that the audiences always followed these chiastic structures. It is more likely that the chiastic structures are there because they provide a convenient way to organize material in one's mind and are an easy way to remember material for dictation or performance.

Such a method of composition also fits quite well with Mark's method of creating meaning through the juxtaposition of episodes without direct commentary. Mark could play around with various episodes that he has at hand to create juxtapositions that he found meaningful.

If one composes in one's mind by placing images on a building, it is easy to remember the structure as one has created it in one's mind. One can move back and forth among the overall structure, large sections, and subsections of the narrative. One can also develop overlapping structures. It seems likely that Mark planned the placement of the three statements of Jesus being the Son or a son of God and developed them in relation to each other. They go at the beginning, middle, and end of the Gospel. There are a number of parallels between the baptism scene and the crucifixion-centurion scene that indicate that they were planned together and that in Mark's mind they explicate each other. The triplet of son-of-God statements does not exactly fit the overall structure for the Gospel that I have proposed, but one can plan out a structure like that and then go back and superimpose it on a previously defined structure to help develop it.

Mark as an Orally Developed Written Composition

If the Gospel of Mark was composed using the architectural memory system, Mark would very likely have presented it from memory several times before committing it to writing, since it was common for authors to polish their works before publication through repeated presentations in front of friendly audiences. Changes could then be made based on the audience reaction and the suggestions that audience members offered. The simplified architectural memory system allows for a great deal of recomposition without completely redoing the structure. He could have started with a simple narrative and reworked it as time went on, adding or dropping material and reworking interrelationships between material as his understanding of the Gospel developed. It seems to me quite unlikely that one would develop all the complex interrelationships among episodes in the Gospel on the first try. The complexity of Mark's narrative suggests that he has presented the material, reflected upon it, worked it over, and further developed it to present Jesus in the way most in keeping with his own understanding.

10

A Prophet Like Moses and Elijah: Popular Memory and Cultural Patterns in Mark

Richard A. Horsley

The way we understand the Gospel of Mark has been changing dramatically in the last thirty years. Once we recognize that the Gospel is a sustained narrative, indeed a complete story with a main plot and several subplots, we can no longer treat individual episodes in isolation. Once we recognize that, in the predominantly oral communication environment of antiquity, stories such as the Gospel of Mark were performed before communities of people, even after they were written down, we can no longer project the assumptions and typical approaches of literary study that assumes a writer at a desk and an individual reader. And once we recognize that only a tiny literate elite possessed written copies of texts, we can no longer assume that our sources for the reconstruction of ancient history can be treated as if they were documents in modern archives. The composition-performance and the appropriation of the Gospel of Mark were embedded in a broader cultural memory in which written scrolls were one among many media of communication.

Werner Kelber was one of the first to explore Mark's Gospel as a dramatic story. He then almost single-handedly pioneered the recognition of the difference between and relation of orality and literacy and the implications for Mark and other New Testament literature. More recently he has been the first to discern the importance of studies of cultural memory in other fields and how understanding memory will further change the way we approach the composition and use of Mark and other Gospels.[1] Presupposing the impact of Kelber's innovation in these three interrelated areas (see the introduction),[2] I would like to pursue some of the implications of Kelber's insights into the importance of cultural memory for fuller appreciation of the Gospel of Mark.

The Complexities of
Israelite Cultural Memory

Since memory is always social-cultural, it is necessary to focus both on the particular social-cultural memory involved in Mark and on the way in which memory works in the composition and performance of the Gospel in its historical social context. Insofar as the contents of the Gospel are inseparable from its form, it is clear that the overall story and most of its component episodes were embedded not merely in the memory of Jesus and the Synoptic tradition but more deeply in Israelite cultural memory. The principal settings—Galilee, Judea, Jerusalem, the Temple—are sites laden with and bearers of Israelite culture memory, and the principal characters come into conflict over customs, rituals, festivals, and religious and economic practices central to Israelite memory. Jesus is represented as acting out roles reminiscent of some of the prime heroes in Israel's history. The past that the Gospels are appropriating for purposes of present community concerns is that of Israel as well as Jesus' ministry. The latter is embedded in the former and cannot be separated from it.

Insofar as the Gospel (however widely available in written form) was being orally performed, moreover, its reception and its hermeneutics were oral/aural. While established Gospel studies in particular and New Testament studies in general are ill-equipped to understand orally performed narratives, help is readily available from related fields that have given considerable thought to the practice and theory of oral performance in relation to and comparison with written texts. In striving to appreciate Mark's story as oral performance I have found most compelling the work of John Miles Foley, who draws on ethnography of speaking, ethnopoetics, and sociolinguistics in developing his own theory of immanent art. Key for my explorations of Mark and other orally derived texts are the interrelated components of the *text* itself, the performance *context,* and the way the text metonymically references the cultural *tradition.*[3] Kelber, who interacts closely with Foley, stated the importance of "extra-textual" *tradition* in both the production and reception of a text in comprehensively strong terms as a circumambient context or "biosphere in which speaker and hearers live, . . . an invisible nexus of references and identities from which people draw sustenance, . . . and in relation to which they make sense of their lives."[4] In attempting to appreciate a Gospel in oral performance, we are thus no longer searching for the meaning of the text, but attending to *the work that a text does in a community of people.* We are focused squarely on the historical social context in attempting to understand the work done by an orally performed text *as it (metonymically) references the tradition.* The cultural tradition of a community is the key to appreciating how a text-in-performance did its work.

But we are now faced with serious problems as we attempt to investigate the Israelite cultural memory/tradition in which Jesus' ministry (and pre-Markan Gospel materials) were embedded and the way that tradition was metonymically referenced by the performed text. In the field of New Testament studies, it has simply been assumed that Israelite tradition/cultural memory was virtually identical with and known through the medium of the (Hebrew) Bible—the Law and the Prophets. It has also simply been assumed that ancient Judeans and Galileans dealt with the cultural memory that they presumably knew via the biblical text mainly in fragmentary units of a verse, a proverb, a law, a motif, or even a phrase. Recent research, however, has demonstrated that these assumptions of standard Gospel studies, which are deeply rooted in print culture, are quite unwarranted and simply anachronistic. We can focus on three interrelated areas of this recent research.

First, literacy in Judea and Galilee was limited mainly to circles of scribes and priests concentrated in Jerusalem and the Herodian administrations. Moreover, scrolls were both cumbersome and expensive. Thus about the only people who had direct knowledge of the nascent Hebrew scriptures were scribes and priests connected with the Temple in Jerusalem or the dissident scribal-priestly community at Qumran, who left the Dead Sea Scrolls. It seems highly unlikely that Judean and Galilean villagers, the vast majority of the populace, who could neither afford expensive, cumbersome scrolls nor read them, would have had direct knowledge of the nascent Hebrew scriptures. Villagers and townspeople presumably knew of the existence of "the writings" (scripture) kept mainly in the Temple in Jerusalem. They shared with scribal circles a reverence for the aura and authority that surrounded the written word on those huge, heavy scrolls. Yet it seems highly unlikely that the nonliterate Galilean villagers, among whom memories of Jesus' mission were originally cultivated in the context of Israelite cultural memory, would have had direct contact with scrolls of the Law and the Prophets. The distinctive account in Luke 4:16-21 that portrays Jesus reading from a scroll of Isaiah has been shaped by Luke from knowledge of practices in assemblies (*synagōgai*) of the Jewish diaspora.

It has simply been assumed that references in the Gospel of Mark to "the writing" or "it is written" (often accompanied by an ostensible citation of or allusion to a particular passage) indicate that a "biblical" or "scriptural" text is being quoted.[5] Closer examination suggests that the statements in Mark that "it is written" do not mean that a literate author was consulting a written text.[6] Rather, "it is written" refers to the existence, "up there somewhere," of written scrolls with supposed authority to which Jesus' opponents, the scribes and Pharisees, have access and supposedly know only too well. Most (but not all) of these references are polemical, throwing the authority of "the writing" or the written version back in the faces of the scribal groups who supposedly know them. The Gospel of Mark knows of the existence of "the writing." But it is not at all clear that the narrator is quoting from direct knowledge of a written scroll.

Second, the written text of the Law and the Prophets was not standardized among scribal-intellectual circles who possessed written scrolls until well into the second century CE or later. Scholars who have spent a lifetime poring over the scrolls of books found among the Dead Sea Scrolls that were later included in the Hebrew Bible are concluding that two or three different textual traditions coexisted in the same scribal community at Qumran.[7] Those different textual traditions, moreover, were still unstable, still undergoing development in the form of continuing interpretation-composition in the process of being recopied. In addition to the different textual traditions of the books of the Pentateuch and prophetic books, moreover, there were alternative versions of Israel's history, the Torah, and prophetic lore (and *not* just "rewritten Bible/Torah") in books that were not later included in the Hebrew Bible, such as the *Biblical Antiquities* of Pseudo-Philo, *Jubilees*, the *Temple Scroll*, 4QMMT, and the different sections of the book of *Enoch*. Thus even in scribal circles different versions of Israelite cultural tradition competed for authority. If there were different, competing versions of Israelite tradition in scribal circles, which possessed written scrolls, how many more might there have been in popular circles, which did not? We should not conclude that the peasantry was ignorant of Israelite tradition. They simply cultivated their own versions that would have been influenced only indirectly by the written versions of the scribal elite.

In the Gospel of Mark most of the references and allusions to Israelite tradition do not make an explicit connection with a particular passage in a nascent scriptural text. Jesus does a number of Moses-like or
Elijah-like acts, but with no reference to particular passages in Exodus or
Numbers or 1 and 2 Kings. Jesus commandeers a donkey for his ride into
Jerusalem, but with no explicit reference to Zech 9:9. Where reference is
made to "it is written," moreover, the references turn out, for example, to
be combinations of sayings by different prophets (1:2-3; 11:17). It is difficult, if not impossible, moreover, to determine that a particular version
of the nascent scripture is being "quoted," for example, the Septuagint or
the Masoretic or another textual tradition. At the time, even in scribal
circles, different versions of Israelite tradition existed, including versions
of books long since written on scrolls; therefore, it seems far more likely
to imagine that the Gospel of Mark drew on multiple forms and versions
of Israelite tradition. The reference to the story of David and his com-
panions eating "the bread of the presence," which names Abiathar rather
than Ahimelech as high priest at the time (2:23-28), evidently did not
depend directly on either the Septuagint or the proto-Masoretic version,
but on yet another of multiple versions of the tradition of David's career.
The dispute between Jesus and the scribes and Pharisees in Mark 7:1-13,
moreover, is not between the "written Torah" and the "oral Torah," as earlier Protestant interpreters supposed. It was rather explicitly between the
Pharisees' "tradition of the elders" and the fundamental covenantal "commandment of God," which would have been widely known and recited
orally in Israel for generations.

Third, even the literate elite, the scholars of scribal circles such as
the Pharisees and Qumranites, depended as much or more on oral cultivation and memory than they did on their precious but cumbersome
scrolls. Modern biblical scholars, working under the assumptions of print
culture, project pictures of the ancient scribes, Pharisees, and rabbis in
their own image as eagerly engaged in study and interpretation of sacred
(biblical) written texts. That picture does not fit with evidence from our
sources. Ironically, we have been aware for some time that the Pharisees
cultivated orally "traditions of the elders" (Mark 7) that were not written yet, they claimed, derived from Sinai every bit as much as had the
laws written in the books of Moses. The scribal-priestly community
at Qumran that left the Dead Sea Scrolls also had extensive rules and
regulations, "laws and ordinances," that are couched in language similar
to that in legal material of the Pentateuch, but these are not quotations
of or explicit interpretations of the latter. In later rabbinic circles the

Torah was learned by recitation rather than by poring over the lettering on scrolls. The "text" was thus available in rabbis' memory.

As Martin Jaffee has pointed out, if we look closely at the self-descriptions of how the Qumran community proceeded in common meetings, it is clear the members recited their scriptures orally. According to their regulations for a gathering of ten (or more), "The congregation shall watch in community for a third of every night of the year, to recite the scroll [*sepher*] and to search the ordinance [*mishpat*] and to bless together" (1QS 6.6-8). To translate the Hebrew with "to read" and "to study" conforms their procedure anachronistically to modern print culture, especially biblical study. Their practice was clearly oral recitation of some text committed to memory (some version of Deuteronomy?), a performance of some collection of regulations (some version of ordinances like those transcribed in 1QS or CD?), along with oral delivery of communal blessings. As Jaffee points out, the scriptural text was inscribed in their memory as much as it was on their scrolls. Even scribal-priestly circles, the literate elite, thus cultivated their cultural tradition in oral forms that were not explicit interpretations of scripture. And while some parts of their cultural tradition had been written on scrolls and perhaps thus somewhat stabilized, their cultivation of even those parts depended on memory and oral recitation. Among the nonliterate villagers, of course, Israelite cultural tradition would have depended almost completely on oral communication, on social memory cultivated orally, without writing.

In the Gospel of Mark, most of those numerous references and allusions to figures and incidents in Israelite tradition can most easily have derived from oral cultivation of Israel's cultural memory. Stories of Moses, Elijah, David, and other heroes would have been widely known and cultivated and not confined to the proto-scriptural and other texts produced and used by the scribal-priestly elite. Covenantal principles or psalms, and probably many prophetic sayings, would have been widely known and cultivated in ways not confined to written texts.

Research in these three interrelated areas has thus undermined the previous assumptions of Gospel studies. What were previously imagined as "people of the book" did not have their knowledge of Israelite tradition primarily from the Hebrew Bible. The work of Kelber and others has fostered a much fuller appreciation of the importance of Israelite cultural memory for the development, composition, and use of the Gospel of Mark. But especially for the ordinary people among whom the Gospel developed and was recited, the written scrolls of books that were later included in the (Hebrew) Bible, which modern scholars had

assumed were *the* medium through which Jesus-followers knew Israelite tradition, played a relatively peripheral role in their cultural memory.
Their cultural memory depended rather on extra-textual media, or variant
versions of stories, songs, rituals, and customs that were cultivated orally.

Israelite cultural memory was far more complex than it has appeared
previously from scholarly concentration on scriptural books. That, in turn,
suggests that our approach to Israelite cultural memory and the central
importance it played in the emergence and use of the Gospels will need
to be correspondingly complex. In the limited context of this chapter I
will briefly explore two main theses: that Israelite cultural memory was
contested in a struggle between official and popular tradition, hegemonic
and anti-hegemonic memory, and that Israelite cultural memory operated
in certain prominent patterns, at least at the popular level at which Mark
was produced and performed.

Popular versus Official Tradition

The difference between the literate scribal circles who possessed written
texts and the nonliterate villagers who did not points to a deeper division in Israelite cultural memory. It has been standard in Gospel studies
to posit "Judaism" as the context in which Jesus and his followers were
involved and out of which the Gospel tradition developed. Essentialist constructs such as "Judaism," however, do much to obscure historical
differences exposed by recent research. The source for what constituted
"Judaism" has been the Hebrew Bible (Old Testament). Since it is highly
unlikely that the vast majority of Judean and Galilean villagers had direct
knowledge of the books that became the Hebrew Bible, however, we cannot use those books as the only sources for their cultural memory and
social identity. Nor can we assume that the oral versions of Israelite tradition cultivated by villagers existed merely at an innocuous cultural level
without political-economic import and implications. We cannot posit a
unitary ancient Jewish cultural memory as if the same social identity were
expressed and attested somehow by all the various versions. Ancient Israelite cultural memory was more complex. The difference between elite
versions of Israelite tradition and popular versions corresponded to and
expressed a fundamental political-economic division in ancient society.

The emphasis that memory is social and closely related to group
identity in recent studies of cultural memory focuses attention on the
historical social context of Mark and the community that shaped and

used it. Attending to the story as a whole, moreover, rather than individual verses and "pericopes" in isolation, exposes the fundamental political conflict central to the dominant plot of the Gospel's narrative: Jesus and his followers, in carrying out a renewal of Israel, stand opposed to and opposed by the Jerusalem high priestly rulers; their representatives, the Pharisees; and their patron, the Roman governor. This fundamental conflict parallels the division noted in recent research on orality and literacy.

The political-economic-religious conflict between Jerusalem rulers and their scribal representatives, on the one hand, and the Galilean villagers, on the other, corresponds to the cultural difference between those who command literacy and written texts and the nonliterate. These divisions, moreover, are not merely literary artifice but were fundamental historical divisions in that society. They are indicated also in documents produced by the literate elite, such as the histories of Josephus. These other Judean documents from the time portray the same fundamental divide and persistent conflict between the wealthy and powerful rulers, with their intellectual-scribal retainers, on the one side, and the subsistence villagers from whom they expropriated taxes, tithes, and tribute, on the other. This makes it all the more likely that in the story of Jesus and his followers the community whose identity was being reinforced by the cultural/social memory that both shaped the story and was referenced by it also was embedded in sharp conflict with powerful rulers and their literate representatives. The cultural dimension, the social memory, corresponded to and was embedded in a historical political-economic-religious conflict, a conflict that had existed for centuries during which different cultural memories and social identities had developed.

The Temple in Jerusalem, headed by the high priesthood, had been set in place and maintained by imperial regimes as an instrument of their rule and taking of tribute. According to the limited sources we have for the second temple period (for example, Ezra, Nehemiah, Sirach), the wealthy and powerful aristocracy oppressed the peasants of Judea, despite the efforts of imperial governors such as Nehemiah or scribal sages such as Ben Sira to mitigate the worst effects. The imperial attempt to suppress increasing resistance in the 170s and 160s BCE only served to provoke the Maccabean Revolt against the Empire and the high priestly aristocracy. Galilean villagers did not come under the Jerusalem high priestly regime's control until about one hundred years before Jesus' birth, at which point they were required by the Jerusalem high priesthood to submit to "the laws of the Judeans."

The Romans only intensified the fundamental divide between rulers and ruled when they imposed the military strongman Herod as king and then his heirs as rulers in various districts of his realm. Herod created a new set of high priestly families loyal to his own regime and the Romans. Our principal sources for Judean and Galilean history in Roman-Herodian times indicate that the period was framed by widespread popular revolts, a three-year struggle against Herod's conquest of his Rome-bestowed realm; revolts at his death in every district of his kingdom; and the great revolt of 66–70 CE. The period was further punctuated, moreover, by persistent protests by both scribal circles and Jerusalem crowds and by distinctive Israelite movements among the peasantry.

Because of the fundamental political-economic-religious conflict in Judea and Galilee, it is difficult to discern what if any forces or factors might have provided some sort of social cohesion between Judeans and their Jerusalem rulers. Even less does there appear to have been a common cultural memory shared by the Jerusalem rulers and Galilean villagers, who, during Jesus' lifetime and the following generation, were no longer under the jurisdiction of the Temple-state and its laws, after only a century of Jerusalem rule. It seems likely, in fact, that cultural memory worked as much as a source of division and conflict as it did as a source of cohesion.

How this continuing conflict between rulers and ruled, between the Jerusalem high priestly families, on the one hand, and the Judean and Galilean peasants, on the other, worked itself out in terms of cultural memory can be seen, for example, in celebration of the foundational memory of the exodus in the annual Passover festival. The ritual reliving of the exodus in the Passover celebration was originally celebrated in households. Started presumably under king Josiah in the late seventh century BCE (1 Kings 23), celebration of the Passover was centralized in Jerusalem as a pilgrimage festival. The centralization of the celebration in the Temple was a way of associating the memory of the people's formative event of liberation from oppressive foreign rule with Jerusalem, as well as a source of revenue for the high priesthood and the Jerusalem economy. At least in late-second-temple times, however, the thousands of Judean peasants and the smaller number of Galileans who came to Jerusalem as pilgrims for the Passover festival were still celebrating the people's liberation from foreign rule. Josephus provides abundant evidence that the Passover was the occasion for popular protests against Herod's oppression of the people by control and manipulation of the high priesthood, in part. The people also knew very well that, after Herod's death, the high priests were appointed by and collaborated with the Roman governors during the first century. Not surprisingly, the pilgrims' celebration of the Passover had potential as a time of protest against Roman and high priestly rule. Recognizing the threat, the Roman governors habitually brought troops into the city and posted them on the porticoes of the Temple complex as a show of force, further exacerbating the structural conflict. Cumanus even unleashed the troops against Passover demonstrators (Josephus, *Jewish Antiquities* 20.105-12).[8]

The memory of exodus, as perpetuated primarily in the Passover festival, was thus hardly the constitutive memory for the identity of all Judeans (and Galileans) as a unified people. Because of the paucity of our sources, we have little idea of how the priestly aristocracy thought of the exodus, presumably the focus of the festival over which they presided in the Temple. Certainly Moses and his leadership of the exodus is dwarfed by the extensive praise of Aaron and God's eternal covenant with the Zadokite/ Aaronid priesthood in Ben Sira's hymn to the great ancestral heroes and officers (Sirach 44–50). For the villagers who came as pilgrims to the festival in Jerusalem, the Passover was a way of expressing their resentment of and struggle against their rulers—that is, what this "constitutive memory" was about in the first place. It is surely significant that the one point we know of where memory of the exodus plays a central role among scribal groups is the Qumranites' opposition to and withdrawal from Jerusalem high priestly rule, as articulated in their Community Rule.

It is just such discrepancies between the ways in which Israelite tradition was understood, interpreted, and acted upon by popular groups and movements, on the one hand, and in scribal literature and rulers' behavior, on the other, that has led me to adapt the anthropological distinction between the "great tradition" and the "little tradition." In other agrarian societies anthropologists have noticed the difference between the ways the ruling elite and the peasants understand and use the cultural tradition that they share in various degrees. In the work of James C. Scott that is most helpful, I believe, for study of ancient Judean history and the Gospels, the "little tradition" refers to "the distinctive patterns of belief and behavior which are valued by the peasantry." The "great tradition" refers to the corresponding patterns among the aristocracy and their intellectual-scribal retainers, sometimes to a degree embodied in written documents.[9] Depending on the historical development of the traditions, there is considerable parallel and a degree of interaction among them. Despite their overlaps and interaction, however, Scott insists that each of these parallel traditions "represents a *distinct* pattern of belief and practice."[10]

The differences would vary with such factors as residence, income, consumption, language, education, juridical status, and ethnicity. In terms of such factors the differences between the official Jerusalem tradition and the Israelite popular tradition would have been considerable. Insofar as Galilee had been subject to Jerusalem rule for only a hundred years prior to the lifetime of Jesus and his followers, the Israelite popular tradition in Galilee would have diverged even more from the Jerusalem-based great tradition.

The overlap and interaction between the official and popular traditions in Judea and Galilee can be illustrated again from the exodus and Passover. Stories of Israel's constitutive exodus from bondage under foreign rule into an independent people under the direct rule of its God originated among the early Israelite peasantry. In the broad narratives sponsored by the monarchy and Temple-state, for example—the Yahwist and the Priestly narratives—the exodus was inserted into or framed by the promises to Abraham and its presumed fulfillment in the Davidic monarchy and Solomonic temple and Aaronid high priesthood. Stories of prophetic leaders such as Moses, Joshua, and Elijah and of popularly acclaimed kings such as Saul and the young David originated among people struggling for independence from oppressive rulers. They were then later inserted into—and their explosive potential blunted by—broader narratives that served to legitimate royal or priestly regimes in Jerusalem. Thereafter, the exodus, and its celebration in the Passover festival, represented something very different in the great tradition of Jerusalem elites and the little tradition of the Judean and Galilean peasantry.

In the Gospel of Mark itself, the Passover festival celebrating the exodus is the occasion for Jesus' forceful prophetic condemnation of the Temple and high priesthood (11:15-17; 12:1-9; and so forth) and the Jerusalem rulers' and their Roman patron's actions to "destroy" (Mark 14:2) the threat to their position by the representative of the popular tradition. Elsewhere, Mark's story portrays repeated conflicts between the official and the popular traditions. This comes out explicitly in Jesus' debates with the Pharisees, for example, when the Pharisees' "traditions of the elders" provide for the economic support of the Temple through the device of the dedication of peasant property and produce to the Temple, to which Jesus responds with the basic "commandment of God" that insists that local produce be retained for local needs ("honor father and mother," Mark 7:1-13).

Studies of cultural/social memory discern an important difference in collective memory that corresponds to a considerable extent to the difference between great and little traditions found by anthropologists in complex agrarian societies. Classic work on collective memory tended to focus on the social identity and cohesion of large-scale social systems, in part because of the Durkheimian roots of Maurice Halbwachs and his pioneering reflections. More recent analysis of social memory, however, includes attention to anti-hegemonic memory as well as hegemonic memory.[11] In a large-scale society, peasants, industrial laborers, women, and minority groups usually have a distinctive social memory of their own that usually differs considerably from the official memory of the dominant culture. In fact, what purports to be the official memory of a society is often the hegemonic culture of the group that controls the media of cultural production. But underneath the officially propagated cultural memory are "vernacular" and "folk" memories (among others) that enable subordinated groups to maintain a degree of social identity not completely controlled by the dominant culture.[12]

Critical studies of popular memory also recognize that, like the great and little traditions, official and popular memories are engaged in an ongoing process of interaction. Or, more to the point, anti-hegemonic memory is engaged in a persistent process of contestation and resistance with hegemonic memory. To focus on popular culture as something in itself, as if it had sole claim on authenticity, would only essentialize it, just as the dominant culture has previously been essentialized as *the* culture of a nation or people. That would only obscure the ongoing struggle between dominant and subordinate groups over memory that is more often than not sharply contested.[13]

The differences and ongoing struggle between official and popular traditions or between hegemonic and anti-hegemonic cultural memory discerned in other societies at other times can provide considerable illumination of the Gospel of Mark. Throughout the story, in episode after episode, Israelite memory is contested. In Mark's story, which emerged from and in regular performance and articulated the identity of a Jesus movement, Jesus repeatedly engaged in actions that resonate with the people's memory of Moses and Elijah and in declarations that oppose the Pharisees' attempt to control local life according to their own official memory of what constitutes proper observance of Sabbath and offerings to the Temple. Most obvious and dramatic of all, perhaps, is Jesus' confrontation with the high priest and elders in Jerusalem at the climax of the story. In a series of disputes, he recites prophetic sayings and traditional images from their own scriptures against them to insist repeatedly that they stand condemned by God for persistent oppression of the people (Mark 11:12—12:40).

Prominent Patterns in Israelite Cultural Memory
That Inform Mark's Gospel

In Gospel studies, we have been trained to focus on and to seek the meaning of textual fragments, of particular "pericopes" or individual verses. We then look, among other things, for possible references or allusions to particular verses, laws, motifs, and so on in the Hebrew Bible and other Judean literature. Our research tools are even codified by chapter and verse. We then tend to assume that the producers and users of Mark and other Gospels did the same, that is, that they appropriated Hebrew Bible literature mainly in fragmentary units, such as verses, sayings, laws, and motifs.

There are several reasons why this assumption and this procedure are inappropriate. One is that, as Kelber and others have explained, the Gospel of Mark itself was almost certainly composed and read or performed aloud as a whole story rather than in fragmentary units, one or two at a time. As explained above, moreover, recent research on orality and literacy in the ancient world and on the development of variant textual traditions in Judea at the time indicates that the producers and users of Mark's Gospel probably did not have direct contact with the books of the Hebrew Bible. And, as suggested by the previous point, scrolls of proto-scriptural books written in Hebrew were almost certainly not the primary means by which Judean and Galilean villagers and Greek-speaking Syrian villagers who joined Jesus movements knew and cultivated Israelite cultural tradition.

It is necessary to seek an approach to the importance of cultural memory in Mark more appropriate to the Gospel understood as a whole story produced and used in a predominantly oral communication environment. Hebrew biblical books and other Judean literature are indeed our primary sources for Israelite tradition at that time, especially for the great tradition concentrated in Jerusalem. And modern scholarly reference works, often now available electronically and codified by chapter and verse, are still invaluable research tools. But we have no good basis for believing that ancient Galileans and Judeans and Syrians knew and cultivated their Israelite cultural memory primarily in fragments such as individual sayings, lines of poetry or song, or other "biblical" verses. Fragments such as proverbs, laws, customs, poetic lines, and prophetic sayings communicated nothing without a broader meaning context. There are thus good reasons for looking for broader patterns of communication and meaning in cultural memory as well as attending to the fragments that may lead us to them. Indeed, in attempting to appreciate the Gospel of Mark as a whole story I have become convinced that we can discern some broader patterns of Israelite cultural memory operative across the narrative.

It has long been seen, for example, that the several dialogues in Mark 10:1-45 have a certain coherence. They all include a formulaic statement, for example, of "sentences of holy law." And they may all go together as aspects of instruction and discipline for the communities Mark addresses. Two of the four dialogues, however, make explicit references to Israelite tradition. Are we to imagine that a sequence of dialogues in Mark's story have a coherence but that no such coherence existed in the Israelite tradition that it references? Although we can no longer assume that Israelite tradition/memory was confined to the biblical literature and parallel Judean texts, this literature does provide many of our principal sources for it. And if we but look in biblical literature and other Judean texts, we can find a coherent pattern that parallels and illuminates the perceived coherence among the dialogues in Mark 10. Over a generation ago, Hebrew Bible scholars discerned a previously unrecognized pattern in the Covenant given on Sinai in Exodus 20 and Joshua's covenant renewal speech in Joshua 24 by comparisons with ancient Hittite suzerainty treaties.[14] The same basic pattern was then recognized in and behind the covenant renewal texts from Qumran (the Community Rule and the Damascus Rule).[15] Recognizing this pattern in the Mosaic covenant then enables us to discern the same pattern of covenant renewal in the longest speech of Jesus in the series of speeches paralleled in the Gospels of Matthew and Luke (Q/Luke 6), in the first long discourse in Matthew (Matthew 5–7), and to a degree in *Didache* 1–6.[16]

As suggested by the explicit citation of the covenantal principles in the dialogue in Mark 10:17-31 and the focus on one of those principles in Mark 10:2-12, the same covenantal pattern underlies and informs the whole series of dialogues in Mark 10.[17] It seems that there were relatively stable patterns in the Israelite cultural tradition to which Mark's narrative makes reference. Indeed, the Mosaic covenantal pattern provides further continuity in Mark's story, as it did in Israelite tradition. The recitation of "Honor your father and mother" as a paradigmatic basic "commandment of God" in Mark 7:1-13, referencing again the Ten Commandments, and Jesus' offering and sharing of the cup of "my blood of the covenant" in the Last Supper, referencing the covenant ceremony on Sinai in Mark 14:22-25, locate Jesus' mission directly in the deep-running covenantal tradition of Israel. Drawing attention to particular chapters and verses in the Hebrew biblical text helps us, but the whole of the covenantal pattern and covenantal tradition is far greater than the sum of its proof-text parts.

And the appearance of the same covenantal pattern in the Qumran Rules and the discourses in Q, Matthew, and the *Didache*, without explicit citations of covenantal passages in nascent scriptural texts, suggests that the pattern was operative in the social memory cultivated in scribal circles and village communities.

In seeking to discern broader cultural patterns operative in Judean and Galilean society around the time of Jesus, however, we should exercise caution not to combine motifs and images from a variety of sources into a synthetic scheme or concept of our own making. That is what has happened, for example, in the standard Christian scholarly construct of Jewish "messianic expectations." The synthetic Christian scholarly projection of expectations of "the Messiah" began to break down when closer investigations indicated that different texts spoke of different figures as agents of future deliverance, whether a prophet, a messiah, a "son of man," or even God as direct intervener. Subsequent Christian texts fused images of these separate figures in various ways, as doctrines of Christology began to emerge. Then, in the 1960s and 1970s, scholars were surprised to discover that late-second-temple Judean literature in fact attested very little by way of expectations of a messiah and displayed virtually no expectation of an eschatological prophet or a prophet like Moses. Essentialist constructs such as "Judaism" had been blocking scholarly recognition that the cultural elite that produced Judean literature were not particularly interested in such figures remembered for their actions against foreign and domestic rulers.

The nonliterate peasantry in Judea, Galilee, and Perea, however, produced numerous concrete movements led by charismatic leaders acclaimed as "king." Although he avoids the term "messiah," it is clear from Josephus's accounts that these movements were modeled on the Israelite resistance to Philistine occupation led by the young David. In the Deuteronomistic History accounts, David's followers from tribe of Judah and then all the Israelites anointed ("messiahed") him "king" (2 Sam 2:4; 5:2). Since, in the imperial Israelite monarchy attested by the royal Psalms, the anointing was done in a formal ceremony with pomp and circumstance (see especially Psalms 2 and 110), those accounts may well reflect older popular tradition. The Judean, Galilean, and Perean peasants who formed the movements led by "kings" against Roman rule, however, do not appear to be dependent on the texts of the Jerusalem great tradition. That there were so many such movements led by popularly acclaimed kings in various areas of Israelite heritage and over so many generations, from 4 BCE to the great revolt in 66–70 CE to the Bar Kokhba Revolt in 132–135, suggests that these movements were informed by persistent and distinctive popular Israelite memory. They had their own versions of Israelite tradition, which provided a ready-made "script" for active resistance to Roman rule and to the Herodian kings and high priests whom the Romans set in power over them.[18]

The Gospel of Mark seems to be informed by this popular Israelite memory but is sharply critical of it. Jesus is declared "son of God" or "messiah" at the beginning, middle, and end of the story. But when Peter declares that Jesus is the messiah and then immediately rebukes him for having to go up to Jerusalem to be killed, Jesus rebukes him right back: "Get behind me, Satan." And at the end of the story Jesus is labeled "king of the Judeans" by Pilate and the Roman soldiers and "king of Israel" by the high priests, that is, by the rulers who, threatened by his mission, are desperate to destroy him. Particularly in Jesus' rebuke of Peter and in his admonition to James and John, who ask for positions of power when Jesus comes into his kingdom, one senses that the Gospel of Mark may be reacting against the "script" of messianic movements of insurrection that were deeply embedded in popular Israelite cultural memory of the time. Perhaps that very "script" had come to play a role in branches of the Jesus movement.

More central to the main plot of the Gospel, however, are memory of Moses as the prophet of Israel's formation and memory of Elijah as the prophet of Israel's renewal. The memory of Moses' and Elijah's work in the founding and renewal of Israel is instrumental to the main plot of Mark's story, which has Jesus spearheading renewal of Israel over against its rulers and their Roman sponsors. Most obvious are the two sequences of episodes in which Jesus performs sea crossings and wilderness feedings, exorcisms and healings, like Moses and Elijah, respectively (4:35—8:26). Shortly thereafter, Jesus appears on the mountain with both Moses and Elijah (9:2-8). Like both Moses and Elijah, Jesus spends a time of preparation in the wilderness before launching his mission (1:9-20). Just as Elijah commissioned Elisha to continue his mission to renew Israel in opposition to oppressive domestic and foreign rulers (the twelve tribes explicitly symbolized in the twelve stones of the altar, and so forth), so Jesus calls and commissions disciples to help implement his similar mission (3:13-19; 6:6-13; etc.; again with much explicit symbolization by twelve disciples, baskets of leftovers, years of hemorrhage, and so on). Finally, as noted in connection with the broader covenant pattern in Mark, as if a new Moses, Jesus delivers a covenant renewal discourse and presides over a renewed covenant meal in his final meal with the disciples (10:1-45; 14:22-25).

Mark's narrative, however, gives no indication that any of the particular episodes involved in this new-Moses-and-new-Elijah pattern correspond with or make explicit allusions to particular passages involving
Moses in Exodus or Numbers or Elijah in 1 and 2 Kings. There are no
quotations of or allusions to proto-scriptural books. Given what we are
learning about the fluid state of those books in the first century CE, we can
conclude that it seems unlikely that the episodes were explicit references
to texts. The books that were later included in the Hebrew Bible and/or
the books of the Septuagint, moreover, were not the only, and probably
not the principal, source of Israelite cultural memory.

One medium of the cultural memory of Israelite prophets was monuments constructed evidently by the high priestly or Herodian rulers and
tended by the scribes and/or Pharisees, as suggested by Jesus' woes against
the latter in Q/Luke 11:47-51. The many recitations in a wide range of
biblical literature (including many Psalms) of various sequences of Moses'
wondrous acts of deliverance, including his command of the Red Sea
waters and the water from the rock and manna in the wilderness, suggest
widespread oral recitations in Israelite society, some of which were preserved once they were written down in the Psalter (see also 1 Cor 10:1-13).
Among scribal-priestly circles, cultural memory of Moses was carried both
in oral tradition and in texts that were later not included in the Hebrew
Bible. Some of these are now known from the Dead Sea Scrolls. At the
popular level, memory of key figures such as Moses, the prophetic liberator
and founder of Israel, and Elijah, the great hero of the people's renewal,
would have been cultivated orally in village communities. For example,
that the stories of Elijah's and Elisha's healings and other wondrous actions
in 1 and 2 Kings appear in a style so different from the rest of the Deuteronomic history has suggested to some that they reflect popular narratives. If such narratives continued to be cultivated in village communities,
particularly in the northern Israelite territories where those prophets were
so prominent, it would help explain how the portrayals of Jesus' healings
are so reminiscent of stories of Elijah's and Elisha's healings without any
indication that they are closely patterned on the literary accounts in 1 and
2 Kings.

What is far more striking, in terms of attestations of a pattern in
popular Israelite culture that lies behind and emerges in Mark's story of a
peasant prophet who is spearheading the renewal of Israel, are the several
concrete cases of prophets active in Judea and Samaria right around the
time of Jesus' mission.[19] Each of these prophets led followers in anticipation of a new divine act of deliverance. Like a new Moses, a Samaritan

prophet led people up Mount Gerizim, where, he declared, they would find the precious remains of the tabernacle from Mount Sinai. Like a new Moses and/or Joshua, Theudas led his people out to the Jordan river to cross into (or from) the wilderness. The prophet who returned to Judea "from Egypt," stepping into a role like that of Joshua at Jericho, led his followers up to the Mount of Olives, from which they would witness the collapse of the walls of Jerusalem and the disappearance of the Roman garrison. The fact that, according to Josephus, there were many such movements, all clearly patterned after the formative actions of deliverance led by Moses and/or Joshua, offers clear evidence of a general and widespread popular memory of these heroic Israelite prophets of old and the people's liberation and entry into land that they spearheaded. These multiple movements led by prophets like Moses and/or Joshua right around the time of Jesus suggest the active presence of a distinctively Israelite cultural pattern that provides the script followed in Mark's story of Jesus engaged in a renewal of Israel over against the rulers.[20]

That Judean and Galilean villagers' cultural memory was focused on the figures of Moses, Joshua, and Elijah and on the events of their leadership of Israel in times of crisis fits a common pattern found among other peoples by students of cultural/social memory. The latter find that a group or people invests only certain events with extraordinary significance. In their ongoing social life, a process of selection, emphasis, condensation, and reconfiguration continues to refine and redefine such key events and figures. These "constitutive memories" ("what must not be forgotten")[21] then leave lasting marks on communities or people, defining their identities and normative values.[22] Focal, or "constitutive," memories can become linked into a master narrative that is all the more effective in shaping social identity. This is apparently one of the key effects of Israelite cultural memory in the Gospel of Mark as well as in the (other) popular prophetic movements at the time.

An Analogy: Cultural Patterns in the Cevenols' Memory of the Camisards

It is difficult for biblical interpreters trained in the assumptions of print culture to understand how memory works in a predominantly oral society. Because we are members of the intellectual elite who have received training in the dominant culture, it is difficult for us to appreciate anti-hegemonic memory in which resistance to the dominant culture is rooted. Perhaps an analogy from a different society and different time might be helpful for understanding Mark's story and the movement in which it was produced and used. The case of the Cevenol peasants in southwestern France, studied by social historians, can provide a sense or how anti-hegemonic social memory works among peasant societies in circumstances somewhat similar to those of the ancient Galileans and Syrians who used Mark.

While conducting research in the mountains of Cevennes, the French historian Philippe Joutard discovered from conversations with contemporary peasants in the area that their group identity and their periodic active resistance to the state was intensely focused on and shaped by their memory of the Camisard revolts of 1702–4.[23] When local enforcement of the Revocation of the Edict of Nantes (effectively outlawing Protestants) began in Cevennes, preachers provoked violent resistance led by local leaders. Mainly by guerrilla action they held off the armies of Louis XIV for two years. After establishment historians and even the Protestant elite had condemned them as religiously fanatical bandits and rebels, nineteenth-century Romantic Protestant historians produced glowing accounts of the Camisard uprising and its leaders. Joutard and his team of oral historians discovered, however, that contemporary Cevenol peasants' memory of the Camisards had roots far deeper and more integral to their identity than the accounts of the Protestant historians. While their memory had been shaped to a degree by having read such histories, Cevenol peasants' accounts of the Camisard heroes and uprising focused on local skirmishes and episodes, including the experiences of family ancestors.

> These accounts are essentially structured by village and family memory, even though it is clear that all informants see the wars as being experienced by the Protestant community as a whole; they are in this respect independent of nineteenth century historiography, and many of them seem indeed to derive directly from eighteenth-century experience, which had remained underground, commemorated in oral culture.[24]

Joutard and his students learned that stories of Camisard exploits had been told to children much as folktales were told in other areas of Europe. Many of these children's stories and others, far from being mere legends, it turns out, are verifiable from eighteenth-century documents with regard to the historical information about persons and events that they carry. Others are unverifiable and probably contain little reliable historical memory. That so many are verifiable suggests that information from such stories can supplement what is known from written documents regarding the Camisard uprising.

More important for my purposes here is the role or effect of the popular memory of the Camisards, what some theorists of cultural memory have called anti-hegemonic memory. These stories strongly informed the Cevenol Protestants' identity as a community of resistance to attacks and interference in its affairs by the French state and other outsiders. Memory of the Camisard resistance fed further resistance, which continued into the late twentieth century. Subsequent actions and movements of resistance in which Cevenol Protestants became involved, whether the French Revolution, the Republic, the Resistance during World War II, and support of the Left, were understood in terms of their memory or reliving of the Camisard uprising and leadership.

Cevenol Protestants' memory, moreover, differed significantly from the dominant French national memory in terms of relative importance ascribed to events. As with other peasant villagers, even though they had supported the Revolution, memory of revolutionary events in Paris were far less important for them than memory of their lords' oppressive practices during the *ancien regime*. Napoleon and World War I were hardly even blips on the screen of their memory, even though these were peasants who had been through the state-sponsored schools, where they read the standard history books. What university historians, Paris journalists, and French national school curricula deemed the important great events of history, however, were not simply accepted as important and assimilated into the Cevenol peasantry's memory. On the contrary, the Protestant mountain villagers understood themselves as communities of resistance to the dominant order, their own identity formed by their memory of the Camisard prophets and their sustained uprising.

Although the Cevenol peasants interviewed by Joutard and his associates were literate, living as they were in a highly literate dominant society and having themselves attended school, their collective memory was clearly dependent more on orality than on writing. Their patterned memory and the collective identity it provided were shared and sustained mainly in orally narrated stories, many focused on the exploits and episodes of the Camisard resistance that had taken place in the mountain areas where their ancestors had lived. Particular memories and reminders of the Camisard lore, moreover, were carried and cultivated in the course of local and relatively fluid conversational discourse that would be virtually impossible to document (short of ethnographers living in a village as participant observers).

Comparisons and Further Reflections

This brief survey of the social memory of the Camisards among the Cevenol peasants provides a comparative example of how Gospel scholars
can imagine Galileans and Judeans working from Israelite memory. Three
points seem particularly pertinent.

First, the way in which popular memory of the Camisards worked
among the Cevenol peasants can enable students of Jesus and the Gospels
to imagine how popular memory of Moses, Joshua, and Elijah worked
among ancient Galileans and Judeans. Although the Protestant peasants
of the Cevennes were literate and had even read written accounts of the
Camisards, their own memory of their heroes of resistance depended on
local oral communication. Ancient Galileans and Judeans, however, were
nonliterate and did not even have access to written documents. Their cultural memory was thus far more dependent on oral cultivation of Israelite
tradition in their village communities. Even if they did have contact with
the scribal and Pharisaic representatives of the Temple and high priesthood, their cultural memory was probably not heavily influenced by it, if
we judge from the Cevenol analogy. Their memory of Israel's formative
events under Moses and Joshua was independent and surely differed in
significant ways from the great tradition in Jerusalem. What the book of
Jubilees or Josephus regarded as great events may not have mattered much
to them, except in their general deleterious effects in military devastation
and increased taxation. Even if the media of the Galilean and Judean
peasants were children's stories and narratives with legendary embellish-
ments, such stories carried the gist of serious historical memory if, again,
we go by what Joutard and his colleagues found in the Cevennes.

Second, just as stories of the Camisard resistance had become basic
for the social identity of Protestant villagers in the Cevennes, so apparently had memory of the actions of Moses and Joshua and Elijah become
basic for the social identity of ancient Galileans and Judeans (and Israelites before them). The Cevenols understood themselves as a separate
people defending their communities against attacks by hostile outside
rulers, as had their Camisard heroes. Similarly, Galilean and Judean and
Samaritan peasants understood themselves as distinctive peoples properly
independent of foreign rule under the sole kingship of God, as established
under the leadership of Moses and Joshua and reestablished through the
prophetic movement led by Elijah and Elisha. Memory of Moses and
Joshua, perhaps also of Elijah and Elisha, may have been so fundamental
as to be constitutive of Galilean and Judean villagers' social identity and

then for the Markan community that derived from the origins of the Jesus movement in Galilee.

Third, out of their identity as communities of resistance to outside rule grounded in memory of the Camisards, in every new situation of attack and resistance the Cevenols understood themselves to be repeating or reenacting the Camisards' resistance. Similarly, the ancient Galileans and Judeans understood their own resistance to the oppressive rule of the Romans and their high priestly or Herodian clients as repetitions of the formative actions taken by Moses, Joshua, and Elijah. Indeed, their memory of Elijah was shaped somewhat to the memory of Moses in key respects, such as the time of preparation in the wilderness for leading the liberation or renewal of Israel against oppressive rulers.

A couple of observations that James Fentress and Chris Wickham make in their general discussion of "class and group memories" may open up further insights for interpreters of the Gospels. First, "events can be remembered more easily if they fit into the forms of narrative that the social group already has at its disposal."[25] Analogously, Jesus' healings were more easily remembered insofar as they fit the pattern familiar in stories of Elijah's healings, and Jesus' Last Supper fit the pattern familiar from the covenant ratification ceremony presided over by Moses on Sinai. Second, "memories can be analysed as narratives; but they also have functions, and can be analysed . . . as guides to social identity."[26] Similarly, both the Israelite memories of Moses, Joshua, and Elijah and those of Jesus take the form of narratives. The narrative is more than just a literary pattern, however: it is a memory that may figure in the very identity of a group, such as the Galilean or Judean peasantry generally, or a Jesus movement in particular. This insight meshes with what emerges in analysis of oral performance of Mark's story. Studies of cultural/social memory also suggest that the performances of stories is integrally linked with the group identity of performer and audience in historical social context.

Fentress and Wickham's generalizations, however, are as significant for what they fail to maintain as much as for what they do discern about "class memories." First, they do not take into account the persistent pattern of power relations. Why do the Cevenol Protestants continue to focus their memory on the Camisards, from which they derive their identity as a community of resistance? Among other reasons, because the structure of their life vis-à-vis the political economy and culture of the larger society has not changed. Likewise, the recurrence or persistence of oppressive domestic and foreign rule similar to what was remembered in stories of Moses, Joshua, and Elijah set up a continuing or recurring context in which those paradigmatic figures and events of resistance or revolt were again directly applicable. Precisely because of this recurrent or persistent structure of power relations, memory of Moses and Elijah was compelling.

Second, it is not enough to say that new events are more easily remembered if they fit into central or key narratives in the group's shared memory. It must also be taken into account that new events cannot help being experienced according to those central or key stories and prominent patterns of a people's memory. The memory of key events informs and shapes people's experience of events that produce new memory. This is a key insight from study of social memory. The Cevenols experienced the German occupation and local resistance to it as a recurrence of earlier royal repression of their Protestant ways and their resistance.

Similarly, Galilean and Judean peasants experienced Roman, Herodian, and high priestly oppression and repression as a recurrence of Pharaoh, the Canaanite city-state kings, Solomon, and Ahab and Jezebel. Their own resistance was experienced as a recurrence of the exodus and the popular resistance to Ahab and his regime by the "children/sons of the prophets" (benē-nabi'im). Jesus' immediate followers can thus easily have experienced his mission to renew Israel, in such episodes as feedings and covenant-teachings, in terms of Moses' leadership of the exodus and wilderness journey, and his healings and exorcism in terms of Elijah's remarkable acts of healing in his restoration of Israel. That is, studies of social memory such as that of the Cevenols suggest that what was remembered of Jesus' actions and teachings had, to begin with, something to do with the Israelite social memory of his first followers, which was focused on the prophets of Israel's origins and renewal. In terms perhaps strange to Gospel scholars but familiar among students of social memory: memory of the movements led by Moses, Joshua, and Elijah provided the fundamental framework for cognition, organization, and understanding of what was happening in Galileans' interaction with Jesus. Stories of their actions, narrative patterns deeply ingrained in social memory, constituted the very cognitive habits by which Jesus' first followers experienced and understood what was happening in his teaching and action.[27]

Third, memory does not function simply as a guide to social identity. As Fentress and Wickham point out, central to the memory of many peasantries are ways of recounting resistance or even revolt against the state. More than identity is involved in these memories. They are a reservoir of motivation and strength to persist in the struggle to maintain their special way of life over against an often hostile, repressive state.

Sometimes the dominant order has the power simply to impose its view of things or even to destroy the subjected community. Subject people, however, can often generate sufficient power to resist by cultivating their own stories and tradition and view of reality. For peasants subject to conquest, invasion, and economic pressures that cause disintegration of village communities, such as Galileans and Judeans at the time of Jesus, their identity is under attack. Maintaining their identity, which is sustained by their cultural memory, is a matter of constant struggle against the invasive dominant order. No wonder such people identify themselves as communities of resistance. Remembering the great heroes of resistance in the past is a powerful means of maintaining not just an identity of resistance but resistance itself. We can easily imagine that for Judean pilgrims the annual celebration of the Passover under the watchful eyes of the Roman military personnel posted on the Temple porticoes helped reconstitute an identity of resistance, but it also constituted an *act* of resistance, at least in ritual form. Similarly, the very action of celebrating the Lord's Supper in commemoration of the renewal of the Mosaic covenant would have constituted an act of resistance by a community of resistance.

It is thus possible, fourth, that cultural/social memory can have a mobilizing effect on a people,[28] enabling them to reestablish the cooperation and solidarity necessary to resist and perhaps even rebel against the impact and invasion of those who wield power. The active regeneration of cultural memory would thus serve not simply to maintain and reinforce social identity but to restore bonds that may have disintegrated. In the case of new movements, revival of cultural memory can create and secure new bonds among the members. When a people evokes memory of an ideal past of freedom, that evocation can easily inspire resistance to oppression in the present. A people's memory can even supply a kind of program or paradigm according to which they can form a new movement in similar circumstances. Like the Cevenols remembering the Camisards, the Galilean, Samaritan, and Judean memory of Moses and Joshua inspired them to form movements of resistance and renewal in the mid first century CE. The same pattern of social memory of Moses and Joshua and Elijah seems likely to been the inspiration of the Jesus movement. And this could have happened in the interaction of Jesus and his immediate followers as well as among those who subsequently joined Jesus movements such as the one that produced Mark's Gospel.

Fifth, and closely related to the previous points, there is an ongoing dialectic between the dominant culture and subordinate memory. Fentress and Wickham offer a good illustration of this in how standard establishment history books provided at least some of the content of the Cevenol Protestant villagers' memory of the Camisards, most of which, however, was distinctively different in emphasis and focus from great-events history. A similar relationship seems to have existed in ancient Galilee and Judea in the interaction of the great and little traditions. Galileans and Judeans may well have gleaned some of their prophetic tradition through interaction with scribal and Pharisaic representatives of the Jerusalem-based great tradition. As indicated in the Gospel of Mark, insofar as he refers to it polemically, the Galilean prophet Jesus knows of the existence of "the writing." But Mark's Jesus rejects much of its content, such as "the traditions of the elders" and the Deuteronomic code about divorce and remarriage, as oppressive or problematic for Galilean peasant families. And he does this on the basis of "the (basic) commandment of God" (for example, Mark 7:1-13; 10:2-9).

Pulling together all of these interrelated aspects of the role of memory among peasants and popular movements of resistance and renewal, we can return to one of our two basic theses: the recognition that memory of Moses and Elijah or of Jesus' mission and message did not operate in fragments such as aphorisms and discrete stories of healing or wilderness feeding. All memory is social, relational—belonging to groups in certain historical contexts. Particular memories belong to broader patterns of memory. And the latter tend to be centered on and organized around focal memories that are constitutive of group identity and, among peasant groups, resistance. There are abundant indications in our sources that memories of Moses, Joshua, Elijah, and other Israelite prophetic leaders were focal, constitutive of Galileans' and Judeans' social identity and struggle to resist the pressures of the Roman imperial order. These foundational memories provided the broader cultural patterns of popular Israelite memory in which the first and subsequent followers of Jesus could have made sense of what was happening. Jesus' actions and teachings made sense and took their place in a broader narrative that preceded and transcended them. For those who formulated, performed, and heard Mark's narrative, Jesus' actions and teachings were understandable as episodes in a longer story of the renewal of Israel led by a figure whose mission was reminiscent, and fit the pattern, of the prototypes Moses and Elijah in popular Israelite cultural memory.

Abbreviations

ABR	*Australian Biblical Review*
AGJU	Arbeiten zur Geschichte des antiken Judentums und des Urchristentums
BETL	Bibliotheca ephemeridum theologicarum lovaniensium
Bib	*Biblica*
BTB	*Biblical Theology Bulletin*
BZAW	Beihefte zur Zeitschrift für die alttestamentliche Wissenschaft
BZNW	Beihefte zur Zeitschrift für die neutestamentliche Wissenschaft
CBQ	*Catholic Biblical Quarterly*
ExpTim	*Expository Times*
HTR	*Harvard Theological Review*
Int	*Interpretation*
JBL	*Journal of Biblical Literature*
JETS	*Journal of the Evangelical Theological Society*
JSNT	*Journal for the Study of the New Testament*
JSNTSup	Journal for the Study of the New Testament: Supplement Series
JSOTSup	Journal for the Study of the Old Testament: Supplement Series
JTS	*Journal of Theological Studies*
LCL	Loeb Classical Library

NovT	*Novum Testamentum*
NTS	*New Testament Studies*
PW	Pauly, A. F. *Paulys Realencyclopädie der classischen Alter-tumswissenschaft*. New ed. G. Wissowa. 49 vols. Munich, 1980.
SBL	Society of Biblical Literature
SBT	Studies in Biblical Theology
SUNT	Studien zur Umwelt des Neuen Testaments
TRE	*Theologische Realenzyklopädie*. Edited by G. Krause and G. Müller. Berlin, 1977–.
VT	*Vetus Testamentum*
WMANT	Wissenschaftliche Monographien zum Alten und Neuen Testament
ZAW	*Zeitschrift für die alttestamentliche Wissenschaft*
ZNW	*Zeitschrift für die neutestamentliche Wissenschaft und die Kunde der älteren Kirche*

Notes

Introduction

1. K. L. Schmidt, a nineteenth-century scholar, characterized the Gospel in this way.

2. Werner H. Kelber's *Mark's Story of Jesus* (Philadelphia: Fortress Press, 1979), pioneering the reading of Mark as a complex overall narrative, is also a model of concise and lucid presentation to ordinary readers.

3. Werner H. Kelber, "The Two-Source Hypothesis: Oral Performance, the Poetics of Gospel Narrativity, and Memorial Arbitration," paper presented at the Society of Biblical Literature 2003 Annual Meeting, Atlanta, p. 21; Steven D. Moore, *Literary Criticism and the Gospels: The Theoretical Challenge* (New Haven: Yale University Press, 1989).

4. See especially Werner H. Kelber, *The Oral and the Written Gospel: The Hermeneutics of Speaking and Writing in the Synoptic Tradition, Mark, Paul, and Q* (Philadelphia: Fortress Press, 1983); Albert Bates Lord, *The Singer of Tales*, Studies in Comparative Literature 24 (Cambridge: Harvard University Press, 1960); Eric A. Havelock, *Preface to Plato*, A History of the Greek Mind, vol. 1 (Cambridge: Harvard University Press, 1963); and Walter Ong, *Orality and Literacy: The Technologizing of the Word*, New Accents (New York: Methuen, 1982).

5. The conclusions of William V. Harris, *Ancient Literacy* (Cambridge: Harvard University Press, 1989), were basically confirmed by those who

reviewed and supplemented his survey of the limits and uses of literacy in the Roman Empire. See also Pieter J. J. Botha, "Greco-Roman Literacy as Setting for New Testament Writings," *Neotestamentica* 26 (1992): 195–215.

6. See especially Catherine Hezser, *Jewish Literacy in Roman Palestine* (Tübingen: Mohr Siebeck, 2001), and pertinent references there.

7. Werner Kelber, "Jesus and Tradition: Words in Time and Words in Space," *Semeia* 65 (1994): 141.

8. Ibid., 140.

9. Among many important books and articles by John Miles Foley, see especially *Immanent Art: From Structure to Meaning in Traditional Oral Epic* (Bloomington: Indiana University Press, 1991); *Singer of Tales in Performance*, Voices in Performance and Text (Bloomington: Indiana University Press, 1995); *How to Read an Oral Performance* (Urbana: University of Illinois Press, 2002).

10. Martin S. Jaffee, *Torah in the Mouth: Writing and Oral Tradition in Palestinian Judaism, 200 BCE–400 CE* (New York: Oxford University Press, 2000).

11. Joanna Dewey, "Oral Methods of Structuring Narrative in Mark," *Interpretation* 53 (1989): 32–44; idem, "The Gospel of Mark as Oral/Aural Event: Implications for Interpretation," in *The New Literary Criticism and the New Testament*, ed. Elizabeth Struthers Malbon and Edgar V. McKnight, JSNTSup 109 (Sheffield: Sheffield Academic, 1994), 145–63; idem, "The Survival of Mark's Gospel: A Good Story?" *JBL* 123 (2004): 495–507; Pieter J. J. Botha, "Mark's Story as Oral Traditional Literature: Rethinking the Transmission of Some Traditions about Jesus," *Hervormde Teologiese Studies* 47 (1991): 304–31; idem, "The Historical Setting of Mark's Gospel: Problems and Possibilities," *JSNT* 51 (1993): 27–55; Richard A. Horsley, *Hearing the Whole Story: The Politics of Plot in Mark's Gospel* (Louisville, Ky.: Westminster John Knox, 2001); Whitney Shiner, *Proclaiming the Gospel: First-Century Performance of Mark* (Harrisburg, Pa.: Trinity Press International, 2003).

12. See especially Antoinette Clark Wire, *Holy Lives, Holy Deaths: A Close Hearing of Early Jewish Storytellers*, SBL Monograph Series 1 (Atlanta: SBL, 2002); Holly Hearon, *The Mary Magdalene Tradition: Witness and Counter-Witness in Early Christian Communities* (Collegeville, Minn.: Michael Glazier, 2004).

13. The papers from the first conference, in South Africa, have been published in two volumes: Jonathan A. Draper, ed., *Orality, Literacy, and Colonialism in Southern Africa*, Semeia Studies 46 (Atlanta: SBL, 2003); and *Orality, Literacy, and Colonialism in Antiquity*, Semeia Studies 47 (Atlanta: SBL, 2004).

14. Werner H. Kelber, "Memory's Desire and the Limits of Historical Criticism," *Oral Tradition* 17 (2002): 55–86, and "Two-Source Hypothesis."

15. Frances A. Yates, *The Art of Memory* (Chicago: University of Chicago Press, 1966); Mary Carruthers, *The Book of Memory: A Study in Medieval Culture* (Cambridge: Cambridge University Press, 1990); and Janet Coleman, *Ancient and Medieval Memories: Studies in Reconstruction of the Past* (Cambridge: Cambridge University Press, 1992).

16. Jan Assmann, *Das kulturelle Gedächtnis: Schrift, Erinnerung, und politische Identität in frühen Hochkulturen* (Munich: Beck, 1992); Aleida Assmann, *Erinnerungsräume: Formen und Wandlungen des kulturellen Gedächtnises* (Munich: Beck, 1999); Maurice Halbwachs, *The Collective Memory* (New York: Harper & Row, 1980); and idem, *On Collective Memory* (Chicago: Chicago University Press, 1992).

17. Kelber, "Memory's Desire," 55–56; "The Words of Memory: Christian Origins as MnemoHistory—A Response," in *Memory, Tradition, and Text: Uses of the Past in Early Christianity*, ed. Alan Kirk and Tom Thatcher, Semeia Studies 52 (Atlanta: SBL, 2005), 222–23, 226, 238–39.

18. Kelber, "Memory's Desire," 56.

19. Jan Assmann, "Collective Memory and Cultural Identity," *New German Critique* 65 (1995): 125–33.

20. Kelber, "Two-Source Hypothesis," 27.

21. Ibid.

22. Kelber responds comprehensively to the essays in Kirk and Thatcher, eds., *Memory, Tradition, and Text*.

23. Holly E. Hearon, *The Mary Magdalene Tradition: Witness and Counter-Witness in Early Christian Communities* (Collegeville, Minn.: Liturgical, 2004).

24. Jaffee, *Torah in the Mouth*.

25. In addition to the volumes listed in note 13 above, Jonathan A. Draper, ed., *The Didache in Modern Research*, ADJU 37 (Leiden: Brill, 1996); and Richard A. Horsley with Jonathan A. Draper, *Whoever Hears You Hears Me: Prophets, Performance, and Tradition in Q* (Harrisburg, Pa.: Trinity Press International, 1999). His most accessible previous study of George Khambule is "The Closed Text and the Heavenly Telephone: The Role of the *Bricoleur* in Oral Mediation of Sacred Text in the Case of George Khambule and the Gospel of John," in *Orality, Literacy, and Colonialism in Southern Africa*, 57–89.

26. See notes 16 and 19 above.

27. See the works in note 9 above.

28. *Flavius Philostratus: Heroikos*, trans. and ed. Ellen Bradshaw Aitken and Jennifer K. Berenson McLean, Writings from the Greco-Roman World, vol. 1 (Atlanta: SBL, 2001), and *Philostratus's Heroikos: Religion and Cultural Identity in the Third Century CE* (Atlanta: SBL, 2004); see also Ellen B. Ait-

ken, *The Poetics of the Passion: Jesus' Death in Early Christian Memory* (Göttingen: Vandenhoeck & Ruprecht, 2004).

29. Jens Schröter, *Erinnerung an Jesu Worte: Studien zur Rezeption der Logienüberlieferung in Markus, Q, und Thomas*, WMANT 76 (Neukirchen-Vluyn: Neukirchener, 1997).

30. See Vernon K. Robbins, *Jesus the Teacher: A Socio-Rhetorical Interpretation of Mark* (Philadelphia: Fortress Press, 1984); *New Boundaries in Old Territory: Forms and Social Rhetoric in Mark* (New York: Peter Lang, 1994); and *Exploring the Texture of Texts: A Guide to Socio-Rhetorical Interpretation* (Valley Forge, Pa.: Trinity Press International, 1996).

31. Whitney Taylor Shiner, *Follow Me!: Disciples in Markan Rhetoric* (Atlanta: Scholars, 1995), and *Proclaiming the Gospel: First-Century Performance of Mark* (Harrisburg, Pa.: Trinity Press International, 2003).

32. Horsley with Draper, *Whoever Hears You Hears Me*; and Horsley, *Hearing the Whole Story*.

1. The Implications of Orality for Studies of the Biblical Text

1. A shorter version of this chapter was first presented at a panel in honor of Werner Kelber at the 2003 meeting of the Society of Biblical Literature. The text of that presentation appears in *Oral Tradition* 19 (2004): 96–107. For another approach to this topic see John D. Harvey, "Orality and Its Implications for Biblical Studies: Recapturing an Ancient Paradigm," *JETS* 45 (2002): 99–109.

2. The significance of Kelber's work is signaled by the fact it appears in the bibliography of nearly every study on this topic produced since that time. It's absence would be seen as a glaring omission.

3. Paul J. Achtemeier, *"Omne Verbum Sonat:* The New Testament and the Oral Environment of Late Western Antiquity," *JBL* 109 (1990): 17–19. Frank D. Gilliard modifies Achtemeier's conclusion that reading aloud was the *exclusive* practice in the ancient world, while agreeing that it was the common practice ("More Silent Reading in Antiquity: *Non Omne Verbum Sonabat,"JBL* 112 [1993]: 689–94).

4. There is debate at present regarding the pronunciation of Koine Greek. Margaret Dean offers this observation, quoting W. S. Allen (*Vox Graeca: A Guide to the Pronunciation of Classical Greek* [3rd ed.; Cambridge: Cambridge University Press, 1987], 8): "In the study of a 'dead' language there is inevitably a main emphasis on the written word. But it is well to remember that writing is secondary to speech, and, however much it may deviate from it, has speech as its ultimate basis" (in Dean, "The Grammar of

Sound in Greek Texts: Toward a Method for Mapping the Echoes of Speech in Writing," *ABR* 44 [1996]: 53 n. 2).

5. Ibid., 54.

6. Ibid., 58.

7. Bernard Brandon Scott and Margaret E. Dean, "A Sound Map of the Sermon on the Mount," in *Treasures New and Old: Contributions to Matthean Studies*, ed. David R. Bauer and Mark Allan Powell, Symposium Series 1 (Atlanta: Scholars, 1996), 311–78.

8. Scott and Dean name two studies of aural structural features in relation to the Hebrew Bible: H. Parunak, "Oral Typesetting: Some Uses of Biblical Structure," *Bib* 62 (1981): 153–68, and Thomas P. McCreesh, *Biblical Sound and Sense, Poetic Sound Patterns in Proverbs 10–29*, JSOTSup 128 (Sheffield: JSOT, 1991).

9. Richard A. Horsley and Jonathan A. Draper do undertake some analysis of aural signals in Q in their book, *Whoever Hears You Hears Me: Prophets, Performance, and Tradition in Q* (Harrisburg, Pa.: Trinity Press International, 1999).

10. Scott and Dean, "Sound Map," 361–68.

11. Ibid., 369.

12. Werner H. Kelber, *The Oral and the Written Gospel: The Hermeneutics of Speaking and Writing in the Synoptic Tradition, Mark, Paul, and Q*, Voices in Performance and Text (Bloomington: Indiana University Press, 1997 [1983]), 67.

13. Joanna Dewey, "Mark as Aural Narrative: Structures as Clues to Understanding," *Sewanee Theological Review* 36 (1992): 47.

14. Ibid., 48–49.

15. Dewey, "Oral Methods of Structuring Narrative in Mark," *Int* 43 (1989): 40.

16. Dewey, "Mark as Aural Narrative," 49.

17. Dewey notes that the Gospel of Mark could be performed in one and a half hours, which she judges as short in terms of ancient oral performance standards (ibid., 47).

18. Pieter J. J. Botha, "Mark's Story as Oral Traditional Literature: Rethinking the Transmission of Some Traditions about Jesus," *Hervormde Teologiese Studies* 47 (1991): 318–19.

19. Ibid., 320–21.

20. Ibid., 322, 323.

21. Ibid., 324.

22. Kelber, *The Oral and the Written Gospel*, 140–83.

23. John D. Harvey, *Listening to the Text: Oral Patterning in Paul's Letters* (Grand Rapids, Mich.: Baker Books, 1998).

24. Casey Wayne Davis, *Oral Biblical Criticism: The Influence of the Principles of Orality on the Literary Structure of Paul's Epistle to the Philippians*, JSNTSup 172 (Sheffield: Sheffield Academic, 1999).

25. I am indebted here to John Foley's critique of the term "orality": without tradition, "orality" refers to all spoken discourse ("Words in Tradition, Words in Text: A Response," *Semeia* 65 [1994]: 170). I also acknowledge that I do not use "orality" with any kind of precision in this chapter, in large part because neither do my sources.

26. Antoinette Clark Wire distinguishes the letters of Paul from traditional oral literature, noting that Paul's letters speak for a particular individual and, reflecting Greek higher education in rhetoric, use "a genre allowing a very polemical address with the intent to disrupt and persuade" ("Performance, Politics, and Power: A Response," *Semeia 65* [1994]: 133).

27. Kelber, *The Written and the Oral Gospel*, 19.

28. Antoinette Clark Wire, *Holy Lives, Holy Deaths: A Close Hearing of Early Jewish Storytellers*, SBL Monograph Series 1 (Atlanta: Scholars, 2002), 4.

29. Joanna Dewey, "The Gospel of Mark as Oral/Aural Event: Implications for Interpretation," in *The New Literary Criticism and the New Testament*, ed. Edgar V. McKnight and Elizabeth Struthers Malbon (Valley Forge, Pa.: Trinity Press International, 1994), 154–55. See also J. A. Loubser, "Orality and Pauline 'Christology': Some Hermeneutical Implications," *Scriptura* 47 (1993): 43.

30. Dewey, "Mark as Aural Narrative," 55.

31. Dewey, "Oral Methods of Structuring Narrative," 43.

32. Vernon K. Robbins, "Progymnastic Rhetorical Composition and Pre-Gospel Traditions: A New Approach," in *The Synoptic Gospels*, ed. Camille Focant (Leuven: Leuven University Press, 1993), 116.

33. "To organize the oral mainstream into a linear scheme, and to declare it an unbroken trajectory toward textuality is to eye it through the distorting lens of hindsight" (Kelber, *The Oral and the Written Gospel*, 33).

34. Eduard Nielson, *Oral Tradition: A Modern Problem in the Old Testament*, SBT 11 (Chicago: Allenson, 1954), 34–35. See also Achtemeier, *"Omne Verbum Sonat,"* 10.

35. Werner H. Kelber, "Jesus and Tradition: Words in Time, Words in Space," *Semeia* 65 (1994): 162.

36. Gilbert L. Bartholomew, "Feed My Lambs: John 21:15-19 as Oral Gospel," *Semeia* 39 (1987): 74; Thomas E. Boomershine, "Peter's Denial as Polemic of Confession," *Semeia* 39 (1987): 52.

37. For an effort to argue for the origin of a narrative in oral tradition see Holly E. Hearon, *The Mary Magdalene Tradition: Witness and*

Counter-Witness in Early Christian Communities (Collegeville, Minn.: Liturgical, 2004), chapter 3.

38. Ibid., 72–75.

39. Horsley with Draper, *Whoever Hears You Hears Me,* 137–40.

40. James D. G. Dunn, "Altering the Default Setting: Re-envisaging the Early Transmission of the Jesus Tradition," *NTS* 49 (2003): 160–63.

41. James D. G. Dunn, "Jesus in Oral Memory: The Initial Stages of the Jesus Tradition," *SBL Seminar Papers* (2000): 302.

42. Horsley with Draper, *Whoever Hears You Hears Me,* chapter 7.

43. Margaret Mills, "Domains of Folkloristic Concern: Interpretation of Scriptures," in *Text and Tradition: The Hebrew Bible and Folklore,* ed. Susan Niditch, Semeia Studies 32 (Atlanta: Scholars, 1990), 235.

44. Kelber, *The Written and the Oral Gospel,* 176.

45. Beverly Long, "Recent Field Studies in Oral Literature and Their Bearing on Old Testament Criticism," *VT* 26 (1976): 189.

46. Øivind Andersen, "Oral Tradition," in *Jesus and the Oral Gospel Tradition,* ed. Henry Wansbrough, JSNTSup 64 (Sheffield: Sheffield Academic, 1991), 29.

47. By "instability" I do not mean to suggest that the texts were wholly free-form, lacking any core or stable elements, but rather that the performer had considerable latitude to shape the text in particular ways.

48. Loubser, "Orality and Pauline 'Christology,'" 35; Dewey, "Gospel of Mark as Oral/Aural Event," 157–58.

49. Long, "Recent Field Studies," 190–91; Dewey, "Gospel of Mark as Oral/Aural Event," 151.

50. Whitney Shiner, *Proclaiming the Gospel: First-Century Performance of Mark* (Harrisburg, Pa.: Trinity Press International, 2003), 112.

51. Kenneth E. Bailey, "Middle Eastern Oral Tradition and the Synoptic Gospels," *ExpTim* 106 (1995): 366.

52. Shiner, *Proclaiming the Gospel.*

53. Hearon, *Mary Magdalene Tradition,* 19–42, 77–100.

54. Ibid., 99–100.

55. David Rhoads, "Performance Criticism: A New Methodology in Biblical Studies?" (unpublished paper, cited by permission).

56. Ibid., 11.

57. Beverly Long, "Recent Field Studies in Oral Literature and the Question of *Sitz im Leben,*" *Semeia* 5 (1976): 40.

58. Robbins, "Progymnastic Rhetorical Composition," 140; Horsley with Draper, *Whoever Hears You Hears Me,* chapter 7.

59. Wire, *Holy Lives, Holy Deaths,* 18.

60. Ibid., 11–12.

61. Ibid., 12, 10.

62. Ibid., 383.

63. One of the challenges John Foley has posed to scholars working with biblical texts is the need to identify "what expressive forms were there or might there have been in early Christian and Jewish communities where the gospel texts were written?" ("Words in Tradition, Words in Text," 173).

64. Horsley with Draper, *Whoever Hears You Hears Me.*

65. Ibid., 165.

66. Robbins, "Progymnastic Rhetorical Composition," 93–146; Horsley with Draper, *Whoever Hears You Hears Me,* 295.

67. Robert Coote, "The Application of Oral Theory to Biblical Hebrew Literature," *Semeia* 5 (1976), 60–61.

68. This is, of course, an over-simplification. Nonetheless, other theories of transmission may be viewed in one way or another as off-shoots of the theories presented here.

69. Rudolph Bultmann, *History of the Synoptic Tradition,* trans. J. Marsh (New York: Harper & Row, 1963).

70. For example, the connection between content and setting is now understood to be far looser than Bultmann supposed (Long, "Recent Field Studies in Oral Literature and Their Bearing on Old Testament Criticism," 191, 193, 197).

71. See Kelber, *The Oral and the Written Gospel,* 3–8.

72. Birger Gerhardsson, *Tradition and Transmission in Early Christianity* (Lund: Gleerup, 1964); idem, *The Gospel Tradition* (Malmo: Gleerup, 1986); idem, *The Reliability of the Gospel Tradition* (Peabody, Mass.: Hendrickson, 2001); Harald Reisenfeld, *The Gospel Tradition* (Philadelphia: Fortress Press, 1970).

73. Kelber, *The Oral and the Written Gospel,* 8–30.

74. Ibid, 13.

75. Kenneth E. Bailey, "Informal Controlled Oral Tradition and the Synoptic Gospels," *Asia Journal of Theology* 5 (1991): 34–54.

76. Bailey develops these ideas in "Middle Eastern Oral Tradition," 363–67.

77. Kelber, *The Oral and the Written Gospel,* 24.

78. Hearon, *The Mary Magdalene Tradition,* 77–100.

79. Samuel Byrskog, *Story as History, History as Story: The Gospel Tradition in the Context of Ancient Oral History* (Leiden: Brill, 2000), 225.

80. This view is shared by Eduard Nielson, *Oral Tradition,* 30.

81. Byrskog, *Story as History,* 197, 127.

82. Ibid., 139 (here following the work of Margaret Mills).

83. Horsley with Draper, *Whoever Hears You Hears Me*, 7.

84. Andersen, "Oral Tradition," 21.

85. William S. Taylor, "Memory and the Gospel Tradition," *Theology Today* 15 (1959): 172.

86. Richard Rohrbaugh, "The Social Location of the Marcan Audience," *BTB* 23 (1993): 115; Meir Bar-Ilan, "Illiteracy in the Land of Israel in the First Centuries CE," in *Essays in the Social Scientific Study of Judaism and Jewish Society*, ed. S. Fishbane, S. Schoenfeld, and A. Goldschläger, vol. 2 (Hoboken, N.J.: KTAV, 1992), 56; William V. Harris, *Ancient Literacy* (Cambridge: Harvard University Press, 1986), 267.

87. Joanna Dewey, "From Storytelling to Written Text: The Loss of Early Christian Women's Voices," *BTB* 26 (1996): 72.

88. Ibid., 74.

89. Werner H. Kelber, "Orality, Literacy, and Colonialism in Antiquity," in *Orality, Literacy, and Colonialism in Antiquity*, ed. Jonathan A. Draper, Semeia Studies (Atlanta: SBL, 2004), 135.

90. Werner H. Kelber, "Biblical Hermeneutics and the Ancient Art of Communication: A Response," *Semeia* 39 (1987): 101.

91. Harm W. Hollander, "The Words of Jesus: From Oral Tradition to Written Record in Paul and Q," *NovT* 42 (2000): 356.

92. Wire, "Performance, Politics, and Power," 134.

93. Kelber, "Biblical Hermeneutics," 101.

94. Long, "Recent Field Studies in Oral Literature and the Question of *Sitz im Leben*," 188.

95. Wire, *Holy Lives, Holy Deaths*, 383–84.

96. Kelber, "Orality, Literacy, and Colonialism in Antiquity," 136.

97. Kelber, "Jesus and Tradition," 159.

98. Joanna Dewey, "Textuality in an Oral Culture: A Survey of the Pauline Traditions," *Semeia* 65 (1994): 61.

99. Dewey, "The Gospel of Mark as Oral/Aural Event," 152.

2. Gender and Otherness in Rabbinic Oral Culture: On Gentiles, Undisciplined Jews, and Their Women

1. The most convenient and thorough introductory discussion of oral tradition in rabbinic Judaism is that of G. Stemberger, *Introduction to the Talmud and Midrash* (2nd ed.; Edinburgh: T & T Clark, 1995), 33–44. The Hebrew reader will benefit from two recent contributions that appeared too late to inform the present study: Y. Zussman, "'Oral Torah' Means Exactly What It Says: The Impact of an Iota," in *Talmudic Researches: A Collection of*

Essays on Talmud and Related Fields Dedicated to the Memory of Prof. Ephraim E. Urbach, ed. Y. Zussman and D. Rozental (Jerusalem: Magnes, 2005), 1:209–384, and S. Naeh, "The Art of Memory: Structures of Memory and Images of Texts in Rabbinic Literature," in ibid., 2:543–89. The present essay builds upon my own study of rabbinic oral tradition, *Torah in the Mouth: Writing and Oral Tradition in Palestinian Judaism, ca. 200 BCE–400 CE* (New York: Oxford University Press, 2001), 3–12, 65–156. Here I focus upon two matters unaddressed in my book: the way in which the structure of rabbinic monotheism and the character of rabbinic constructions of gender influence rabbinic thinking about oral tradition.

2. There is currently no "general theory" of the nature of the oral traditional process in rabbinic culture in relationship to the surviving genres of written rabbinic literature. Each rabbinic genre—mishnah, midrash, gemara, and so forth—has its own sub-genres, each of which represents its own set of puzzles to anyone who would try to explain how these texts came from the oral tradition into the manuscripts that preserve them. An excellent orientation to recent research is available in D. Stern, ed., *The Anthology in Jewish Literature* (New York: Oxford University Press, 2004), especially the essays by Y. Elman, E. Segal, and D. Stern. See also P. Mandel, "Between Byzantium and Islam: The Transmission of a Jewish Book in the Byzantine and Early Islamic Periods," in *Transmitting Jewish Traditions: Orality, Textuality, and Cultural Diffusion*, ed. Y. Elman and I. Gershoni (New Haven: Yale University Press, 2000). To these may be added the more focused and detailed contributions of Zussman (on the Mishnah specifically) and Naeh (on Tannaitic material more broadly) mentioned in note 1. My most recent attempt to draw a general theoretical framework for pursuing more detailed inquires may be consulted in Martin S. Jaffee, "Rabbinic Authorship as a Collective Enterprise," in *The Cambridge Companion to Rabbinic Literature*, ed. Charlotte Fonrobert and Martin S. Jaffee (Cambridge: Cambridge University Press, forthcoming).

3. The ritual, performative dimension of the rabbinic engagement with oral tradition is explored in S. Fraade, "Literary Composition and Oral Performance in Early Midrashim," *Oral Tradition* 14 (1999): 33–35. See also Martin S. Jaffee, "Oral Transmission of Knowledge as Rabbinic Sacrament: An Overlooked Aspect of Discipleship in Oral Torah," in *Knowledge and Learning in Jewish Tradition*, ed. H. Kreisel (Beersheva: Bar Ilan University Press, forthcoming).

4. See, for example, the discussion of practices that enhance or, to the contrary, impair the power of memory in *b. Horayot* 13b: "Five things cause learning to be forgotten . . . ; five things restore learning. . . ." Small collections of material on the importance of memory in Torah learning appear as well at *Sifre Deuteronomy*, par. 48 and 306, *y. Berakhot* 5:1, 9a, and *b. 'Avodah*

Zarah 19a-b. For a broader discussion of rabbinic preoccupation with textual memory, see M. Swartz, *Scholastic Magic: Ritual and Revelation in Early
Jewish Mysticism* (Princeton: Princeton University Press, 1996), 40–43, now
expansively supplemented by S. Naeh, "The Art of Memory."

5. Zussman, "'Oral Torah,'" 257.

6. The Mishnah's tractate *'Avot* ("The Founders") is distinct from
other mishnaic tractates in that it is concerned exclusively with motivational
and homiletical epigrams rather than legal inquiry. Its first two chapters (*m.
'Avot* 1:1—2:8) are famous for supplying a thumbnail sketch of the chain of
authorities, stemming from Moses to the editors of the Mishnah, responsible
for preserving and transmitting the rabbinic oral tradition. For recent, innovative studies of *Mishnah Avot* in the context of the religious cultures of late
antiquity, see A. Troper, *Wisdom, Politics, and Historiography: Tractate Avot in
the Context of the Graeco-Roman Near East* (Oxford: Oxford University Press,
2004), and J. Schofer, *The Making of a Sage: A Study in Rabbinic Ethics* (Madi-
son: University of Wisconsin Press, 2005).

7. *Ma'alyn 'alav*: Here and in R. Doseti's statement, many texts read:
ma'aleh 'alav hakatuv: "Scripture regards him."

8. Verses from Deuteronomy proved crucial as "tags" upon which early
rabbinic exegetes sought to hang their own conceptions of the importance
of memory in the preservation of Oral Torah. See, for example, *Sifre Deuteronomy* to Deut 11:22ff. and the recent comments of Naeh, "The Art of
Memory," 542–54.

9. The text is cited from the critical edition of S. Sharvit, ed., *Tractate
Avot through the Ages: A Critical Edition, Prolegomena and Appendices* (Jerusalem: Hebrew University Press, 2004), 126–27. Translations of all rabbinic
citations in this essay are my own.

10. S. Naeh, "Art of Memory," 553, offers the provocative suggestion
that the reference in the Mishnah to "intentional" forgetting is an oblique
reference to the technical mnemonic skill of editing a corrupted memorized
text by deletion of the corruption from the memory. While talmudic emenda-
tional terminology, such as *samey mika'n* ("delete from this [the following]")
suggests use of such a mnemonic practice in amoraic circles, I am not convinced the present passage points toward a comparable tannaitic technique.
The amoraic method presupposes memorization of fixed texts and comparison of variant versions. While the Tannaim transmitted these versions, they
show little interest in the sorts of text-critical or meta-textual issues that concern the Amoraim.

11. This and all other citations from the Babylonian Talmud are cited
from the standard printed editions after comparison with major manuscript
variants.

12. Hebrew: *'ammey ha-'arets*; literally, "people of the land." We shall discuss this term in greater detail further on.

13. Hebrew: *'ovdey kokhavim*; literally, "star worshippers." The term is likely to be a censor's improvement upon an earlier text's *goyim* ("Gentiles"). In light of the rabbinic view that virtually all non-Jews were worshippers of false gods, there is little real distinction between the terms. In this essay I shall routinely use the term "Gentiles." For an extensive discussion of rabbinic attitudes toward non-Jewish religions, see R. Goldenberg, *The Nations That Know Thee Not: Ancient Jewish Attitudes towards Other Religions* (New York: New York University Press, 1998).

14. A pointed pun at *b. Berakhot* 18b frames the issue beautifully: "The sons [or disciples] of Rabbi Hiyya went out to the countryside [*kiryata'*: a place where other rabbinic disciples were few and far between], and immediately they forgot (*'iyakar*) their learning (*talmudeiho*), and they struggled to recall it." For other conjunctions of verbs formed of the stem *'qr/'qr* with nouns such as *tlmwd'* (learning) and *gmr'* (tradition), see M. Sokoloff, *'qr/'qr*, s.v., *A Dictionary of Jewish Babylonian Aramaic* (Ramat Gan: Bar Ilan University Press; Baltimore: Johns Hopkins University Press, 2002), 878. On the role of fellow students in helping colleagues to restore their memories, see *b. 'Avodah Zarah* 46b. The ultimate testimony to the crucial role of the discipleship community in supporting the identity of the individual may be adduced in the famous tale of Honi the Circle-Maker (*b. Ta'anit* 23a). Upon awaking after seventy years, Honi returns to his old disciple-circle only to discover that, while his traditions are fondly recalled, no one alive now recognizes him. His famous response: *'o hevruta' 'o metuta'*—"either a study-partner or death!"

15. Compare the set of negations, attested from early rabbinic times, that oblige "a person" each day to praise God for "not making me a Gentile, for not making me an ignoramus (*bwr*), for not making me a woman" (*t. Berakhot* 6:18, ed. Lieberman, 38). By the twelfth century at the latest, the standard version had been incorporated into the private morning benedictions, thanking God "for not making me a Gentile, for not making me a slave, and for not making me a woman" (Maimonides, *Mishneh Torah: Laws of Prayer and Priestly Blessings* 7:6).

16. The groundbreaking essay on the theme of rabbinic masculinity is that of M. Satlow, "'Try to Be a Man': The Rabbinic Construction of Masculinity," *Harvard Theological Review* 89 (1996): 19–40.

17. For comprehensive discussions of rabbinic attitudes toward Gentiles, see G. Porton, *Goyim: Gentiles and Israelites in Mishnah-Tosefta* (Atlanta: Scholars, 1988) and S. Stern, *Jewish Identity in Early Rabbinic Writings*, 1–50. There is much more nuance in rabbinic attitudes toward Gentiles than can

be discussed here. Indeed, this is true of attitudes toward women and non-rabbinic Jews as well. But, as I point out later on, there is some value in focusing on the most extreme positions.

18. I have argued this point in my article "A Rabbinic Ontology of the Written and Spoken Word: On Discipleship, Transformative Knowledge, and the Living Texts of Oral Torah," *Journal of the American Academy of Religion* 65 (1997): 539–49.

19. *Avoth de-Rabbi Nathan Solomon Schechter Edition* with Prolegomenon by M. Kister (New York: Jewish Theological Seminary of America, 1997), 31.

20. L. Finkelstein, ed., *Siphre ad Deuteronomium* (Berlin: Jüdischer Kulturbund in Deutschland, 1939; repr. New York: Jewish Theological Seminary of America, 1969), 408.

21. M. Friedmann, ed., *Midrash Pesiqta Rabbati* (reprint, Tel Aviv: n.p., 1963); S. Buber, ed., *Midrash Tanhuma* (Israel: n.p., n.d.), 2:116–17.

22. The midrashist has forgotten that the Greek rendering of the Hebrew scriptures was produced by Jews and only later became the original form of scripture in Greek-speaking Christian communities. Other rabbinic sources are quite aware of the Jewish origins of the Septuagint. See *b. Megillah* 9a-b.

23. By the sixth century, this competition had resulted in an effort by the Emperor Justinian to ban the study of the oral tradition among the Jews. See A. Baumgarten, "Justinian and the Jews," in *Rabbi Joseph H. Lookstein Memorial Volume*, ed. L. Landman (New York: KTAV, 1980), 37–44.

24. M. Bregman, "Mishnah and LXX as Mystery: An Example of Jewish-Christian Polemic in the Byzantine Period," in *Continuity and Renewal: Jews and Judaism in Byzantine-Christian Palestine*, ed. L. Levine (Jerusalem: Jewish Theological Seminary of America, 2004), 333–42. The original Hebrew version of this essay has now appeared as M. Bregman, "The Mishnah as Mystery," in Zussman and Rozental, eds., *Talmudic Researches*, 1:101–9.

25. See Martin S. Jaffee, "One God, One Revelation, One Community: On the Symbolic Structure of Elective Monotheism," *Journal of the American Academy of Religion* 69 (2001): 753–75; R. Stark, *The One True God* (Princeton: Princeton University Press, 2001), 12–17; and Goldenberg, *The Nations That Know Thee Not*, 81–98.

26. I have argued in *Torah in the Mouth*, 60–61, that rabbinic Judaism seems to have been the first form of Judaism to insist that its post-scriptural oral-performative tradition was integrally connected to the tradition of revelations recorded in the Torah of Sinai.

27. The recent discussion of Beruria is best tracked in the following: D. Goodblatt, "The Beruriah Traditions," *Journal of Jewish Studies* 26 (1975):

68–85; R. Adler, "The Virgin in the Brothel and Other Anomalies: Character and Context in the Legend of Beruriah," *Tikkun* 3 (1988): 28–32, and *Tikkun* 6 (1988): 102–5; D. Boyarin, *Carnal Israel: Reading Sex in Talmudic Culture* (Berkeley: University of California Press, 1994), 181–96; T. Ilan, *Jewish Women in Greco-Roman Palestine* (Peabody, Mass.: Hendrickson, 1996), 197–200.

28. See, for example, the exceptional instance of the sage Abaye's mother, discussed in Charlotte Fonrobert, *Menstrual Purity: Rabbinic and Christian Reconstructions of Biblical Gender* (Stanford: Stanford University Press, 2000), 151–53.

29. C. Hezser, *The Social Structure of the Rabbinic Movement in Roman Palestine* (Tübingen: Mohr Siebeck, 1997), 232.

30. The most ambitious efforts are those of T. Ilan, *Mine and Yours Are Hers: Retrieving Women's History from Rabbinic Literature* (Leiden: Brill, 1997), M. Peskowitz, *Spinning Fantasies: Rabbis, Gender, and History* (Berkeley: University of California Press, 1997), and Fonrobert, *Menstrual Purity*.

31. See Boyarin, *Carnal Israel*, 167–96; Ilan, *Jewish Women*, 190–204.

32. The idealization of the domestic concealment of women is common in rabbinic texts, although the social reality was much more complex, with women involved of necessity in the market and other public settings. See Ilan, *Jewish Women*, 128–29, and M. Peskowitz, *Spinning Fantasies*, 49–76, 95–108.

33. See Hezser, *Social Structure*, 213–24. An excellent discussion of the development of the rabbinic *bet midrash* is available in J. Rubenstein, "Social and Institutional Settings of Rabbinic Literature," in *The Cambridge Companion to Rabbinic Literature*.

34. Some sources acknowledge the occasional presence of women in the House of Study but depict it as a kind of invasive anomaly. See Ilan, *Jewish Women*, 194, and Stern, *Jewish Identity*, 241–46.

35. M. Peskowitz, *Spinning Fantasies*, 73.

36. See also Stern, *Jewish Identity*, 240–41: "The relative exclusion of Jewish women from the experience of circumcision, Torah learning, and other features of Jewish identity must affect the nature of their identity as Israel. . . . If she is excluded from the distinctive praxis of Israel as defined in rabbinic sources, what then is her Jewish identity . . . supposed to consist of?"

37. Conversely, traits defined as feminine are also appropriated by rabbinic males when they are assigned a positive role in the construction of holiness. See Natan Margalit, "Priestly Men and Invisible Women: Male Appropriation of the Feminine and the Exemption of Women from

Time-Bound Commandments," *Association for Jewish Studies Review* 28 (2004): 297–316.

38. It must also be observed that not all Jewish women are as Jewish as those who follow rabbinic Torah. See the seminal essay of Charlotte Fonrobert, "When Women Walk in the Way of Their Fathers: On Gendering the Rabbinic Claim for Authority," *Journal of the History of Sexuality* 10 (2001): 402–12.

39. Useful evaluations of rabbinic attitudes toward the *'ammey ha-'arets* may be consulted in A. Oppenheimer, *The 'Am Ha-aretz: A Study in the Social History of the Jewish People in the Hellenistic-Roman Period* (Leiden: Brill, 1977), 67–117, 170–99; L. Levine, *The Rabbinic Class of Roman Palestine in Late Antiquity* (New York: Jewish Theological Seminary of America, 1989), 117–27; Stern, *Jewish Identity*, 114–23; J. Rubenstein, *The Culture of the Babylonian Talmud* (Baltimore: Johns Hopkins University Press, 2003), 123–42; and C. Hayes, "The 'Other' in Rabbinic Literature," in *The Cambridge Companion to Rabbinic Literature*. A recent, and very promising attempt to move behind the stereotype of the *'am ha-'arets* to a more substantial social reality is offered by S. Miller, *Sages and Commoners in Late Antique 'Eretz Israel: A Philological Inquiry into Local Traditions in the Talmud Yerushalmi* (Tübingen: Mohr Siebeck, 2004).

40. Rubenstein, *The Culture of the Babylonian Talmud*, 124–25, argues that the most contemptuous depictions of non-rabbinic Jews stem from the late, anonymous redactional layer ("stammaitic") of the Talmud and reflect the professionalization of rabbinic knowledge in the emerging academies. The point stands or falls on the cogency of the "stammaitic hypothesis," which holds the twin theses that it is (1) possible to isolate a coherent anonymous literary stratum from a document preserved for several centuries by oral transmission and that (2) such a stratum reveals a consistent and self-identical ideological program. In my view, Rubenstein's observations are subtle, and his literary work most careful, yet I remain convinced that the basic stammaitic approach to rabbinic literary history fundamentally overestimates the degree to which literary strata can be recovered from orally transmitted material. See note 50.

41. These proscriptions are part of a larger set of dress and behavioral codes intended to distinguish disciples of sages from those outside the rabbinic circles. See Levine, *Rabbinic Class,* 47–53.

42. The Talmud's explanation of the rule expresses a concern that bystanders will misconstrue the nature of the conversation. A similar view is expressed in *'Avot of Rabbi Natan*, text A, chapter 2 (to be found on p. 9 of S. Schechter's edition of the document). On the theme of talking to women, see Ilan, *Jewish Women*, 126–27.

43. We have already pointed out the view in *m. Avot* 3:3 that the table, as a symbolic equivalent of the Temple altar, must in rabbinic practice be consecrated by words of Torah.

44. See M. Satlow, "'They Abused Him Like a Woman': Homoeroticism, Gender Blurring, and the Rabbis in Late Antiquity," *Journal of the History of Sexuality* 5 (1994): 12–14, for further discussion of this proscription, in particular in the context of rabbinic discussions of homoerotic relationships among men.

45. I follow here the interpretation of the classic Talmudic commentator Rashi.

46. For summaries of these sources, see Levine, *Rabbinic Class*, 52–53, and Hezser, *Social Structure*, 126–30.

47. See also *b. Shabbat* 114a: "Any disciple of the sages whose garment is stained deserves death." The sullying of the symbol of male honor brings upon the disciple a "social death" in the form of a blemish upon one's masculinity. The point is familiar to us from *m. 'Avot* 3:7-9, with which our discussion began.

48. A handy compendium of classical commentaries on the text is available now in *The Talmud Bavli: The Schottenstein Edition, Tractate Pesachim* (Brooklyn, N.Y.: Mesorah Artskrol, 1997), 2:49b1-3. See in particular the various footnotes to the translated text.

49. Hezser, *Social Structure*, 96–100, points out that the early rabbinic movement seems to have had a high proportion of members whose fathers had been disciples of sages. That is, the movement spread from a core of households.

50. I have translated the text from the standard edition with occasional emendations suggested, on the basis of manuscript variants and early parallels, by the Hebrew study of S. Wald, *BT Pesahim III: Critical Edition with Comprehensive Commentary* (New York: Jewish Theological Seminary of America, 2000), 212ff. For the purposes of his literary-historical work, Wald distinguishes the tannaitic, amoraic, and redactional ("stammaitic") layers of the text. These issues do not bear materially on my discussion, so I do not reproduce Wald's divisions in this translation. See also Rubenstein, *The Culture of the Babylonian Talmud*, 129–35, for whom Wald's strata-analysis plays a crucial role in linking the most hostile formulations to the "stammaitic" editor.

51. This is a reference to Rabbi Judah the Patriarch, the third-century sage widely regarded as the compiler of the Mishnah.

52. So Wald, *BT Pesahim III*, 212, replacing Yohanan.

53. The main texts are *b. Nedarim* 50a and *b. Ketuvot* 62a-b. See the recent discussion of S. Friedman, "A Good Story Deserves Retelling: The

Unfolding of the Akiva Legend," *Jewish Studies Internet Journal* 3 (2004): 55–94 (http://www.biu.ac.il/JS/JSIJ/3-2004/JSIJ-3-2004.pdf).

54. I owe this point to an electronic communication from Charlotte Fonrobert on July 30, 2002.

55. So Wald, *BT Pesahim III*, 212.

56. The most exhaustive discussion of rabbinic perspectives on the Torah as a gift for all of humanity remains, unfortunately, untranslated from the original Hebrew. See M. Hirshman, *Torah for the Entire World* (Tel Aviv: Ha-Kibbutz Ha-Me'uhad, 1999).

57. For a survey of pre-rabbinic Jewish references to putatively oral ancestral traditions, see Jaffee, *Torah in the Mouth*, 44–52.

58. This paper has had a long gestation period and its present appearance has depended upon many kindnesses. I thank in particular Joseph Nagy, Charlotte Fonrobert, Jeffrey Rubenstein, and Hindy Najman.

3. Many Voices, One Script:
The Prophecies of George Khambule

1. Rudolf Bultmann, *The History of the Synoptic Tradition*, trans. J. Marsh (2nd ed.; Oxford: Blackwell, 1968), 108–30.

2. See the summary in Eugene Boring, *Sayings of the Risen Jesus: Christian Prophecy in the Synoptic Tradition* (Cambridge: Cambridge University Press, 1982) 1–9.

3. Boring, *Sayings of the Risen Jesus*.

4. David E. Aune, *Prophecy in Early Christianity and the Ancient Mediterranean World* (Grand Rapids, Mich.: Eerdmans, 1983).

5. Werner H. Kelber, *The Oral and the Written Gospel: The Hermeneutics of Speaking and Writing in the Synoptic Tradition, Mark, Paul, and Q* (Philadelphia: Fortress Press, 1983).

6. Boring, *Sayings of the Risen Jesus*, 245.

7. Kelber, *The Oral and the Written Gospel*, 30.

8. See Jonathan A. Draper, "The Marriage of the Lamb and the Isigodlo in iBandla labancwele of the Zulu Prophet George Khambule," in *The Power of Oral History: Memory, Healing, and Development*, Proceedings of the Twelfth International Oral History Conference, June 24–27, 2002 (Pietermaritzburg: Oral History Project, 2002), 1:15–33; "Worshipping with Angels in the New Jerusalem: George Khambule and *Ibandla Labancwele*," paper presented at the Orality, Literacy, and the World of the Spirit

Conference, Free University of Brussels, 2002; "The Closed Text and the Heavenly Telephone: The Role of the Bricoleur in Oral Mediation of Sacred Text in the Case of George Khambule and the Gospel of John," in *Orality, Literacy, and Colonialism in Southern Africa*, ed. Jonathan A. Draper, Semeia Studies 46 (Atlanta: SBL, 2003), 57–89; "The Ritualization of Memory: The Interface of Written and Oral Tradition in *Ibandla Labancwele* of George Khambule," paper presented at the Colloquium on Orality, Literacy, and Memory, Rice University, October 10–12, 2003; "George Khambule and the Book of Revelation: Prophet of the Open Heaven," *Neotestamentica* 38, no. 2 (2004): 101–24; "World War as a Precursor and Aspect of Globalisation: The Case of George Khambule (1884–1949) and the Book of Revelation," in *Spirits of Globalisation*, ed. Sturla J. Staelsett (London: SCM, forthcoming).

9. For an account of the Edendale settlement see Sheila Meintjes, "Edendale, 1851–1930: Farmers to Townspeople, Market to Labour Reserve," in *Pietermaritzburg 1838–1988: A New Portrait of an African City*, ed. John Laband and Robert Haswell (Pietermaritzburg: University of Natal Press, 1988), 66–69.

10. For accounts and photographs of the participation of black South African volunteers on the Western front see Norman Clothier, *Black Valour: The South African Native Labour Contingent, 1916–1918 and the Sinking of the "Mendi"* (Pietermaritzburg: University of Natal Press, 1987); Ian Gleeson, *The Unknown Force: Black, Indian, and Coloured Soldiers through Two World Wars* (Rivonia, Johannesburg: Ashanti, 1994).

11. *Liturgy* 3, 76–78. All texts of Khambule were written in Zulu and transcribed and translated by a team consisting of J. A. Draper, B. M. Mkhize, M. K. Ntuli, and B. Maseko.

12. *Diary* 3, 118–22.

13. Nomguqo Patricia Dlamini, *Paulina Dlamini: Servant of Two Kings*, ed. Heinrich Filter, trans. S. Bourquin (Pietermaritzburg: University of Natal Press, 1986), 34–35; Magema M. Fuze, *The Black People and Whence They Came* (Pietermaritzburg: University of Natal Press, 1979), 91.

14. Bengt Sundkler, *Zulu Zion and Some Swazi Zionists* (London: Oxford University Press, 1976), 134.

15. Ibid., 143, 159.

16. Ibid., 127.

17. *Diary* 1, *Diary* 3, *Liturgy* 3.

18. *Diary* 2 in part, *Liturgy* 1.

19. *Diary* 2 in part, *Liturgy* 2, *Hymnbook* 1 in part.

20. *Hymnbook* 1 in part.

21. This is embroidered on Mhlungu's stole in a photograph of Khambule and his two women prophets, which is reproduced in Sundkler's *Zulu Zion* opposite page 140. Digital analysis of the original allows much more to be read than may have been available to Sundkler.

22. Peter Berger and Thomas Luckmann, *The Social Construction of Reality: A Treatise on the Sociology of Knowledge* (New York: Doubleday, 1966); see also Draper, "The Ritualization of Memory."

23. *Liturgy* 2, 7.

24. A similar dynamic can be seen at work in the writings of the *AmaNazaretha* church of Isaiah Shembe, which is roughly contemporary with Khambule. It is sometimes difficult to know what comes from Isaiah Shembe and what comes from his son and successor Johannes Galilee Shembe. For a discussion of the problem of sources in the Shembe tradition see R. Papini and I. Hexham, eds., *The Catechism of the Nazarites and Related Writings*, vol. 4 (Lewiston: Edwin Mellen, 2002).

25. *Diary* 3, 118–22.

26. *Liturgy* 3, 52–53.

27. Ibid.

28. *Diary* 1, 51A.

29. *Diary* 1, 47A.

30. Philip Mhlungu, *Report in Zulu on Various Independent Churches at Ethelezini*, Sundkler Archives, Carolina Library, Uppsala, 1941. The text was written in Zulu and was transcribed and translated by J. A. Draper, B. M. Mkhize, M. K. Ntuli, and B. Maseko; 35–38.

31. Mhlungu, *Report*, 44.

32. *Diary* 1, 15A.

33. *Diary* 1, 15A–B.

34. *Diary* 1, 56A.

35. *Liturgy* 3, 86–91; *Diary* 2, 7–12.

36. *Liturgy* 3, 37–40; *Diary* 2, 60–62.

37. *Diary* 1, 6B–7A.

38. *Diary* 1, 15B–16A.

39. *Liturgy* 3, 75–78.

40. *Diary* 1, 9B–12B.

41. *Diary* 1, 48A.

42. *Diary* 1, 15A.

43. *Diary* 1, 34B; *Diary* 1, 55A.

44. For example, *Diary* 1, 52B.

45. *Diary* 2, 118, 120.

46. *Diary* 1, 52A.

47. *Diary* 3, 125.

48. *Diary* 3, 130.

49. *Diary* 1, 41A–B.

50. Sundkler, *Zulu Zion*, 128.

51. Unfortunately, Sundkler died before he had set his archives in order, and they were in considerable disarray.

52. Erica Bourgoignon, *Psychological Anthropology: An Introduction to Human Nature and Cultural Differences* (New York: Holt, Reinhart and Winston, 1979).

53. *Diary* 1, 48A.

54. *Diary* 3, 118–22.

55. *Hymnbook* 3, 38.

56. *Diary* 1, 9A–B.

4. Form as a Mnemonic Device: Cultural Texts and Cultural Memory

1. Benedict Anderson, *Imagined Communities: Reflections on the Origin and Spread of Nationalism*, rev. ed. (London: Verso, 1991).

2. Maurice Halbwachs, *Les Cadres sociaux de la mémoire* (Paris: Alcan, 1925).

3. The literature on this topic is abundant. For a first orientation, see Daniel L. Schacter, *Searching for Memory: The Brain, the Mind, and the Past* (New York: Basic Books, 1996).

4. Michael S. Roth, "We Are What We Remember (and Forget)," *Tikkun* 9, no. 6 (1994): 41–42, 91.

5. George Herbert Mead, *Mind, Self, and Society: From the Standpoint of a Social Behaviorist* (Chicago: University of Chicago Press, 1934).

6. Ernst Cassirer, *Philosophy of Symbolic Forms*, trans. Ralph Manheim, 4 vols. (New Haven: Yale University Press, 1953–96).

7. George Kubler, *The Shape of Time: Remarks on the History of Things* (New Haven: Yale University Press, 1962).

8. See also Horst Kirchner, "Vorgeschichte als Geschichte," *Die Welt als Geschichte* 11 (1951): 83–96, and idem, "Über das Verhältnis des schriftlosen frühgeschichtlichen Menschen zu seiner Geschichte," *Sociologus* 4 (1954): 9–22. I owe these references to Cornelius Holtorf; see especially his article "Towards a Chronology of Megaliths: Understanding Monumental Time and Cultural Memory," *Journal of European Archaeology* 4 (1996): 119–52.

9. Hans Belting, *Likeness and Presence : A History of the Image before the Era of Art*, trans. E. Jephcott (Chicago: University of Chicago Press, 1994).

10. The question of how to interpret the symbolic relation between bread and flesh, wine and blood, decided by the Fourth Lateran Council (1215) in favor of "being," was reopened during the Reformation, when Luther opted for "being" and Zwingli for "meaning."

11. See Kenneth Burke, *Language as Symbolic Action: Essays on Life, Literature, and Method* (Berkeley: University of California Press, 1966).

12. The Greek term *hyphisma*, from *hyphainein* ("to weave"), seems to be a precursor of the Latin notion of *textus* since it has been applied by the Sophists to verbal utterances.

13. Werner H. Kelber, *The Oral and the Written Gospel: The Hermeneutics of Speaking and Writing in the Synoptic Tradition, Mark, Paul, and Q*, Voices in Performance and Text (Bloomington: Indiana University Press, 1997 [1983]), 19, quoting John Colin Carothers, "Culture, Psychiatry, and the Written Word," *Psychiatry* 22 (1959): 312.

14. Konrad Ehlich, "Text und sprachliches Handeln: Die Entstehung von Texten aus dem Bedürfnis nach Überlieferung," in *Schrift und Gedächtnis: Beiträge zur Archäologie der literarischen Kommunikation*, ed. Aleida Assmann, Jan Assmann, and Christof Hardmeier (Munich: Fink, 1983), 24–43.

15. Clifford Geertz, *The Interpretation of Cultures: Selected Essays* (London: Hutchinson, 1975), xxx, understands by "cultural texts" not only written texts but also structured and repeatable performances of high importance for a given society such as the Balinese cock fight. The cultural text is a semiotic unit whose repeated actualization in the form of reading, recitation, or performance informs the identity of the participants in a normative and/or formative way.

16. See Ehlich, "Text und sprachliches Handeln," 30–31.

17. The ritualized form of institutionalizing the extended situation in oral societies creates that particular time structure that Jan Vansina has described as "floating gap" and Maurice Bloch characterized as a combination of sacred cyclical time and profane linear time. Time is divided into, on the one hand, a mythical past that is cyclically repeated and "re-presentified" in the various ritual performances and that remains always at the same distance to the linearly proceeding present and, on the other hand, a recent past that moves along linearly with the present. Where the cultural texts are predominantly codified in written form, the floating gap tends to disappear and the time-structure of the "extended situation" changes from ritual repetition to permanent presence.

18. After William Warburton, *The Divine Legation of Moses* (London, 1738), 1:192–93.

19. See Elizabeth Eisenstein, *The Printing Press as an Agent of Change: Communications and Cultural Transformations in Early Modern Europe* (Cambridge: Cambridge University Press, 1979).

20. Odile Hannes Steck, *Studien zu Tritojesaja*, BZAW 203 (Berlin: de Gruyter, 1991).

21. Paul Zumthor, *Introduction à la poésie orale* (Paris: Editions du Seuil, 1983), 245–61; ET = *Oral Poetry: An Introduction*, trans. Kathryn Murphy-Judy (Minneapolis: University of Minnesota Press, 1990). See also Aleida Assmann, "Schriftliche Folklore: Zur Entstehung und Funktion eines Überlieferungstyps," in *Schrift und Gedächtnis*, 175–93.

22. Michael Fishbane, *Biblical Interpretation in Ancient Israel* (Oxford: Clarendon, 1986).

23. G. Offner, "A propos de la sauvegarde des tablettes en Assyro-Babylonie," *Revue d'Assyriologie et d'Archéologie* 44 (1950): 135–43. The famous formula warning the reader "neither to add nor to subtract" from the written version is found in the Erra epic; see Michael Fishbane, "Varia Deuteronomica," *ZAW* 84 (1985): 350–52.

24. See José Faur, *Golden Doves with Silver Dots: Semiotics and Textuality in Rabbinic Tradition*, Jewish Literature and Culture (Bloomington: Indiana University Press, 1986).

25. Early Christianity, for example, was moving in a world already full of sacred and canonized texts that were sung, not just read, in temples, schools, and homes, and Christianity developed its own cultural texts by ways of oral and literate composition and transmission within the realm of this already existing canon. We can be sure that the early Christians reserved cantillation for the canonical texts of Jewish tradition and transmitted and performed their own texts in ordinary speech. This may be one of the reasons why Paul took to letter writing in order to create a body of normative and formative literature for the emerging movement. Letters would not trespass on the borders of canonized texts because they were to be read aloud—but not sung—to the community. The notion of "extended situation" includes both transmission and performance of cultural texts. Therefore, it is not only the distinction between orality and literacy that matters but also the distinction between discrete styles of performance such as cantillation and recitation.

26. "Symbolic pregnancy" is the English translation of Cassirer's concept of *Prägnanz* by Roger Stephenson, "Eine zarte Differenz: Cassirer on Goethe on the Symbol," in *Symbolic Forms and Cultural Studies: Ernst Cassirer's Theory of Culture*, ed. Cyrus Hamlin and John Michael Krois (New Haven: Yale University Press, 2004), xxx.

5. Memory in Oral Tradition

1. Salih Ugljanin, *The Song of Baghdad*, in *Serbocroatian Heroic Songs*, 14 vols., coll. Milman Parry, trans. and ed. Albert Bates Lord, Publications of the Milman Parry Collection (Cambridge: Harvard University Press, 1953–79), 2:8, lines 1–12.

2. Sources for quotations are as follows: *Homeri opera*, 4 vols., ed. David B. Monro and Thomas W. Allen (3rd ed.; Oxford: Clarendon, 1969); *Widsith*, ed. Kemp Malone (Copenhagen: Rosenkilde and Bagger, 1962); *Beowulf and the Fight at Finnsburg*, ed. Friedrich Klaeber (3rd ed.; Boston: Heath, 1950); *Serbocroatian Heroic Songs: The Wedding of Mustajbey's Son Bećirbey as Performed by Halil Bajgorić*, ed. John Miles Foley, Folklore Fellows Communications, vol. 283 (Helsinki: Academia Scientiarum Fennica, 2004), with eEdition, www.oraltradition.org/zbm; and the unpublished holdings of the Milman Parry Collection of Oral Literature at Harvard University (see Matthew W. Kay, *The Index of the Milman Parry Collection, 1933–35: Heroic Songs, Conversations, and Stories* [New York: Garland, 1995]). All translations are my own.

3. On the Great Divide model and its shortcomings, as well as a more nuanced model for oral tradition, see John Miles Foley, *How to Read an Oral Poem* (Urbana: University of Illinois Press, 2002). On the distinction between autonomous literacy, which assumes a single trajectory from oral tradition to writing and print for all cultures, and ideological literacy, which allows for variant forms of evolution, see Foley, *How to Read an Oral Poem*, 66–69.

4. Dell Hymes, in his "Ways of Speaking," in *Explorations in the Ethnography of Speaking*, ed. Richard Bauman and Joel Sherzer (2nd ed.; Cambridge: Cambridge University Press, 1989), 440, defines registers as "major speech styles associated with recurrent types of situations." See further John Miles Foley, *The Singer of Tales in Performance*, Voices in Performance and Text (Bloomington: Indiana University Press, 1995), 49–53, 82–92, 110–15, 150–75; idem, *How to Read an Oral Poem*, 109–24.

5. *Widsith*, 115.

6. On legendary poets as anthropomorphizations of oral tradition in ancient Greece, medieval England, twentieth-century Bosnia, and contemporary Mongolia, see John Miles Foley, *Homer's Traditional Art* (University Park: Pennsylvania State University Press, 1999), 49–62.

7. Here are the other occurrences of the *wordhord onleac* formula and a systemic variant (*modhord onleac*), with notation of the speaker and addressee in each case:

Andreas 316: wis on gewitte,   wordhord onleac
                wise in mind, he unlocked his word-hoard (Andreas
                to God)
Andreas 610: Ða gen weges weard   wordhord onleac
                Then yet the path's guardian unlocked his word-hoard
                (God to Andreas)
Andreas 172: meotud mancynnes,   modhord onleac
                mankind's measurer, unlocked his mind-hoard
                (God to Andreas)
Beowulf 259: werodes wisa,   wordhord onleac
                the troop's guide, unlocked his word-hoard (Beowulf
                to Wulfgar)

8. Differences among the varieties of language employed in Old English poems are due to a combination of differences among genres, composers, and local dialects (the last probably less important than the first two, based on comparative parallels that show the poetic register to be inherently multidialectal). But without any dependable information about the origins of the untitled, unattributed contents of the Anglo-Saxon poetic canon, we cannot judge the relative significance of these factors. The Old English poetic language is, however, quite similar across the spectrum of different kinds of poetry; see John Miles Foley, "How Genres Leak in Traditional Verse," in *Unlocking the Wordhord: Anglo-Saxon Studies in Memory of Edward B. Irving Jr.*, ed. Mark C. Amodio and Katherine O'Brien O'Keeffe (Toronto: University of Toronto Press, 2003). Compare the analysis of well-collected modern oral traditions, in which the levels of idiolect, dialect, and pan-traditional language can be assessed (e.g., John Miles Foley, *Traditional Oral Epic: The Odyssey, Beowulf, and the Serbo-Croatian Return Song* [Berkeley: University of California Press, 1990], 158–200, 278–328 on South Slavic oral epic).

9. For details, see Foley, *Traditional Oral Epic*, 201–39, 329–58.

10. See especially John Miles Foley, *Immanent Art: From Structure to Meaning in Traditional Oral Epic* (Bloomington: Indiana University Press, 1991), 190–242; on "large words," idem, *How to Read an Oral Poem*, 11–21. See also the concept of "indexed translation," as described in idem, *Singer of Tales*, 181–207.

11. For a full discussion of this traditional "word," see Foley, *Immanent Art*, 214–23.

12. See also the South Slavic verb *turati* ("drive out," "impel"), conventionally used to describe the demanding physical activity of the *guslar*'s oral performance.

13. On the role of music in South Slavic epic, see H. Wakefield Foster, "The Role of Music," in *The Wedding*, ed. Foley.

14. This passage is drawn from my edition-in-progress of Bašić's performance; for details on the recording, see Kay, *Index*, 221, no. 6597a. For a full edition and translation of a South Slavic oral epic from the same region of Stolac in central Hercegovina, see Foley, *The Wedding*, with eEdition, http://www.oraltradition.org/zbm.

15. On the composite nature of "words" in oral tradition, which the singers themselves identify as phrases, scenes, and entire story-patterns (but never the typographically or lexically defined increments we denote by that term), see Foley, *How to Read an Oral Poem*, 11–21.

16. This is the "thesis statement" for the Pathways Project (www.pathwaysproject.org), a multimedia undertaking that consists of a book, *Pathways of the Mind: Oral Tradition and the Internet* (by John Miles Foley [Urbana: University of Illinois Press, 2007]) embedded in a suite of electronic media: a developmental blog (http://www.otandit.blogspot.com), eEditions (http://www.oraltradition.org/zbm), eCompanions (http://oraltradition.org/hrop), a tagged and searchable database, and an aggregator. See the Pathways Project Web site for further details.

6. Tradition in the Mouth of the Hero:
Jesus as an Interpreter of Scripture

1. Richard P. Martin, *The Language of Heroes: Speech and Performance in The Iliad* (Ithaca: Cornell University Press, 1989), 146.

2. Ibid., xiv.

3. Ibid., 231–39. Martin (233–34) cites examples of the near-merger of poet and hero in the epic traditions of the Nyanga in Africa, the Turkic *Körogh* epic, and Burjat performances of the Geser epic in Central Asia. See Daniel P. Biebuyck, "The African Heroic Epic," in *Heroic Epic and Saga: An Introduction to the World's Great Folk Epics*, ed. Felix J. Oinas (Bloomington: Indiana University Press, 1978), 351; Ilhan Basgöz, "The Epic Tradition among the Turkic Peoples," in *Heroic Epic and Saga*, 314–17; G. M. H. Shoolbraid, *The Oral Epic of Siberia and Central Asia* (Bloomington: Indiana University Press, 1975), 2, 24. See also the example of the Irish *Táin*, where the poet Muirgen sings as though he were the hero Fergus himself; this example is discussed in Casey Dué and Gregory Nagy, "Illuminating the Classics with the Heroes of Philostratus," in *Philostratus's Heroikos: Religion and Cultural Identity in the Third Century c.e.*, ed. Ellen Bradshaw Aitken and Jennifer K. Berenson Maclean, Writings from the Greco-Roman World, vol. 6 (Atlanta:

SBL, 2004), 56–57. For a translation of the *Táin*, see Thomas Kinsella, *The Táin: From the Irish Epic Táin Bó Cuailnge* (Oxford: Oxford University Press, 1969).

4. For a review of the recent scholarship on Jesus as a hero, see Jennifer K. Berenson Maclean, "Jesus as Cult Hero in the Fourth Gospel," in *Philostratus's Heroikos*, 195–99. Arguments that patterns for stories about heroes provided models for stories about Jesus include Alan Dundes, "The Hero Pattern and the Life of Jesus," in *In Quest of the Hero*, ed. Robert A. Segal, Mythos (Princeton: Princeton University Press, 1990), 179–223; David E. Aune, "Heracles and Christ: Heracles Imagery in the Christology of Early Christianity," in *Greeks, Romans, and Christians: Essays in Honor of Abraham J. Malherbe*, ed. David L. Balch, Everett Ferguson, and Wayne A. Meeks (Minneapolis: Fortress Press, 1990), 3–19; Harold W. Attridge, "Liberating Death's Captives: Reconsideration of an Early Christian Myth," in *Gnosticism and the Early Christian World: In Honor of James M. Robinson*, ed. James E. Goehring et al. (Sonoma, Calif.: Polebridge, 1990), 103–15; and Gregory J. Riley, *One Jesus, Many Christs: How Jesus Inspired Not One True Christianity, But Many* (San Francisco: HarperSanFrancisco, 1997). On the influence of the biography of the poet-hero, such as Aesop, see Adela Yarbro Collins, "Finding Meaning in the Death of Jesus," *Journal of Religion* 78 (1998): 175–96; and Lawrence M. Wills, *The Quest for the Historical Gospel: Mark, John, and the Origins of the Gospel Genre* (London: Routledge, 1997).

5. On the influence of hero cult on early beliefs about Jesus, see Samson Eitrem, *"Heros,"* PW 8.1 (1913): cols. 1111–45; Arthur Darby Nock, "The Cult of Heroes," *HTR* 37 (1944): 141–74; reprinted in *Essays on Religion in the Ancient World*, ed. Zeph Stewart (Oxford: Oxford University Press, 1972), 2:575–602; and Hans Dieter Betz, "Heroenverehrung und Christusglaube: Religionsgeschichtliche Beobachtungen zu Philostrats *Heroicus*," in *Griechische und Römische Religion*, vol. 2 of *Geschichte—Tradition—Reflexion: Festschrift für Martin Hengel zum 70. Geburtstag*, ed. Hubert Cancik, Hermann Lichtenberger, and Peter Schäfer (Tübingen: Mohr Siebeck, 1996), 119–39; ET = "Hero Worship and Christian Beliefs: Observations from the History of Religion on Philostratus's *Heroikos*," in *Philostratus's Heroikos*, 25–47.

6. See Gregory Nagy, *Pindar's Homer: The Lyric Possession of an Epic Past* (Baltimore: Johns Hopkins University Press, 1990), 29–50; idem, *Poetry as Performance: Homer and Beyond* (Cambridge: Cambridge University Press, 1996), 39–58; Ellen Bradshaw Aitken, *Jesus' Death in Early Christian Memory: The Poetics of the Passion*, Novum Testamentum et Orbis Antiquus SUNT 53 (Göttingen: Vandenhoeck & Ruprecht, 2004), 14–16.

7. On activating the presence of the cult hero through cult, see Gregory Nagy, "The Sign of the Hero: A Prologue," in *Flavius Philostratus: Heroikos*, trans. and ed. Jennifer K. Berenson Maclean and Ellen Bradshaw Aitken, Writings from the Greco-Roman World, vol. 1 (Atlanta: SBL, 2001), xxix.

8. Milman Parry, "Studies in the Epic Technique of Oral Verse-Making, I: Homer and Homeric Style," *Harvard Studies in Classical Philology* 41 (1930): 73–147; idem, *The Making of Homeric Verse: The Collected Papers of Milman Parry*, ed. Adam Parry (Oxford: Oxford University Press, 1987 [1971]). Of the writings of Albert Bates Lord, see particularly *The Singer of Tales*, Studies in Comparative Literature 24 (Cambridge: Harvard University Press, 1960); *Epic Singers and Oral Tradition*, Myth and Poetics (Ithaca: Cornell University Press, 1991); and *The Singer Resumes the Tale*, ed. Mary Louise Lord, Myth and Poetics (Ithaca: Cornell University Press, 1995).

9. Gregory Nagy, *The Best of the Achaeans: Concepts of the Hero in Archaic Greek Poetry* (Baltimore: Johns Hopkins University Press, 1979); *Pindar's Homer*, *Poetry as Performance*.

10. Leonard Muellner, *The Meaning of Homeric Eychomai through Its Formulas*, Innsbrucker Beiträge zur Sprachwissenschaft 13 (Innsbruck: Institut für Sprachwissenschaft der Universität Innsbruck, 1976), and *The Anger of Achilles: Mênis in Greek Epic*, Myth and Poetics (Ithaca: Cornell University Press, 1996).

11. See particularly Nicole Loraux, *L'invention d'Athènes: Histoire de l'oraison funèbre dans la "cité classique,"* Civilisations et sociétés 65 (Paris: Éditions de l'École des hautes études en sciences sociales, 1981); ET = *The Invention of Athens: The Funeral Oration in the Classical City*, trans. Alan Sheridan (Cambridge: Harvard University Press, 1986).

12. Martin, *The Language of Heroes*.

13. Corinne Ondine Pache, *Baby and Child Heroes in Ancient Greece* (Urbana: University of Illinois Press, 2004).

14. Casey Dué, *Homeric Variations on a Lament by Briseis*, Greek Studies (Lanham, Md.: Rowman & Littlefield, 2002).

15. Angelo Brelich, *Gli eroi greci: Un problema storico-religioso* (Rome: Edizioni dell'Ateneo, 1958); Nock, *The Cult of Heroes*; Dennis D. Hughes, "Hero Cult, Heroic Honors, Heroic Dead: Some Developments in the Hellenistic and Roman Periods," in *Ancient Greek Hero Cult: Proceedings of the Fifth International Seminar on Ancient Greek Hero Cult, Göteborg University, April 21–23, 1995*, ed. Robin Hägg (Stockholm: Svenska Institutet I Athen, 1999).

16. See Jennifer K. Berenson Maclean and Ellen Bradshaw Aitken, "Introduction," in *Flavius Philostratus: Heroikos*, lxxii–lxxv. On the regional

interests of Philostratus, see Simone Follet, "Philostratus's *Heroikos and the Regions of the Northern Aegean*," in *Philostratus's Heroikos*, 221–36.

17. See, for example, the range of essays contained in *Philostratus's Heroikos*.

18. Maclean and Aitken, "Introduction," lx–lxii; Nagy, "The Sign of the Hero," xxx–xxxv.

19. For a full discussion of the issues of dating, authorship, and occasion for the *Heroikos*, see Maclean and Aitken, "Introduction," xlv–l, lxxvi–lxxxvii; Aitken, "Why a Phoenician? A Proposal for the Historical Occasion for the *Heroikos*," in *Philostratus's Heroikos*, 267–84; Friedrich Solmsen, "Philostratos," PW 20.1 (1941): cols. 124–77; Friedrich Solmsen, "Some Works of Philostratus the Elder," *Transactions of the American Philological Association* 71 (1940): 556–72.

20. Nagy, "The Sign of the Hero," xxx; Martin, *The Language of Heroes*, xiv.

21. See, for example, Dictys of Crete, *Journal of the Trojan War*; and the discussion in Stefan Merkle, "Telling the Truth of the Trojan War: The Eyewitness Account of Dictys of Crete," in *The Search for the Ancient Novel*, ed. Joseph Tatum (Baltimore: Johns Hopkins University Press, 1994); Ewen L. Bowie, "Philostratus: Writer of Fiction," in *Greek Fiction: The Greek Novel in Context*, ed. J. R. Morgan and Richard Stoneman (New York: Routledge, 1994); Dué and Nagy, "Illuminating the Classics," 53–56.

22. Dio Chrysostom *Troikos [Oration* 11] 38; see also the discussion of the correction of Homer in Francesca Mestre, "Refuting Homer in the *Heroikos* of Philostratus," in *Philostratus's Heroikos*, 127–41; Glen W. Bowersock, *Fiction as History: Nero to Julian* (Berkeley: University of California Press, 1994).

23. Nagy, "The Sign of the Hero," xxx.

24. See Corinne Ondine Pache, "Singing Heroes: The Poetics of Hero Cult in the *Heroikos*," in *Philostratus's Heroikos*, 3–24; and Jennifer K. Berenson Maclean, "The αἶνοι of the *Heroikos* and the Unfolding Transformation of the Phoenician Merchant," in *Philostratus's Heroikos*, 237–50.

25. See, for example, François Bovon, *Luke 1: A Commentary on the Gospel of Luke 1:1—9:50*, trans. Christine M. Thomas, Hermeneia (Minneapolis: Fortress Press, 2002), 153–54; idem, *Luke the Theologian: Thirty-three Years of Research: 1950–1983*, trans. K. McKinney, Pittsburgh Theological Monograph Series 12 (Allison Park, Pa.: Pickwick, 1987), 84–90, 101–8; C. F. Evans, *Saint Luke*, TPI New Testament Commentaries (Philadelphia: Trinity Press International, 1990), 272; Robert C. Tannehill, *The Narrative Unity*

of Luke-Acts: A Literary Interpretation, vol. 1: *The Gospel According to Luke* (Philadelphia: Fortress Press, 1986), 80, 224.

26. Luke 24:30; compare Luke 22:19; see the discussion in Evans, *St. Luke*, 912–13; Tannehill, *Narrative Unity*, 1.289–92.

27. Evans, *St. Luke*, 786–91; Dennis E. Smith, *From Symposium to Eucharist: The Banquet in the Early Christian World* (Minneapolis: Fortress Press, 2003), 262–63, 357–58; Jonathan Brumberg-Kraus, "Symposium Scenes in Luke's Gospel with Special Attention to the Last Supper," (Ph.D. diss., Vanderbilt University, 1991).

28. Harold W. Attridge, "Divine Dialogue in Hebrews," a paper presented at the International Meeting of the Society of Biblical Literature, Rome, July 11, 2001.

29. Aitken, *Jesus' Death*, 130–64.

30. Ellen Bradshaw Aitken, "Wily, Wise, and Worldly: Instruction and the Formation of Character in the Epistle to the Hebrews," in *The Changing Face of Judaism, Christianity and Other Greco-Roman Religions in Antiquity*, ed. Ian Henderson and Gerbern S. Oegema, Studien zu den Jüdischen Schriften aus hellenistisch-römischer Zeit 2 (Gütersloh: Gütersloher, 2006), 294–305.

31. On the composition of Hebrews as indebted to homiletical forms and practices, see Lawrence Wills, "The Form of the Sermon in Hellenistic Judaism and Early Christianity," *HTR* 77 (1984): 277–99; C. Clifton Black, "The Rhetorical Form of the Hellenistic Jewish and Early Christian Sermon: A Response to Lawrence Wills [77:277–299, 1984]" *HTR* 81 (1988): 1–18; Harold W. Attridge, "Paraenesis in a Homily (λόγος παρακλήσεως)," *Semeia* 50 (1990): 211–26; Alistair Stewart-Sykes, *From Prophesy to Preaching: A Search for the Origins of the Christian Homily*, Vigiliae christianae Supplement 59 (Leiden: Brill, 2001), 158–69.

32. The Gospel of John contains considerable material for such an analysis, including many indications of the intimacy of relationship with Jesus developed through cultic devotion, an intimacy that provides the means for understanding Jesus' words; see Maclean, "Jesus as Cult Hero."

33. An earlier version of this chapter was presented in a special session "Hero Cult and Early Christianity" at the Annual Meeting of the Society of Biblical Literature on November 22, 2004, in San Antonio. I thank Jennifer K. Berenson Maclean for her collaboration in organizing the session, as well as for years of discussion on the topic. I am also grateful to the other participants—Corinne Pache, James Skedros, and Elizabeth Penland—for their helpful comments, and to Leonard Rutgers for offering space within

the Late Antiquity in Interdisciplinary Perspective group's activities for such
an exchange of ideas.

7. Jesus and the Canon:
The Early Jesus Traditions in the Context
of the Origins of the New Testament Canon

1. See also Jens Schröter, "'Die Kirche besitzt vier Evangelien, die
Häresie viele,' Die Entstehung des Neuen Testaments im Kontext der früh-
christlichen Geschichte und Literatur," *Bibel und Kirche* 60 (2005).

2. For a recent overview of the origins and reception of the New Testament canon, see Hermann von Lips, *Der neutestamentliche Kanon: Seine
Geschichte und Bedeutung* (Zürich: Theologischer, 2004).

3. See also Heinz Ohme, "Kanon," in *Lexikon der antiken christlichen
Literatur*, ed. Siegmar Döpp and Wilhelm Geerlings (3rd ed.; Freiburg:
Herder, 2002), 422–24; ET = *Dictionary of Early Christian Literature*, trans.
Matthew O'Connell (New York: Crossroad, 2000).

4. Cf. *1 Clem.* 7:2. There the explication of *metanoia* is introduced with
a reference to the "glorious and venerable rule of our tradition" (εὐκλεὴς καὶ
σεμνὸν τῆς παραδόσεως ἡμῶν κανόνα).

5. Thus, for example, Irenaeus, *Adversus haereses* 3.15.1. In this usage
the word is frequently applied in connection with the rejection of "heretical"
teachings, such as those of Marcion or Valentinus; so, for example, Tertullian,
Adversus Marcionem 4.2.5.

6. *1 Clem.* 41:1 speaks of the "rules of . . . ministration" (τῆς λειτουργίας
. . . κανόν) of the community members.

7. In Eusebius we find the note that Hippolytus established a sixteen-
year canon for determining the date of Easter (κανὼν ἑκκαιδεκαέτηρος
περὶ τοῦ πάσχα) (*Historia ecclesiastica* 5.24.6).

8. Thus, for example, by Tertullian, *De praescriptione haereticorum* 13;
De virginibus velandis 1.

9. See also A. M. Ritter, "Glaubensbekenntnis(se) V. Alte Kirche," *TRE*
13 (1984), 405–6; Hans von Campenhausen, "Das Bekenntnis im Urchris-
tentum," *ZNW* 63 (1972): 226–27. Compare Wolfram Kinzig, "'. . . Natum
et passum etc.' Zur Geschichte der Tauffragen in der lateinischer Kirche bis
zu Luther," in Wolfram Kinzig, Christoph Markschies, and Markus Vinzent,
*Tauffragen und Bekenntnis: Studien zur sogenannten "Traditio apostolica," zu den
"Interrogationes de fide" und zum "Römischen Glaubensbekenntnis,"* Arbeiten zur
Kirchengeschichte 74 (Berlin: de Gruyter, 1999), 75–183.

10. Thus, for example, Eusebius reports that Dionysius of Corinth
opposed the heresy of Marcion in a letter to the Nicomedians, referring to

the "canon of truth" (*Historia ecclesiastica* 4.23.4). Later it is said that the early bishops of Asia did not go their own way in regard to the date of Easter but adhered to the "canon of faith" (*Historia ecclesiastica* 5.24.6). In 6.13.3 Eusebius mentions among the writings of Clement of Alexandria an "ecclesiastical canon" (κανὼν ἐκκλησιαστικός). Irenaeus regularly uses the expression "canon of truth"; for Tertullian this can also be called the canon/rule of faith, of God, of church discipline, or of Scripture. See also Hans von Campenhausen, *Die Entstehung der christlichen Bibel*, Beiträge zur historischen Theologie 39 (Tübingen: Mohr, 1968), 333–34; ET = *The Formation of the Christian Bible*, trans. J. A. Baker (Philadelphia: Fortress Press, 1977).

11. Examples include the title of the "Apocryphon of John" and the beginning of the *Gospel of Thomas*, in which the words of Jesus are described as "hidden" or "secret" (λόγοι ἀπόκρυφοι).

12. By contrast, in current usage—for example, in the collection edited by Wilhelm Schneemelcher—"apocrypha" is used neutrally to designate the writings that did not find entry into the canon but nevertheless are important witnesses to the history of early Christianity.

13. The texts are in Theodor Zahn, *Geschichte des neutestamentlichen Kanons*, vol. 2: *Urkunden und Belege zum ersten und dritten Band*, Part 1 (Erlangen: A. Deichert, 1890), 202, 210–12.

14. Hans von Campenhausen has described this process very accurately. See von Campennhausen, *Entstehung*, 379–80: "The Bible was never regarded as the sole source of the Christian faith. . . . The church . . . always lives at the same time and primarily out of tradition. . . . Scripture never suppresses and replaces the . . . church's proclamation, which holds fast to the original 'guideline of truth.' This 'guideline' . . . is not a norm superior to Sacred Scripture, but shares with it the same beginnings in the original preaching of the apostles, and therefore agrees with it in substance."

15. Ernst Käsemann, "Begründet der neutestamentliche Kanon die Einheit der Kirche?" in *Exegetische Versuche und Besinnungen* (Göttingen: Vandenhoeck & Ruprecht, 1964), 1:221.

16. Ibid., 221–23.

17. See also Michael Wolter, "Die Vielfalt der Schrift und die Einheit des Kanons," in *Die Einheit der Schrift und die Vielfalt des Kanons/The Unity of Scripture and the Diversity of the Canon*, ed. John Barton and Michael Wolter, BZNW 118 (Berlin: de Gruyter, 2003), 48–49.

18. Irenaeus, *Adversus haereses* 1.10.1-2, in *Early Christian Fathers*, ed. and trans. Cyril C. Richardson (New York: Macmillan, 1970), 360.

19. In speaking of Gospels that have *become* canonical or apocryphal, I am adopting a highly appropriate formulation by Dieter Lührmann. See his *Fragmente apokryph gewordener Evangelien in griechischer und lateinischer*

Sprache (Marburg: N. G. Elwert, 2000); idem, *Die apokryph gewordenen Evangelien: Studien zu neuen Texten und zu neuen Fragen* (Leiden: Brill, 2004).

20. Of course there are those who reject a preference for Gospels that have been made canonical by reversing the process and uncritically giving the apocrypha preference in regard to the question of the historical Jesus. Hans-Josef Klauck, by contrast, has recently offered a balanced introduction to the apocryphal Gospels: *Apocryphal Gospels: An Introduction*, trans. Brian McNeil (London: T & T Clark, 2003).

21. Recently, for example, by Elaine Pagels, *Beyond Belief: The Secret Gospel of Thomas* (New York: Random House, 2003).

22. On this see my introductions to *The Gospel of Thomas* in Jens Schröter and Hans-Gebhard Bethge, "Das Evangelium nach Thomas," in *Nag Hammadi Deutsch*, ed. Hans-Martin Schenke, Hans-Gebhard Bethge, and Ursula Ulrike Kaiser, vol. 1: *Nag Hammadi Codices I.1–V.1* (Berlin: de Gruyter, 2001), 151–63, and in *Antike christliche Apokryphen*, ed. Christoph Markschies (Tübingen: Mohr, forthcoming).

23. The remarks on this point originated in suggestions I received from Werner Kelber during our conversations in November 2004.

24. Thus, for example, the position of the widely known textbook by Kurt and Barbara Aland, which has also been translated into English: *Der Text des Neuen Testaments: Einführung in die wissenschaftlichen Ausgaben sowie in Theorie und Praxis der modernen Textkritik* (2nd ed.; Stuttgart, 1989), 284: "Only one reading can be the original, no matter how many variants of the passage exist." ET = *The Text of the New Testament: An Introduction to the Critical Editions and to the Theory and Practice of Modern Textual Criticism*, trans. Erroll F. Rhodes (Grand Rapids, Mich.: Eerdmans, 1987).

25. Two of the most important contributions to this development are David C. Parker, *The Living Text of the Gospels* (Cambridge: Cambridge University Press, 1997), and Eldon J. Epp, "The Multivalence of the Term 'Original Text' in Textual Criticism," *HTR* 92 (1999): 245–81.

26. The edition of the New Testament published in Cambridge in 1881–82 by B. F. Westcott and F. J. A. Hort bore the title *The New Testament in Its Original Greek*.

27. Thus von Campenhausen, *Entstehung*, 169: "This complex [i.e., the Jesus traditions and the Gospel literature] constitutes the starting point of 'canonical' development and will form the first focus of the later 'New Testament.'"

28. For what follows see also Jens Schröter, "Anfänge der Jesusüberlieferung: Überlieferungsgeschichtliche Beobachtungen zu einem Bereich urchristlicher Theologiegeschichte," *NTS* 50 (2004): 58–70.

29. This is especially evident in the Gospel of John, where we find antic-ipations of the time after Easter embedded even within the description of Jesus' earthly activity (cf. John 2:22; 7:39; 12:16; 20:9). Only after Jesus has been glorified can his words and the scriptures be understood; only when he has returned to the Father will he send the Paraclete (John 14:16, 26; 15:26; 16:7, 13). On the basis of this post-Easter perspective, Jesus can even say that his going away is good for the disciples, because otherwise the Paraclete would not come (16:7).

30. This teaching could be introduced without attribution to an author-ity (e.g., in Paul and 1 Peter), affirmed under the authority of James, the brother of the Lord (Letter of James), or be regarded as "The Teaching of the Apostles" (*Didache*).

31. This is evident in the expression "beginning of the Gospel" (ἀρχὴ τοῦ εὐαγγελίου) in Mark 1:1—independently of the question of whether it should apply to the Gospel of Mark as a whole or to the appearance of the Baptizer that is described immediately afterward.

32. *Didache* 8:2: μηδὲ προσεύχεσθε ὡς οἱ ὑποκριταί, ἀλλ᾽ ὡς ἐκέ-λευσεν ὁ κύριος ἐν τῷ εὐαγγελίῳ αὐτοῦ, οὕτως προσεύχεσθε.

33 Thus, for example, the expression in 4:4 has thematic links to Luke 12:4-5 // Matt 10:28; Acts 4:19 (cf. 5:29), while that in 15:4 is related to Acts 20:35.

34. If the Pastoral Letters were written only after Marcion's "canon" existed (thus again recently von Lips, *Kanon*, 51–53, modifying von Campenhausen's thesis), the time of writing would not be far from that of *2 Clement*.

35. First Timothy, where the saying is applied to the presbyters, agrees with the Lukan wording; the *Didache* agrees with the Matthean.

36. See also Jürgen Roloff, *Der erste Brief an Timotheus*, Evangelisch-katholischer Kommentar 15 (Neukirchen-Vluyn: Neukirchener, 1988), 305–6, n. 409.

37. It cannot be clearly determined whether the author of *2 Clement* used a written Gospel containing explicitly quoted words of the Lord. Speak-ing for this are, for example, Helmut Koester, *Ancient Christian Gospels: Their History and Development* (Philadelphia: Trinity Press International, 1990), 17–18, 353; Lührmann, *Fragmente*, 132–37; Andreas Lindemann, *Die Cle-mensbriefe*, Handbuch zum Neuen Testament 17, Die Apostolischen Väter 1 (Tübingen: Mohr Siebeck, 1992), 194. Compare von Lips, *Kanon*, 37.

38. See also Koester, *Gospels*, 66–71.

39. There is a thorough discussion of the passage in Parker, *Living Text*, 31–48.

40. See also Lührmann, *Evangelien*, 191–215, as well as the Appendix on the history of tradition, 221–28. Lührmann connects this with Eusebius's remark about a story told by Papias concerning a woman accused of many sins. According to Eusebius this episode is drawn from the *Gospel of the Hebrews*, from which Didymus might later have taken it.

41. Other significant examples to which the same applies include the ending of the Gospel of Mark and the address of the Letter to the Ephesians.

42. This is not to say—and let me make this absolutely clear—that the prayer could not have originated with Jesus. There are, rather, a number of good reasons to suppose that it did. Here, in contrast, the issue is the process of tradition, which shows itself to have been quite free and not aimed at the preservation of the one original form.

43. See also the corresponding chapter in Parker, *Living Text*, 49–74.

44. See also Koester, *Gospels*, 353.

45. See also Klauck, *Evangelien*, 36–40; Lührmann, *Fragmente*, 142–53; and http://www.user.uni-bremen.de/~wie/Egerton/Egerton_home.html.

46. See also Lührmann, *Evangelien*, 125–43.

47. See also Klauck, *Evangelien*, 110–18; Lührmann, *Fragmente*, 72–95; Uwe-Karsten Plisch, *Verborgene Worte Jesu—verworfene Evangelien: Apokryphe Schriften des frühen Christentums* (Berlin: Evangelische Haupt-Bibelgesellschaft und von Cansteinsche Bibelanstalt, 2002), 17–25; and http://www.earlychristianwritings.com/gospelpeter.html; http://www-user.uni-bremen.de/~wie/texteapo/Petrus_einleit.html.

48. For discussion of these fragments and further aspects of the tradition history of the *Gospel of Peter*, see Lührmann, *Evangelien*, 55–104.

49. See Klauck, *Evangelien*, 142–62; Plisch, *Verborgene Worte*, 93–122; and http://home.epix.net/~miser17/Thomas.html; http://de.wikipedia.org/wiki/Thomasevangelium.

50. For the Greek fragments see Lührmann, *Fragmente*, 106–31; idem, *Evangelien*, 144–81.

51. See Klauck, *Evangelien*, 207–18; Plisch, *Verborgene Worte*, 137–42; and http://www.thenazareneway.com/the_gospel_of_mary_magdalene.htm.

52. For these, see Lührmann, *Fragmente*, 62–71; idem, *Evangelien*, 105–24.

53. See Judith Hartenstein, *Die zweite Lehre: Erscheinungen des Auferstandenen als Rahmenerzählungen frühchristlicher Dialoge*, Texte und Untersuchungen 146 (Berlin: Akademie, 2000), 157–58.

54. I will remark, only in passing, that the evaluation of many apocryphal writings in some parts of present Jesus research is also problematic because it reclaims later, often anti-Jewish traditions for Jesus himself and

thus arrives at an image of Jesus that is not very plausible historically. Clearly different in direction, by contrast, are the depictions of Jesus by, for example, E. P. Sanders, *The Historical Figure of Jesus* (London: Allen Lane/Penguin, 1993), and Seán Freyne, *Jesus, a Jewish Galilean: A New Reading of the Jesus Story* (London: T & T Clark, 2004).

55. This title is found as a *subscriptio* in the *Gospel of Thomas* and in the *Gospel of Mary*, in the form "Gospel according to . . ." A "so-called Gospel of Peter" is mentioned by Eusebius in connection with a letter of Bishop Serapion to the community at Rhossus (*Historia ecclesiastica* 6.12.3-6).

56. Justin, *Apologia* 66.3. The former also appears at 67.3 and many times in *Dialogus cum Tryphone*.

57. Here I am adopting formulations from Parker, who characterizes the Gospels as follows: "The terminology which I adopt here is to characterise the text of the Gospels as a free, or perhaps as a living, text." Earlier he writes, "the concept of a Gospel that is fixed in shape, authoritative, and final as a piece of literature has to be abandoned" (*Living Text*, 200, 93). Epp, "Multivalence," 278 and n. 106, uses these formulations to characterize the canon.

58. Luke emphasizes that he "investigated everything . . . from the very first" (παρηκολουθηκότι ἄνωθεν πᾶσιν), that he did so carefully (ἀκριβῶς), and that he then wrote an orderly account (καθεξῆς σοι γράψαι).

59. Καθὼς παρέδοσαν ἡμῖν οἱ ἀπ' ἀρχῆς αὐτόπται καὶ ὑπηρέται γενόμενοι τοῦ λόγου. Thus, he is already looking forward, beyond the Gospel, to the Acts of the Apostles.

60. Eusebius, *Historia ecclesiastica* 3.39.15-16.

61. Ibid., 3.39.4: "For I did not imagine that things out of books would help me as much as the utterances of a living and abiding voice" (Eusebius, *The History of the Church from Christ to Constantine*, trans. and ed. G. A. Williamson [Harmondsworth: Penguin, 1965], 150).

62. Eusebius, *Historia ecclesiastica* 3.24.5-7.

63. Thus C. E. Hill, "What Papias Said about John (and Luke): A 'New' Papian Fragment," *JTS* 49 (1998): 582–629.

64. In Acts 20:29-30, within Paul's farewell speech, Luke mentions "savage wolves" who will threaten the flock from without, as well as men from within the community who will distort the truth in order to entice the disciples to follow them. Papias speaks of people who teach "commandments from other sources" (ἀλλότριαι ἐντολαί) rather than the truth (Eusebius, *Historia ecclesiastica* 3.39.3).

65. According to Eusebius, *Historia ecclesiastica* 6.25.11-14.

66. The first magisterial establishment of the authoritative writings was that of Trent—again in circumstances of theological controversy. To

that extent William Wrede's dictum that the canon was established by the "authority of the bishops and theologians" of the second to fourth centuries is in error. See his "Über Aufgabe und Methode der sogenannten neu-testamentlichen Theologie," in *Das Problem der Theologie des Neuen Testaments*, ed. Georg Strecker (Göttingen: Vandenhoeck & Ruprecht, 1975 [1897]), 85.

67. See T. C. Skeat, "The Oldest Manuscript of the Four Gospels?" *NTS* 43 (1997): 1–34; Graham N. Stanton, "The Fourfold Gospel," *NTS* 43 (1997): 322–23.

68. Irenaeus, *Adversus haereses* 3.11.7-9. It appears that here Irenaeus is already using an older document that associated the four Gospels with the vision of the four living creatures in human form from Ezekiel 1 and the reception of that figure in Revelation 4. See T. C. Skeat, "Irenaeus and the Four-Gospel Canon," *NTS* 34 (1992): 194–99.

69. Origen, *Homiliae in Lucam* 1.1.

70. See n. 61 above.

71. The same is true of the other New Testament writings, but here we continue to restrict our discussion to the Gospels.

72. Bart D. Ehrman, *The Orthodox Corruption of Scripture: The Effect of Early Christological Controversies on the Text of the New Testament* (New York: Oxford University Press, 1993), n. 276. See also the summary of his findings in his *Lost Christianities: The Battle for Scripture and the Faiths We Never Knew* (Oxford: Oxford University Press, 2003), 215–27.

73. Kurt Aland, "Der neue 'Standard-Text' in seinem Verhältnis zu den frühen Papyri und Majuskeln," in *New Testament Textual Criticism: Its Significance for Exegesis; Essays in Honour of Bruce M. Metzger*, ed. Eldon J. Epp and Gordon D. Fee (Oxford: Clarendon, 1981), 274–75.

74. Parker, *Living Text*, 208: "The quest for a single original text of the Gospels is driven by the same forces that have sought a single original saying of Jesus behind the different texts of different Gospels. Both quests are dubious."

75. Ibid., 188: "While early Christianity may have come to make lists of authoritative books, there were no authoritative copies of them."

76. Ibid., 196, 204: "That a Greek New Testament contains what it does is so natural to us that we need to be particularly careful to remember how much more a theoretical than a real entity the Greek New Testament was until the invention of printing. . . . There is a sense in which there is no such thing as either the New Testament or the Gospels. What is available to us is a number of reconstructions. . . . Some of these reconstructions are manuscripts. . . . Others are printed texts like Nestle–Aland."

8. The Interface of Orality and Literature
in the Gospel of Mark

1. See, for example, Paul Achtemeier, "*Omnes verbum sonat*: The New Testament and the Oral Environment of Late Western Antiquity," *JBL* 109 (1990): 3–27; Pieter J. J. Botha, "Mark's Story as Oral Traditional Literature: Rethinking the Transmission of Some Traditions about Jesus," *Hervormde Teologiese Studies* 47 (1991): 304–41; idem, "Letter Writing and Oral Communication in Antiquity: Suggested Implications for the Interpretation of Paul's Letter to the Galatians," *Scriptura* 42 (1992): 17–34; Joanna Dewey, "Textuality in an Oral Culture: A Survey of the Pauline Traditions," *Semeia* 65 (1994): 37–65; idem, "The Gospel of Mark as an Oral-Aural Event: Implications for Interpretation," in *The New Literary Criticism and the New Testament*, ed. E. S. Malbon and E. V. McKnight, JSNTSup 109 (Sheffield: Sheffield Academic, 1994), 145–63.

2. Werner H. Kelber, *The Oral and the Written Gospel: The Hermeneutics of Speaking and Writing in the Synoptic Gospels, Mark, Paul, and Q*, Voices in Performance and Text (Bloomington: Indiana University Press, 1997 [1983]).

3. John Miles Foley, *Oral Formulaic Theory and Research* (New York: Garland, 1985); *The Theory of Oral Composition: History and Methodology*, Folkloristics (Bloomington: Indiana University Press, 1988); *Traditional Oral Epic: The Odyssey, Beowulf, and the Serbo-Croatian Return Song* (Berkeley: University of California Press, 1990); *Immanent Art: From Structure to Meaning in Traditional Oral Epic* (Bloomington: Indiana University Press, 1991); idem, "Word-Power, Performance, and Tradition," *Journal of American Folklore* 105 (1992): 275–301; "Words in Tradition, Words in Text: A Response," *Semeia* 65 (1994): 169–80; *The Singer of Tales in Performance*, Voices in Performance and Text (Bloomington: Indiana University Press, 1995).

4. Jonathan A. Draper, "Wandering Radicalism or Purposeful Activity? Jesus and the Sending of Messengers in Mark 6:6-56," *Neotestamentica* 29, no. 2 (1995): 187–207; idem, *The Didache in Modern Research*, AGJU 37 (Leiden: Brill, 1996); Richard A. Horsley with Jonathan A. Draper, *Whoever Hears You Hears Me: Prophets, Performance, and Tradition in Q* (Harrisburg, Pa.: Trinity Press International, 1999).

5. Vernon K. Robbins, "Picking Up the Fragments: From Crossan's Analysis to Rhetorical Analysis," *Forum* 1, no. 2 (1985): 31–64, http://www.religion.emory.edu/faculty/robbins/Pdfs/Fragments.pdf; Burton L. Mack and Vernon K. Robbins, *Patterns of Persuasion in the New*

Testament (Sonoma, Calif.: Polebridge, 1989), http://www.religion.emory.edu
/faculty/robbins/Patterns.html; Burton L. Mack, *Rhetoric and the New Testament*, Guides to Biblical Scholarship (Minneapolis: Fortress Press, 1990);
Vernon K. Robbins, "Progymnastic Rhetorical Composition and Pre-Gospel
Traditions: A New Approach," in *The Synoptic Gospels: Source Criticism and
the New Literary Criticism*, ed. Camille Focant, BETL 110 (Leuven: Leuven University Press, 1993), 120–21, http://www.religion.emory.edu/faculty
/robbins/Pdfs/Progymnastic.pdf; idem, "The Present and Future of Rhetorical Analysis," in *The Rhetorical Analysis of Scripture: Essays from the 1995
London Conference*, ed. S. E. Porter and T. H. Olbricht, JSNTSup 146 (Sheffield: Sheffield Academic, 1997), 24–52, http://www.religion.emory.edu
/faculty/robbins/future/future24.html.

   6. Werner H. Kelber, "Jesus and Tradition: Words in Time, Words in
Space," *Semeia* 65 (1994): 139–67; "Modalities of Communication, Cognition, and Physiology of Perception: Orality, Rhetoric, Scribality," *Semeia* 65
(1994): 193–216.

   7. Robbins, "Progymnastic Rhetorical Composition," 120–21.

   8. Ronald F. Hock and Edward N. O'Neil, *The Chreia in Ancient Rhetoric: The Progymnasmata*, Texts and Translations 27, Graeco-Roman Religion
Series 9 (Atlanta: Scholars, 1986), 95.

   9. Whitney Shiner, *Proclaiming the Gospel: First-Century Performance of
Mark* (Harrisburg, Pa.: Trinity Press International, 2003).

   10. Ibid., 7.

   11. Quintilian, *Institutio oratoria* 10.1.16-19 (LCL), quoted in Shiner,
Proclaiming the Gospel, 3.

   12. Foley, "Words in Tradition," 170.

   13. Vernon K. Robbins, "Oral, Rhetorical, and Literary Cultures: A
Response," *Semeia* 65 (1994): 75–91.

   14. Kelber, "Jesus and Tradition," 159.

   15. Robbins, "Oral, Rhetorical, and Literary Cultures," 80. See Vernon
K. Robbins, "Writing as a Rhetorical Act in Plutarch and the Gospels," in
*Persuasive Artistry: Studies in New Testament Rhetoric in Honor of George A.
Kennedy*, ed. Duane F. Watson (Sheffield: JSOT), 157–86; Bernard Bran-
don Scott and Margaret E. Dean, "A Sound Mapping of the Sermon on
the Mount," *SBL Seminar Papers* 32 (1993): 672–725; Margaret E. Dean,
"The Grammar of Sound in Greek Texts: Toward a Method for Mapping the
Echoes of Speech in Writing," *ABR* 44 (1996): 53–70.

   16. Vernon K. Robbins, "Rhetorical Composition and Sources in the
Gospel of Thomas," in *Society of Biblical Literature 1997 Seminar Papers* (Atlanta:
Scholars, 1997), 86–114.

   17. Foley, *Singer of Tales*, 49–53, 82–92, 110–15, 150–75.

18. Ibid., 50, citing Dell Hymes, "Ways of Speaking," in *Explorations in the Ethnography of Speaking*, ed. Richard Bauman and Joel Sherzer (2nd ed.; Cambridge: Cambridge University Press, 1989), 440.

19. Foley, *Singer of Tales*, 50, citing M. A. K. Halliday, *Language as Social Semiotic: The Social Interpretation of Language and Meaning* (Baltimore: University Park Press, 1978), 111.

20. This translation of the *Gospel of Thomas* is from John S. Kloppenborg, Marvin W. Meyer, Stephen J. Patterson, and Michael G. Steinhauser, *Q-Thomas Reader* (Sonoma, Calif.: Polebridge, 1990).

21. For analysis of one dramatic instance of embedded recitation from the writings in Mark, see Vernon K. Robbins, "The Reversed Contextualization of Psalm 22 in the Markan Crucifixion: A Socio-Rhetorical Analysis," in *The Four Gospels 1992: Festschrift Frans Neirynck*, ed. F. van Segbroeck, C.M. Tuckett, G. Van Belle, J. Verheyden, BETL 100 (Leuven: Leuven University Press, 1992), 2:1161–83, http://www.religion.emory.edu/faculty/robbins/Pdfs/ReversedPs22Mark15.pdf.

22. Shiner, *Proclaiming the Gospel*, 162–65, 184–87.

23. Ibid., 164.

24. Scholars know, of course, that this "voice of Isaiah" is a merger of Exod 23:20 with Mal 3:1.

25. *Ho rhētheis* in Matt 3:3 is a divine passive (see also Matt 1:22; 2:15, 17; 4:14).

26. John 1:22-23 is an interesting alternative to all of the Synoptic Gospels, since it presents John the Baptist interpreting himself as the voice about which Isaiah spoke. In other words, in the Gospel of John the interface of oral and written is internal to the narrational voice of the Baptist himself.

27. Craig A. Evans, *Mark 8:27—16:20*, Word Biblical Commentary 34B (Nashville: Thomas Nelson, 2001), 228–30.

28. Ibid., 229–30.

29. Ibid., 229.

30. See Mark 2:25-26; 7:6-8; 9:11-13; 11:17-18; 12:35-37; 14:20-21, 27-28; see also 4:11-12; 15:34.

31. Vincent Taylor, *The Gospel according to Mark* (London: Macmillan, 1963), 476.

32. Ibid.

33. See Richard Valantasis, *The Gospel of Thomas* (London: Routledge, 1997), 143–50.

34. Matthew 21:43 is most probably a later addition; comparison of the Synoptic Gospels with one another brings focus on the parable itself in relation to Ps 118:22-23, rather than the extended dynamics of the narration internal to each Gospel.

35. It is likely that Matt 21:44, which is another recitation from the writings, has been added from Luke in later manuscripts. Therefore, this recitation is discussed only in the section below on the Lukan version of the story.

36. There are at least four instances in Mark that are either inaccurate or uncertain: (1) wording from Isaiah in Mark 1:2-4; (2) Abiathar as high priest when David gets the bread of presence (Mark 2:26); (3) the presence "in writings" that the Son of Man is to go through many sufferings and be treated with contempt (Mark 9:12); and (4) the presence "in writings" that people will do to Elijah "whatever they please" (Mark 9:13).

9. Memory Technology and the Composition of Mark

1. Werner H. Kelber, *The Oral and the Written Gospel: The Hermeneutics of Speaking and Writing in the Synoptic Tradition, Mark, Paul, and Q*, Voices in Performance and Text (Bloomington: Indiana University Press, 1997 [1983]).

2. Whitney Shiner, *Proclaiming the Gospel: First-Century Performance of Mark* (Harrisburg, Pa.: Trinity Press International, 2003).

3. Werner H. Kelber, "Biblical Hermeneutics and the Ancient Art of Communication: A Response," *Semeia* 39 (1987): 97–105; "Narrative as Interpretation and Interpretation of Narrative: Hermeneutical Reflections on the Gospels," *Semeia* 39 (1987): 107–33; "Modalities of Communication, Cognition, and Physiology of Perception: Orality, Rhetoric, and Scribality," *Semeia* 65 (1994): 193–216; "The Quest for the Historical Jesus from the Perspective of Medieval, Modern, and Post-Enlightenment Readings, and In View of Ancient Oral Aesthetics," in John Dominic Crossan, Luke Timothy Johnson, and Werner H. Kelber, *The Jesus Controversy: Perspectives in Conflict* (Harrisburg, Pa.: Trinity Press International, 1999).

4. Parry's essays have been collected in Milman Parry, *The Making of Homeric Verse: The Collected Papers of Milman Parry*, ed. Adam Parry (Oxford: Oxford University Press, 1971); Albert Bates Lord, *The Singer of Tales*, Studies in Comparative Literature 24 (Cambridge: Harvard University Press, 1960). The investigations of Parry and Lord had a significant influence on the works of Walter Ong and Eric Havelock, who were in turn important sources for the view of orality in Kelber's *The Oral and the Written Gospel* and for most discussions of orality among biblical scholars since that time.

5. Lord, *The Singer of Tales*, 30–123.

6. Kelber, *The Oral and the Written Gospel*, 44–139.

7. Pieter J. J. Botha, "Mark's Story as Oral Traditional Literature: Rethinking the Transmission of Some Traditions about Jesus," *Hervormde Teologiese Studies* 47 (1991): 304–31.

8. Ibid., 322.

9. Ibid., 317–19.

10. Lord, *The Singer of Tales*, 130.

11. Botha, "Mark's Story," 319–22.

12. Ibid., 319–22.

13. Robert Fowler, *Loaves and Fishes: The Function of the Feeding Stories in the Gospel of Mark*, SBL Dissertation Series 54 (Chico, Calif.: Scholars, 1981), 68–90.

14. Lord, *The Singer of Tales*, 25, 36.

15. A recent discussion of memory systems is found in Jocelyn Penny Small, *Wax Tablets of the Mind: Cognitive Studies of Memory and Literacy in Classical Antiquity* (London: Routledge, 1997), 81–137. This work also contains excellent discussions of the nature of ancient books and libraries, the process of writing and reading, and composition technique. For other discussions of memory in antiquity, see Frances A. Yates, *The Art of Memory* (Chicago: University of Chicago Press, 1966); Bromley Smith, "Hippias and a Lost Canon of Rhetoric," *The Quarterly Journal of Speech Education* 12 (1926): 129–45; L. A. Post, "Ancient Memory Systems," *The Classical Weekly* 15 (1932): 106–10; Donald E. Hargis, "Memory in Rhetoric," *Southern Speech Communication Journal* 17 (1951): 114–24; W. W. Meissner, "A Historical Note on Retention," *Journal of English and Germanic Philology* 59 (1958): 229–36; Wayne E. Hoogestraat, "Memory: The Lost Canon?" *The Quarterly Journal of Speech* 46 (1960): 141–47; G. B. Matthews, "Augustine on Speaking from Memory," *American Philosophical Quarterly* 2 (1965): 157–60; Thomas H. Olbricht, "Delivery and Memory," in *Handbook of Classical Rhetoric in the Hellenistic Period, 330 BC–AD 400*, ed. S. E. Porter (Leiden: Brill, 1997), 159–67; Heinrich Lausberg, *Handbook of Literary Rhetoric: A Foundation for Literary Study*, trans. M. T. Bliss, A. Jansen, and D. E. Orton (Leiden: Brill, 1998), 478–80. On the relationship of written texts, memory, and performance in classical Greece, see Rosalind Thomas, *Literacy and Orality in Ancient Greece* (Cambridge: Cambridge University Press, 1992), 113–27.

16. Quintilian, *Institutio oratoria* 11.2.44-45; 11.2.48-49.

17. Ibid., 11.2.32-35.

18. Cicero, *De oratore* 2.86.351–88.360; *Rhetorica ad Herennium* 3.16-24; Quintilian, *Institutio oratoria* 11.2.11-31. The system is fully explained in Yates, *Art of Memory*, 1–26, and Small, *Wax Tablets*, 81–116. Yates shows how the system was developed throughout European history.

19. Cicero, *De oratore* 1.34.157.

20. H. I. Marrou, *A History of Education in Antiquity*, trans. G. Lamb (New York: Mentor Books, 1964), 210–15, 363–64, 366.

21. Many of these observations about composition are based on the excellent discussion found in Small, *Wax Tablets*, 177–201.

22. Pliny the Younger, *Letters* 9.36 (LCL), cited in Small, *Wax Tablets*, 181.

23. Quintilian, *Institutio oratoria* 10.6.1–2 (LCL), cited in Small, *Wax Tablets*, 182.

24. Small, *Wax Tablets*, 185–87, citing T. J. Luce, *Livy: The Composition of His History* (Princeton: Princeton University Press, 1977), 144; C. B. R. Pelling, "Plutarch's Method of Work in the Roman Lives," *Journal of Hellenic Studies* 100 (1980): 91–92; Andrew R. Dyck, "The Fragments of Heliodorus Homericus," *Harvard Studies in Classical Philology* 95 (1993): 1–64.

25. Luce, *Livy*, 144.

26. Pelling, "Plutarch's Method," 92; Small, *Wax Tablets*, 185.

27. Shiner, *Proclaiming the Gospel*, 115–16.

28. Ibid.

10. A Prophet Like Moses and Elijah:
Popular Memory and Cultural Patterns in Mark

1. References to Werner Kelber's books and articles have profoundly influenced many New Testament scholars; see citations in the introduction.

2. I am also attempting to build on the important work of others such as John Miles Foley, Jan Assmann, and Martin Jaffee, cited in the introduction. I owe a special debt of gratitude to Alan Kirk and Tom Thatcher for leading me into the study of social memory; for a bibliography, see Alan Kirk and Tom Thatcher, eds., *Memory, Tradition, and Text: Uses of the Past in Early Christianity*, Semeia Studies 52 (Atlanta: SBL, 2005).

3. More fully explained in Richard A. Horsley, *Hearing the Whole Story: The Politics of Plot in Mark's Gospel* (Louisville, Ky.: Westminster John Knox, 2001); and Richard A. Horsley with Jonathan A. Draper, *Whoever Hears You Hears Me: Prophets, Performance, and Tradition in Q* (Harrisburg, Pa.: Trinity Press International, 1999), especially chapter 7.

4. Werner H. Kelber, "Jesus and Tradition: Words in Time and Words in Space," *Semeia* 65 (1994): 159.

5. The standard modern scholarly assumption is stated explicitly by Burton A. Mack, *A Myth of Innocence: Mark and Christian Origins* (Philadelphia: Fortress Press, 1988), 321–23: "Mark was a scholar. A reader of texts and a writer of texts. . . . Mark's Gospel was composed at a desk in a scholar's study lined with texts." Recent research on the limited literacy and availability of scrolls in antiquity make this appear as an anachronistic projection of modern scholarly print culture.

6. As explained in Horsley with Draper, *Whoever Hears You Hears Me*, 140–44; and Horsley, *Hearing the Whole Story*, 231–35.

7. Eugene Ulrich, *The Dead Sea Scrolls and the Origins of the Bible* (Grand Rapids, Mich.: Eerdmans, 1999).

8. Discussed in Richard A. Horsley, *Jesus and the Spiral of Violence: Popular Jewish Resistance in Roman Palestine* (Minneapolis: Fortress Press, 1995), 94–99.

9. James C. Scott, "Protest and Profanation: Agrarian Revolt and the Little Tradition," *Theory and Society* 4 (1977): 3–32, 159–210; applied to Jesus and Gospel materials in Horsley and Draper, *Whoever Hears You Hears Me*, especially chapter 5; Horsley, *Hearing the Whole Story*; and Richard A. Horsley, ed., *Hidden Transcripts and the Arts of Resistance: Applying the Work of James C. Scott to Jesus and Paul*, Semeia Studies (Atlanta: SBL, 2004).

10. Scott, "Protest and Profanation," 18.

11. Jan Assmann, *Das kulturelle Gedächtnis: Schrift, Erinnerung, und politische Identität in frühen Hochkulturen* (Munich: Beck, 1992), 72–80, 294–97; Kirk, "Social and Cultural Memory," in *Memory, Tradition, and Text*, 17.

12. John Bodnar, *Remaking America: Public Memory, Commemoration, and Patriotism in the Twentieth Century* (Princeton: Princeton University Press, 1992); Michael Schudson, *Watergate in American Memory: How We Remember, Forget, and Reconstruct the Past* (New York: Basic Books, 1992); Jeffrey K. Olick, "Collective Memory: The Two Cultures," *Sociological Theory* 17 (1999): 337–38.

13. Jeffrey K. Olick, "Social Memory Studies: From 'Collective Memory' to the Historical Sociology of Mnemonic Practices," *Annual Review of Sociology* 24 (1998): 126–27.

14. See, for example, George Mendenhall, "The Covenant Forms in Israelite Tradition," *Biblical Archaeologist* 17 (1954): 50–76; Delbert Hillers, *Covenant: The History of a Biblical Idea* (Baltimore: Johns Hopkins University Press, 1969).

15. Klaus Baltzer, *The Covenant Formulary* (Philadelphia: Fortress Press, 1971).

16. Horsley with Draper, *Whoever Hears You Hears Me*, chapter 9.

17. Horsley, *Hearing the Whole Story*, chapter 8.

18. See further Richard A. Horsley, "Popular Messianic Movements Around the Time of Jesus," *CBQ* 46 (1984): 471–95.

19. Fuller discussion and documentation in Richard A. Horsley, "'Like One of the Prophets of Old': Two Types of Popular Prophets at the Time of Jesus," *CBQ* 47 (1985): 435–63, and idem, "Popular Prophetic Movements at the Time of Jesus, Their Principal Features and Social Origins," *JSNT* 26 (1986): 3–27.

20. Fuller analysis and argument in Horsley, *Hearing the Whole Story*, chapter 10.

21. Assmann, *Das Kulturelle Gedächtnis*, 30.

22. Kirk, "Social and Cultural Memory," 7, 11.

23. See the studies of Philippe Joutard, *La Legend des Camisards* (Paris, 1977); and G. Lewis, "A Cevenol Community in Crisis: The Mystery of 'l'homme à moustache,'" *Past and Present* 109 (1985): 144–75; "social memory" analysis by James Fentress and Chris Wickham, *Social Memory* (Oxford: Blackwell, 1992) 87–114.

24. Fentress and Wickham, *Social Memory*, 92.

25. Ibid., 88.

26. Ibid.

27. Kirk, "Social and Cultural Memory," 15; Fentress and Wickham, *Social Memory*, 51; Michael Schudson, "The Presence in the Past versus the Past in the Present," *Communication* 11 (1989): 112; Yael Zerubavel, *Recovered Roots: Collective Memory and the Making of Israeli National Tradition* (Chicago: University of Chicago Press, 1995), 229.

28. Kirk, "Social and Cultural Memory," 17, citing Schudson, "Presence in the Past," 111; Roy Rosensweig and David Thelen, *The Presence of the Past: Popular Uses of History in American Life* (New York: Columbia University Press, 1998), 75; Fentress and Wickham, *Social Memory*, 108–9.

Contributors

Ellen Bradshaw Aitken, Associate Professor of Early Christian History and Literature at McGill University, is the author of *Jesus' Death in Early Christian Memory: The Poetics of the Passion* (Vandenhoeck & Ruprecht, 2004), as well as the co-editor and translator (with Jennifer K. Berenson Maclean) of the *Heroikos* of Flavius Philostratus (SBL, 2001). She is currently working on a book on the Epistle to the Hebrews in the context of Flavian Rome, in addition to various projects relating to early Christianity and hero cult.

Jan Assmann, Professor Emeritus of Egyptology at Heidelberg University and Honorary Professor of Cultural Studies and the Theory of Religion at the University of Constance, has developed foundational theory of cultural memory, most significantly for biblical studies, in *Das kulturelles Gedächtnis: Schrift, Erinnerung, und politische Identität in frühen Hochkulturen* (C. H. Beck, 1992). His books translated into English include *Moses the Egyptian: The Memory of Egypt in Western Monotheism* (Harvard University Press, 1997), *The Search for God in Ancient Egypt* (Cornell University Press, 2001), *The Mind of Egypt: History and Meaning in the Time of the Pharaohs* (Harvard University Press, 2003), and *Death and Salvation in Ancient Egypt* (Cornell University Press, 2005).

Jonathan A. Draper, Professor of New Testament at the School of Religion and Theology, University of KwaZulu-Natal, Pietermaritzburg, is author (with Richard A. Horsley) of *Whoever Hears You Hears Me: Prophets, Performance, and Tradition in Q* (Trinity Press International, 2000), and editor of *The Didache in Modern Research* (Brill, 1997); *The Eye of the Storm: Bishop John William Colenso and the Crisis of Biblical Interpretation* (T. & T. Clark, 2004); *Orality, Literacy, and Colonialism in Southern Africa* (Brill, 2004); and *Orality, Literacy, and Colonialism in Antiquity* (Scholars Press, 2004).

John Miles Foley, W. H. Byler Distinguished Chair in the Humanities, Curators' Professor of Classical Studies and English, and founding Director of the Center for Studies in Oral Tradition and the Center for Research at the University of Missouri, Columbia, is a specialist in the world's oral traditions, especially the ancient Greek, medieval English, and contemporary South Slavic traditions. Among his major publications, and perhaps the most pertinent to biblical studies, are *Immanent Art* (Indiana University Press, 1991), *The Singer of Tales in Performance* (Indiana University Press, 1995), and *How to Read an Oral Poem* (University of Illinois Press, 2002).

Holly E. Hearon, Associate Professor of New Testament at Christian Theological Seminary, Indianapolis, is the author of *The Mary Magdalene Tradition: Witness and Counter-Witness in Early Christian Communities* (Liturgical Press, 2004), which received an award from the Catholic Press Association, and editor of (and contributor to) *Distant Voices Drawing Near: Essays in Honor of Antoinette Clark Wire* (Liturgical Press, 2004), along with many articles. Her current research is focused on the intersection of women, Christian origins, and orality in the ancient world, and social memory theory.

Richard A. Horsley is Distinguished Professor of Liberal Arts and Study of Religion at the University of Massachusetts, Boston. Among his many books are *Whoever Hears You Hears Me: Prophets, Performance, and Tradition in Q* (with Jonathan A. Draper; Trinity Press International, 1999), *Hearing the Whole Story: The Politics of Plot in Mark's Gospel* (Westminster John Knox Press, 2001), and *Jesus and Empire: The Kingdom of God and the New World Disorder* (Fortress Press, 2003).

Martin S. Jaffee, Professor of Jewish Studies at the University of Washington, is a widely respected scholar of rabbinic literature. His essay "Oral Tradition in the Writing of Rabbinic Oral Torah: On Theorizing Rabbinic Orality" (*Oral Tradition* 14 [1999], 3–32) and his book *Torah in the Mouth: Writing the Oral Tradition in Palestinian Judaism 200 BCE–400 CE* (Oxford University Press, 2001) opened up a new understanding of rabbinic learning and teaching in terms of the oral-written communication of rabbinic culture.

Vernon K. Robbins is Professor of New Testament and Comparative Sacred Texts in the Department and Graduate Division of Religion, Winship Distinguished Research Professor at Emory University, and Professor Extraordinary at the University of Stellenbosch, South Africa. With *Jesus the Teacher* (Fortress Press, 1984) he launched socio-rhetorical criticism in New Testament studies. In *The Tapestry of Early Christian Discourse* (Routledge, 1996) and *Exploring the Texture of Texts* (Trinity Press International, 1996), he presented programmatic strategies for the approach. A festschrift in his honor, *Fabrics of Discourse* (ed. David B. Gowler; Trinity Press International, 2004), contains essays displaying socio-rhetorical interpretation.

Jens Schröter, Professor of New Testament at the University of Jena, is author of a number of New Testament studies including *Erinnerung an Jesu Worte: Studien zur Rezeption der Logienüberlieferung in Markus, Q, und Thomas* (Neukirchener, 1997), and *Konstruktion von Wirklichkeit* (de Gruyter, 2004).

Whitney Shiner, Associate Professor of Christian Origins, George Mason University, is author of *Proclaiming the Gospel: First-Century Performance of Mark* (Trinity Press International, 2003) and *Follow Me! Disciples in Markan Rhetoric* (SBLDS 145; Scholars Press, 1995).